Who Decides the Budget?

A Political Economy Analysis of the Budget Process in Latin America

Mark Hallerberg,
Carlos Scartascini,
and Ernesto Stein

Editors

IDB

Inter-American Development Bank

Co-published by
David Rockefeller Center for Latin American Studies
Harvard University
1730 Cambridge Street
Cambridge, MA 02138

Distributed by
Harvard University Press
Cambridge, Massachusetts
Phone: U.S.A. and Canada, 1-800-405-1619; all others, 1-401-531-2800
E-mail: orders@triliteral.org

London, England
Phone: +44(0) 1243-779777; Fax: +44(0) 1243-843303
E-mail: *cs-books@wiley.co.uk*

Produced by the IDB Office of External Relations

Cataloging-in-Publication data provided by the Inter-American Development Bank Felipe Herrera Library

Who decides the budget? a political economy analysis of the budget process in Latin America / Mark Hallerberg, Carlos Scartascini and Ernesto Stein, editors.

p. cm.
Includes bibliographical references.
ISBN: 978-1-59782-089-9

1. Expenditures, Public. 2. Latin America—Appropriations and expenditures. 3. Fiscal policy—Latin America. I. Hallerberg, Mark. II. Scartascini, Carlos G., 1971-. III. Stein, Ernesto. IV. Inter-American Development Bank. V. David Rockefeller Center for Latin American Studies.

HJ7664.5 .W837 2009 LCCN: 2009926933
336.8 W837--dc22

Contents

Acknowledgments

The initial inspiration for this volume came from a study realized by Carlos Scartascini and Ernesto Stein on the budget process in Bolivia and their work with colleagues on related topics, particularly Pablo Spiller and Mariano Tommasi, in *Policymaking in Latin America: How Politics Shapes Policies* and *The Politics of Policies: Economic and Social Progress in Latin America (2006 Report)*. Components of the frameworks of those publications, particularly the actor-centered approach and general equilibrium perspective, became the basis for the conceptual structure of this volume, in this case applied to decisions made on the allocation of public resources in the budget process.

This volume is part of a larger agenda of the Research Department of the Inter-American Development Bank (IDB) to examine the topics of political institutions and policy outcomes in Latin America. This agenda includes—among other products—the aforementioned books, a forthcoming publication that looks at the role of political actors and the arenas in which decisions are made, and the analysis of the policymaking process in two even broader areas: the set of policies that affect a country's productivity and fiscal reforms.

The volume consists of studies taken on by eight different interdisciplinary country teams under the auspices of the IDB and United Kingdom Department for International Development (DfID), as well as significant background and lessons drawn from two other country studies. These studies were conceived as part of the execution of two projects, one that focuses on the Southern Cone Countries, coordinated by Carlos Scartascini and Ernesto Stein (with the extensive input of Eduardo Fernández-Arias), and another that includes the Andean Countries, coordinated by Carlos Scartascini, Ernesto Stein, and Fidel Jaramillo. Mark Hallerberg joined the project at a later stage and was instrumental in transforming a collection of working papers into the cohesive set of chapters that follow.

The process of compiling this volume was highly interactive, with ample opportunities for cross-fertilization among the authors of the country chapters, as well as frequent give and take (in both directions) between these authors and the project coordinators. We are greatly indebted to the authors of the country studies and would also like to highlight the work of Cristóbal Aninat and Joaquín Vial, who participated in an in-depth study of the budget process in Chile, which was ultimately not included in this volume because of space limitations. The above-mentioned study on Bolivia by Scartascini and Stein was excluded for similar reasons. Both studies are discussed in the text and are fundamental to the overall product.

Seminars organized by the IDB in Buenos Aires, Bogotá, Quito, and Washington, D.C. to support this project were important focal points in the interactive process. In each one of these events, the authors and coordinators received feedback from an all-star roster of economists, political scientists, country authorities, and policymakers. The close relationship with country authorities (we received comments from a mix of some of the current and/or former ministers, deputy ministers, budget directors, and legislators in each country) has substantially enriched the analysis, ensured the precision of the arguments made in terms of factual accuracy, and increased the relevance of its policy implications.

We would like to thank the following individuals for their help in organizing the seminars and their invaluable support during the early stages of this project (from the initial calls for proposals to the completion of the drafts): Margarita Aneiva, Jesús Bengoechea, Norelis Betancourt, Adriana Cabrera, Carla Carpio, Irene Cartin, Raquel Gomez, Maria Helena Melasecca, and Mariela Semidey. Eduardo Fernández-Arias and Fidel Jaramillo's roles were vital in their ability to generate interest and participation of policymakers and to mobilize support within the Bank.

We are grateful for the assistance of Carlos Santiso who was instrumental in bringing this project to the attention of DfID, which made our successful collaboration possible. Our colleagues at DfID deserve special gratitude, particularly Ernesto Jeger (and his associates), who accompanied us along the process and financed several of the country studies, events, and related costs. DfID also helped plan and finance two seminars in London that were crucial for the dissemination of the findings of the studies to European scholars, who in turn provided invaluable feedback.

We would also like to recognize our colleagues at the IDB, Emory University, and the Hertie School of Government for their support, encouragement, and feedback. Within the IDB, we want to especially recognize the following individuals: Sixto Aquino, Juan Blyde, Guillermo Calvo, Francesca Castellani, Santiago Levy, Eduardo Lora, Steve Quick, Alicia Ritchie, Orlando Reos, and Ricardo Santiago. We are particularly grateful for the encouragement of Sara Calvo and Neile Quintero to write the original paper on Bolivia and the research assistance of Gabriel Filc, who also managed the interaction with the country teams in several stages of the process. Martin Ardanaz provided valuable assistance by putting together some of the material in the introductory chapter.

Apart from those already recognized above, many others deserve recognition for their valuable comments throughout the project phases, particularly James Alt, Barry Anderson, José Arista, Jorge Baldrich, Orazio Bellettini, David Booth, Mauricio Bugarin, Jaime Carrera, Sergio Clavijo, Paolo de Renzio, Patrick Dunleavy, Alejandro Grisanti, Pablo Guidotti, Edward Hedger, Peter Heller, Simon Hix, Robert Inman, Juan Pablo Luna, Diego Mancheno, Mario Marcel, Ricardo Martner, Olga Núñez Sánchez, Alfredo Ramón Pardo Acosta, Michael Penfold, Carolina Rentería, Jesús Rodríguez, Allen Schick, Aaron Schneider, Nelson Shack, Martus Tavares, Mariano Tommasi, Gerardo Uña, Joachim Wehner, and one anonymous referee. We would also like to recognize participants in the previously mentioned seminars and other seminars at LACEA, ISNIE, MPSA, APSA, LSE, ODI, the World Bank, and the IDB, in which some of the studies were presented.

Along with those previously mentioned, the authors of the country studies would like to especially thank the following individuals for their helpful comments and discussions: Rodolfo Acuña, Raúl Ayala, Luis Babino, Cristina Baus, Damián Bonari, Alejandro Bonvecchi, Andrés Borensztein, José Buttner, Luis Miguel Chiriboga, Paul Elguezabal, Shirley Herreño, José Hidalgo, Julio Mejía, Juan Muñoz, Tom Mustillo, Claudia Marcela Numa, Daniela Oleas M., Federico Ortega, Santiago Ortiz, Fernando Paciello, Guillermo Perry, Carolina Reed, Oswaldo Rodriguez, Flora Rojas, José Rosero, Enrique Sosa, Walfa Tellez, Luis

Tonelli, and Marco Varea. The authors are also grateful to the various workshop participants and interviewees who gave generously of their time and knowledge.

Ideas evolve into successful books thanks to capable editorial support. For her invaluable support in this area, we would like to acknowledge Rita Funaro. For pulling everything together, we are most grateful to the main editor, Sarah Schineller, as well as the publications team at the IDB, led by Rafael Cruz and including Cathy Conkling-Shaker, Gerardo Giannoni, Elisabeth Schmidt, and Dolores Subiza. Finally, we would like to thank Ejti Stih for giving us permission to use her painting for the cover. Several reasons made this painting the obvious choice: it is a remarkable work of art; it captures faithfully the spirit of the book; and it has the same source of inspiration that ignited the process that led to this publication: policymaking in Bolivia.

About the Authors

Emmanuel Abuelafia, Country Economist in the Caribbean Country Department of the Inter-American Development Bank. At the time of writing for this volume, he was an analyst at CIPPEC, Argentina.

Vicente Albornoz, Director of CORDES, Ecuador.

Lee Alston, Professor of Economics at the University of Colorado, Boulder.

M. Caridad Araujo, Economist in the East Asia and the Pacific Region Department of the World Bank.

Sergio Berensztein, Professor in the Department of Political Science and International Studies at Universidad Torcuato di Tella, Argentina.

Mario Bergara, President of the Central Bank of Uruguay. At the time of writing for this volume, he was Professor in the Department of Economics of Universidad de la República, Uruguay.

Miguel Braun, Executive Director of CIPPEC, Argentina.

Mauricio Cárdenas, Senior Fellow and Director of the Latin American Initiative at Brookings Institution and President of LACEA. At the time of writing for this volume, he was Executive Director of Fedesarrollo, Colombia.

Luis Carranza, Minister of Finance and Professor at the University of San Martín De Porres, Perú.

Daniel Chasquetti, Adjunct Professor in the Department of Political Science at Universidad de la República, Uruguay.

Jorge F. Chávez, graduate student in economics at Pennsylvania State University. At the time of writing for this volume, he was a Researcher at the Instituto Peruano de Economía, Peru.

Abelardo Daza, Visiting Professor at IESA, Venezuela.

Luciano di Gresia, Assistant Professor in the Department of Economics at Universidad de la Plata, Argentina. At the time of writing for this volume, he was an analyst at CIPPEC, Argentina.

Mark Hallerberg, Professor of Public Management and Political Economy at the Hertie School of Governance. He also maintains an affiliation with Emory University.

Andrés Mejía Acosta, Research Fellow in the Institute of Development Studies of the University of Sussex.

Carolina Mejía, Researcher at Fedesarrollo, Colombia.

Marcus Melo, Professor of the Doctoral Program in Political Science (PPGA) at Universidade Federal de Pernambuco, Brazil.

José R. Molinas, Senior Economist in the Poverty Division of the Latin America and the Caribbean Region Department at the World Bank. At the time of writing for this volume, he was the Director of Instituto Desarrollo, Paraguay.

Juan Andrés Moraes, Adjunct Professor in the Department of Political Science at Universidad de la República in Uruguay.

Bernardo Mueller, Professor in the Department of Economics at the University of Brasilia, Brazil.

Mauricio Olivera, Researcher at Fedesarrollo, Colombia.

Carlos Pereira, Assistant Professor in the Department of Political Science at Michigan State University.

Aníbal Pérez-Liñán, Associate Professor of Political Science at the University of Pittsburgh.

José Manuel Puente, Professor in the Center of Public Policy at IESA, Venezuela.

Germán Rios, Director of Competitiveness Programs at Corporación Andina de Fomento and Assistant Professor at Universidad Católica Andres Bello.

Alesia Rodríguez, independent consultant. At the time of writing for this volume, she was a Researcher at IESA, Venezuela.

Carlos Scartascini, Senior Research Economist in the Research Department of the Inter-American Development Bank.

Ernesto Stein, Regional Economic Advisor for Central America, Mexico, Panama and Dominican Republic (CID) at the Inter-American Development Bank. At the time of writing for this volume, he was the Lead Research Economist in the Research Department of the Inter-American Development Bank

José Valderrama, international consultant currently working for the World Bank.

1 

A New Framework

Carlos Scartascini and Ernesto Stein

THE POLITICS OF THE BUDGET PROCESS

In the same way that children decide how to allocate their allowance between candies and toys, societies decide how to allocate scarce public resources between competing uses. The budget is the main tool used to allocate such resources, and it is in the context of the budget process that politicians must make trade-offs among different policy priorities.

Traditional welfare economics assumes that budget decisions are made by a social planner with the ability and knowledge to maximize social welfare. His or her decision would take into account the benefits and costs of each alternative and select the level and composition of spending that makes everybody better off (Arrow, Sen, and Suzumura, 2002). While this approach to modeling budget policymaking, which delivers "first-best" outcomes, is useful as a benchmark for comparison, the approach is not a good representation of the actual way in which fiscal (or other) decisions are made in the public arena. Rather than the domain of a single welfare-maximizing policymaker, budget decisions are the result of a collective process that involves a variety of political actors, each with his or her own motivations and incentives. Actors involved in budget negotiations have their own views about the needs of society and the benefits and costs of certain policies. They may also have incentives to support different programs according to their aspirations and their roles in the political process. For example, legislators may be enticed to bring benefits to their constituency in order to increase their chances of reelection; line ministers could be interested in fostering publicly funded projects in their domain; and the president may want to increase expenditures before the next election to boost his popularity.

Given the prevailing preferences of the participants, institutional arrangements can either exacerbate or contribute to resolving a number of potential problems. For example, the concentration of budget power in the hands of the president may exacerbate electoral budget cycles. Yet a decentralized budget process in which legislators have considerable power may lead to excessive spending if programs with local benefits are financed from a common pool of resources.

From the discussion above, it is easy to see that political institutions, such as whether or not the president can seek reelection, or whether legislators are elected in large districts under proportional representation or in small districts under majority rule, may affect the incentives of budget participants and thus have an effect on budget outcomes. Similarly, budget institutions that lay out the rules of interaction of the different participants in the budget process, or place constraints on budget outcomes, can also influence these outcomes. Not surprisingly, there is ample literature that examines the impact of political and budgetary institutions on fiscal outcomes. This literature tends to find that political and budget institutions do matter for explaining fiscal outcomes.

Political economy explanations of fiscal outcomes build on the idea that fiscal decisions are the result of political processes that involve actors with varied interests over policy outcomes. These interactions take place mainly between politicians and voters and between politicians that represent diverse interests or constituencies. The problems that may arise from these interactions have been summarized as principal-agent problems and cooperation problems (including the common pool resource problem) (Tommasi, 1998; von Hagen, 2006).[1]

Principal-agent problems refer to the inconsistencies between the incentives or goals of the agent (an elected official) and those of the principal (the people who elected the official). For example, politi-

[1] While in this chapter a twofold classification is followed, there are other ways to review the literature. For example, Alesina and Perotti (1995) discuss the field's main contributions of the 1980s and early 1990s along the lines of different political economy models of budget deficits (e.g., opportunistic politicians, intergenerational redistribution, coalition governments, geographically dispersed interests, etc.). Similarly, Drazen (2002) offers various mechanisms that explain why the political system may yield a bias towards deficits (e.g., electoral cycles, "fiscal illusion," bureaucratic behavior, etc.).

cians might allocate spending differently than how the individuals who voted them into office would have selected, and bureaucrats may do the same with regard to the politicians' preferences (Hallerberg, 2003). These problems are exacerbated when the agent can hide information from the principal (Strøm, 2000). Often, the agent uses such privileged information to carry out actions that the principal would not have allowed if the principal had all of the facts.

A classic example of a **cooperation problem** is the well-known common pool problem (Ostrom, 1990).[2] In fiscal policy, the common pool is the budget that political players draw upon—financed from a general tax fund—to generate concentrated benefits (such as targeted public policies) (Hallerberg, Strauch, and von Hagen, 2009). In standard models, politicians care most about their constituencies when making budget decisions and do not internalize the additional burden for other districts. Consequently, spending is higher than it would otherwise be if each political agent had to bear the whole cost of the policies that he or she proposes for his or her district. The common pool problem can worsen if each player considers a smaller fraction of the total tax burden (Hallerberg and Marier, 2004). In this context, certain institutional characteristics, particularly those that determine the degree of fragmentation of the decision-making bodies, may affect government size. Some examples are the type of political regime, the organization of the executive branch, and the electoral rules. Basically, less-fragmented decision bodies—which are usually presented under presidential executives, smaller and more compact cabinets, and majoritarian electoral systems—tend to present fewer cooperation problems, hence they have better fiscal outcomes.[3]

The way the actors interact in the budget process is not independent of the institutional framework in which they make decisions. Their interactions are particularly affected by the budget institutions, which impose

[2] In this chapter, cooperation problems refer to the game played by multiple political actors with heterogeneous preferences that maximize objectives that, to some extent, include the welfare of their constituencies.

[3] Available literature on this topic is quite profuse. Some of the relevant studies include for political regime: Persson and Tabellini (2000, 2003), Cheibub (2006), Neto and Borsani (2004); for cabinets: Grilli, Masciandaro, and Tabellini (1991), Kontopoulos and Perotti (1999), Bawn and Rosenbluth (2006); and for electoral systems: Lizzeri and Persico (2001), Milesi-Ferretti, Perotti, and Rostagno (2002), Persson and Tabellini (2003), Stein, Talvi, and Grisanti (1998), Scartascini and Crain (2002), Hallerberg and Marier (2004).

restrictions on their actions and define the rules of engagement among them.[4] Therefore, certain outcomes, such as high deficits, may be restricted by devising the right set of institutions, for example, by introducing limits on the outcomes of the process (numerical restrictions) and providing greater power in budget negotiations to those with incentives to keep finances under control (a more hierarchical budget process). The evidence gathered through the mix of literature on this topic, independent of the region of the world that it pertains to, leads to consistent findings.[5]

More traditional institutional literature, usually based on cross-country analysis, has been successful in explaining certain regularities and is a very useful point of departure for the analysis herein. A weakness of this literature, however, is that it fails to explore thoroughly the specific settings faced by key actors in different countries, which may affect their incentives and roles, and ultimately, the budget outcomes. Put another way, the presence of open-list proportional representation electoral rules in a country is certainly relevant for determining the incentives of legislators. But this feature of political institutions may produce different outcomes depending on the way it interacts with other features of the political and budgetary institutional setting. For example, while an open-list proportional representation electoral rule may lead to pork barrel in Brazil, it may not have the same effect in Ecuador, where the constitution disallows budgetary programs with geographically localized benefits. Thus, while available literature has uncovered interesting regularities regarding the electoral system's impact on fiscal outcomes, there is still a need for a more nuanced approach, particularly if the goal is to use the findings of the literature as the basis for policy recommendations. In this volume, a new approach is introduced based on the following premises:

- **The budget process should not be examined as part of an isolated and technical discussion**. On the contrary, the budget process constitutes a fundamental element of the broader policy-

[4] Budget institutions are the set of rules, procedures, and practices according to which budgets are drafted, approved, and implemented (Alesina and Perotti, 1996).

[5] For the United States: Eichengreen (1992), Bohn and Inman (1996), Alt and Lowry (1994), Poterba (1997). For Europe: von Hagen (1992), von Hagen and Harden (1995), Hallerberg and Marier (2004), Yläoutinen (2004), Hallerberg, Strauch, and von Hagen (2009). For Latin America: Alesina et al. (1996), Stein, Talvi, and Grisanti (1998), Filc and Scartascini (2007).

making process. Nearly all government laws affect present or future expenditures, and thus they have implications for budget negotiations. In turn, budget negotiations tend to offer the possibility for politicians to cement support and compensate losers. In fact, as some of the country studies in this volume will illustrate, some reforms can be achieved only during budget negotiations.

- **Budget outcomes cannot be fully explained on the basis of one or two political or institutional dimensions, however important these dimensions may be.** A good understanding of the workings of the budget process requires a systemic view that pays attention to multiple institutional and political dimensions, as well as the interaction between them. Similarly, budget processes and their impact cannot be understood fully by focusing on the incentives and actions of one particular type of actor—for example, a legislator—alone. A good understanding of the process requires attention to a broader set of actors and the interaction among them. For example, a legislator's actions are affected not only by the electoral system that establishes how he or she is elected into office, but also by the powers of the president, the role of political parties and their linkages with voters and interest groups, and even the role of the judiciary. Therefore, looking only at the electoral system may reveal only a small fraction of the story.
- **It is important to look beyond formal rules and incorporate the study of actual practices into the analysis.** As the subsequent chapters will show, in the Latin American countries of focus in this volume, actual practices may differ significantly from the written rules. While laws and regulations help determine the behavior of actors and thus affect budget outcomes, so do informal budget practices that are not written into law. A sole focus on formal rules would lead to a very incomplete characterization of the workings of the budget process and its impact on fiscal outcomes.
- **While budget processes have an important impact on fiscal sustainability, they can also affect other equally important dimensions of fiscal outcomes.** While most analyses have focused on fiscal sustainability variables such as budget deficits and debt—which have also been the main objective of reforms—it is also important to study, particularly in democratic settings, the

ability to increase budget efficiency (and effectiveness) of public expenditures, respond to shocks, and ensure that people's preferences are taken into account.

A MORE NUANCED APPROACH

Based on the limitations presented above, the new framework offered in this chapter builds on the very profuse available literature on budget processes, fiscal policy, and institutions in Latin America. It also adds emphasis to the role of actors, the role of the budget process as facilitator of exchanges in the policymaking process, the differences between formal rules and actual practices, and other relevant budgetary outcomes beyond sustainability.

Actors Are at the Center Stage

As the opening paragraphs of this chapter indicate, budget decisions are the result of the actions of the agents involved in fiscal decision making, who act according to the incentives they face and the rules that govern their interaction. Consequently, in the new framework developed herein, the actors are at the core, and this framework relies on identifying each of the actors, their incentives at each stage of the budget process, and the particular institutional context in which they play out the game. Therefore, it is important to determine not only which are the roles of the president and the legislature in the formal budget process, which tend to be fairly similar across countries, but also the way in which these two actors actually interact in practice, which varies significantly from country to country. It is equally important to ascertain the interactions of other actors in practice, such as the cabinet, civil society, and the business sectors.

In order truly to understand the budget processes and be able to use this knowledge as a basis for policy recommendations, it is essential to perform in-depth country studies, such as those included as chapters of this volume. The incorporation of the specific actors and their incentives at the core of the analysis, in place of a focus on de jure institutions, may allow reformers to avoid unintended outcomes that end up being worse than the status quo.

For example, consider the case of the elimination of the "parliamentary slush funds" (*auxilios parlamentarios*) in Colombia in the 1990s.[6] The budgetary rules in place before the 1991 constitution was ratified in Colombia allowed transfers to be made to lawmakers through parliamentary slush funds, which lawmakers could appropriate discretionally. Lawmakers could use these funds for projects with high political returns. These slush funds served as "tokens of exchange" when the president had to negotiate key votes with legislators. The constitutional elimination of these predetermined and transparent slush funds may have had the intention of increasing the efficiency of public spending, but their abolition took place in the context of a fragmented party system and a president with low partisan power. The continued need for the government to build coalitions gave rise to transfers that were not just less transparent, but also much greater in value, an undesirable result that was very different from the result anticipated.[7] This episode is also representative of another feature of budget processes that we will come back to later in this chapter: the fact that political actors do not always play by the written rules.

The Role of the Budget Process in the Policymaking Process

The previous example from Colombia shows that to understand certain budgetary outcomes and decisions and why some reforms are effective (and/or are adopted) in some countries but not in others, it is important to keep in mind that the budget process is part of a broader policymaking process.[8] Fiscal outcomes are not necessarily the product of decisions

---

[6] The analysis of this case is based on the work of Hommes (1996), Vargas (1999), and Echeverry, Bonilla, and Moya (2004). For a complete analysis of the decision-making process in Colombia, which explains the negotiations between the executive and legislative branches, see Chapter 4 in this volume.

[7] "This episode of Colombian budgetary history is illustrative because the abolition of a budgetary institution, considered undesirable at a given moment, multiplied its value by eight, made it illegal and forced it under the table, without accountability or assignment of responsibilities" (Echeverry, Bonilla, and Moya, 2004: 23). The relevance that parliamentary slush funds gained in the political debate prompted President Uribe to include their elimination as an explicit point of his campaign and in the 100 points of his democratic manifesto.

[8] IDB (2005), Stein and Tommasi (2007), and Spiller, Stein, and Tommasi (2003) are good sources for details on the specifics of the policymaking process from which we have borrowed the overall framework of analysis.

made by technocrats acting solely in the fiscal arena, but the result of a complex web of interactions among government officials, legislators, economic actors, and civil society. In fact, the budget process is at the heart of this broader process, for a variety of reasons. First, funding for any policy with expenditure implications has to go through the budget. Therefore, a number of negotiations that relate to other policymaking spheres—from education to trade policy to infrastructure development—end up being played out within the budget arena. Second, budget resources can be used as a token of exchange—resources for policies. Thus, these resources can help governments build coalitions, as shown in the country study of Brazil in this volume (Chapter 3), or they can be used to compensate potential losers who may otherwise block important policy initiatives, as shown in the country study of Uruguay in this volume (Chapter 8). Finally, reforms to the budget process may facilitate or hinder possibilities of cooperation in other policy areas.

As a consequence of the role that the budget process plays in policymaking, some budget reforms have been passed not necessarily to improve the sustainability or efficiency of fiscal outcomes, but rather to gain additional power in the overall policymaking process. For example, in 2006 the Argentine Congress endowed the executive branch with "superpowers" in the execution of the budget.[9] This prerogative, usually a last-resort measure to be used during a profound crisis, was granted at a moment of relative fiscal largesse in the country. The main objective was to provide the president with tools to build political coalitions through discretionary budget allocations.

Understanding the role of the budget process in the overall policymaking process implies understanding the actors' incentives from a "general equilibrium" perspective, which in turn has two further implications.[10] First, it is important to look at the budget process as part of a larger machinery. As the above examples illustrate, decisions in the fiscal arena respond to a fiscal logic as well as other political needs of the relevant actors.

[9] Argentine Law 26.124 provides the president (through the chief of cabinet) with the ability to change the budget allocations at will during the budget cycle. By that norm, any excess revenues can be allocated by the executive branch without consulting with Congress. For more information, see http://infoleg.mecon.gov.ar/infolegInternet/anexos/115000-119999/118648/norma.htm.

[10] Filc, Scartascini, and Stein (2005) also look at this issue by considering the feedback effects between the budget process and the policymaking process.

Second, it implies the need to account for the actions and results in each stage of the overall budget process. As such, the behavior of each actor in each one of the stages—budget drafting, approval, execution, and control—depends on the rules and the conduct stages (see Box 1.1).[11] For example, the government may have discretion to spend any "unexpected" additional resources, and then, during the drafting of the budget, it may have incentives to underestimate revenues, as is the case currently in Argentina. If, as in Brazil, the president has the discretion to cut individual budget items during budget execution when revenues fall below "expectations" (and thus has a tool to punish legislators who do not support his legislative agenda), then during the drafting stage he will have incentives to overestimate revenues. Similarly, if Congress knows that the executive branch has broad discretion over budgetary allocations during the execution stage (as tends to be the case in Paraguay, for example), then it may have no incentives to work on relevant changes to the budget during the approval stage, even when, according to the formal rules, it has the prerogative to do so.

Actual Practices

It is important to understand not only the *formal rules* of engagement between the actors, but also the *actual practices* that shape the budget process. While most studies assume that formal rules are complied with, the evidence gathered in this volume and related literature shows that this is often not the case. Some actors de facto go beyond the prerogatives granted to them by the constitution and the laws, thus contradicting the letter—or at least the spirit—of the law. Some actors do not play the role they are supposed to play (for example, auditing agencies in most countries), and others do not comply with some types of rules—for example, the numerical rules regarding spending, debt, or deficits. Within Latin America, the extent to which budget participants disregard the letter of the law varies from country to country. Chile, at the compliant end of the range, has been following a numerical structural balance rule, and did so even before it was part of a formal law.

[11] The actors play a "sequential game": their actions in one stage are not independent of their actions, or those of the other actors, in the rest of the stages.

BOX 1.1 The Game the Actors Play

One way to analyze the role of each actor in each stage of the budget process and to evaluate the "sequential game" mentioned in the note 11 is to examine the detailed budget data that corresponds to each stage of the budget process. For example, to assess change, a designated indicator measured in each stage helps to evaluate the ratio of changes (increases, decreases, and reallocation). For the first stage, approval, the indicator is

$$C_{BL} = \frac{\sum_{i=1}^{N} \left| B_i - L_i \right|}{2}.$$

Here, B_i is the participation of item *i* in total spending presented in the executive budget proposal, and L_i is the participation of item *i* in total spending approved in the budget law. Similar coefficients are used for the other stages (changes to the budget during the year and execution of the budget).

These indicators help identify where changes take place, which actors (according to their roles in the process) have more influence, and whether budget execution is close to the original spending plans (and hopefully to careful initial planning).

For example, the following figure, based on average changes made to the budget between 1997 and 2005, shows that in most of the countries in Latin America, Congress plays a minor role in the budget process—changes during approval are not very high, as the first bar illustrates—and that the changes Congress introduces can generally be reversed by the executive during execution—as the last bar shows. For example, in Bolivia during this period Congress made almost no changes during the approval stage, but the executive reallocated more than 15 percent of the total budget during execution.

Changes to the Budget at Each Stage
(average, 1997–2005)

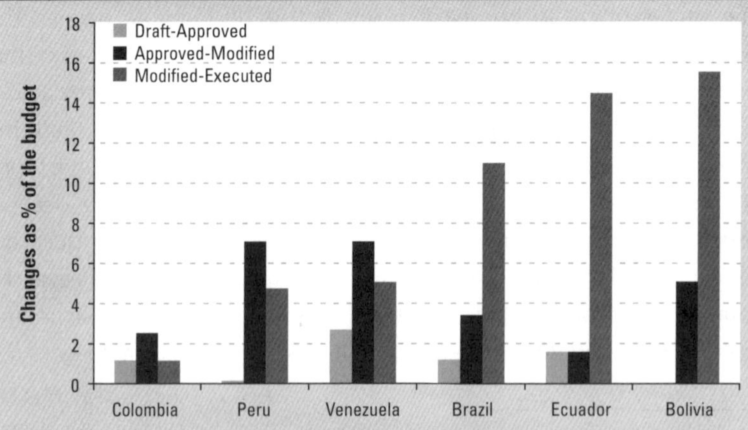

Examples of actors circumventing the restrictions imposed by formal fiscal institutions abound. For example, even though most legislatures are restricted in their capacity to increase public expenditures above the limits presented by the executive's proposal, they often find ways to work around them. In Ecuador, to increase expenditure on certain items, lawmakers, aware that debt service obligations would have to be met anyway, reallocated money from debt services to other items and thus created additional financing needs. In Bolivia, Congress increased expenditure by raising collection estimates of the government as additional sources of revenue. Such revenue estimates have generally been excessive, far above what could be attributed to uncertainty regarding the performance of economic variables. For example, in 1998 the Bolivian Congress increased the estimates of expected gains in efficiency of the tax collection agency and customs by 50 percent to create a cushion for additional spending. In fact, there were no gains in efficiency and the deficit for that year exceeded 4 percent, even though the executive branch underexecuted the budget by more than 3 percent. These types of strategies are not restricted to the legislative branch. Establishing limits on the legislative branch—or alternatively on the executive branch—may have no effect if there is a lack of political and social control over revenue estimates. And these controls may hardly ever become implemented if the only way to achieve political exchanges is to increase—or promise to increase—state expenditure.

One particular case of formal rules that are not always followed in practice is the numerical-rule component of fiscal responsibility laws, which typically combine numerical rules on deficit, expenditures or debt with other procedural and transparency-related rules to achieve better fiscal results. For example, numerical targets on deficit and expenditure in the fiscal solvency law implemented in Argentina in 1999 were not met: the 1999 and 2000 deficits exceeded the established limits, and the law was amended to permit a new deficit reduction scheme. Even this revision did not lead to compliance: in 2001 the deficit was almost 15 percent higher than the new limit and over six times the limit established for that year in the original law.

Peru has only recently complied (partially) with the numerical rules component of its Fiscal Responsibility Law (FRL). The country complied with the soft constraint of reducing fiscal deficit during an economic boom and lessening the impact of electoral cycles (during a cycle with no president seeking reelection). However, Peru has not complied with the "harder" constraint in times of largesse: keeping expenditures from increasing beyond the limits in the law (GDP growth plus 3 percent).

MEASURING FISCAL PERFORMANCE

Fiscal responsibility laws became a widespread reform in Latin America in the late nineties as most countries were trying to improve their access to financial markets (Filc and Scartascini, 2007). Financial restrictions that followed the Asian Crisis had a profound impact on the cash-strapped countries in the region, which forced Latin American governments to pursue reforms that would allow them to restrict expenditures and (politically induced) deficits in the future in order to ensure the sustainability of their fiscal accounts.

The focus on these issues is not new. With the development of the public choice tradition, the literature started to focus on the reasons why politically motivated government actions may not necessarily ensure long-term welfare, particularly decisions regarding the sustainability of fiscal deficits (Buchanan and Wagner, 1977). More recent literature has dealt with the issues of government size and fiscal balances as a response to the negative fiscal results observed in many countries.

The concept of fiscal **sustainability** refers to evaluating whether current debt levels in a country can be serviced given the government's current fiscal position. Consequently, fiscal sustainability has usually been examined through the evolution of deficits and debt (and its structure) alongside government revenues, liabilities, and assets.[12]

While it is crucial to look at the overall fiscal stance of governments, other dimensions are important for a comprehensive analysis of budget matters, particularly because some actors may have certain objectives in mind that may or may not be complementary to sustainability. For example, it seems that a certain level of disenchantment

[12] The devil of the sustainability analysis is in the details and certain issues that are not relevant for developed countries, such as the currency composition of public debt and exposure to large external shocks, are important for developing countries. For a comprehensive account of these issues, see IDB (2006).

of the population with the results of democracy in Latin America can be traced back to their discontent with the allocation of public monies.[13] Even though fiscal results have improved substantially in most countries, the allocation of expenditures seemingly has not followed the same path, and the outcomes of public policies have not improved in the same relative terms.

Consequently, it makes sense to expand the focus of more recent literature that has concentrated on issues of sustainability to include other dimensions such as **efficiency, adaptability** or **flexibility,** and **representativeness** of the budget. Thus, for this volume each chapter has followed its own definition of these variables according to the approach that best reflects the problems or issues relevant for the country being studied and the data available.[14]

In this introductory chapter, **efficiency** is evaluated from two perspectives: allocative and technical efficiency. This reveals the extent to which public resources are allocated to the most important needs and whether or not they are used in a cost-effective manner. In some chapters in this volume, efficiency is evaluated according to outcomes, such as the scope of education coverage and quality. For example, the study on Peru (Chapter 7) analyzes the impact of expenditures on outcomes and the efficiency losses of certain programs.[15]

In other chapters, efficiency is evaluated according to the processes through which certain outcomes are reached. In other words, given that a central interest of this project is to look at the role of the actors, the perspective herein analyzes whether or not the actors make decisions based on actual analysis of benefits and costs—which may not need to be

[13] In a simple quantitative exercise for Latin America, satisfaction with democracy seems to be better explained by the performance of the government (taxes are well spent, government expenditures are not wasteful, and government is effective overall) than by the performance of the economy (GDP per capita growth and average growth).

[14] The interest in analyzing issues beyond sustainability is not new. Early on, two strands of the public choice literature ventured a little farther. One strand looked at the role of politics and policymaking in redistribution (Meltzer and Richard, 1980, 1981; Peltzman, 1980; Stigler, 1970), while the other examined the role of the bureaucracy and efficiency in the production of public goods (Niskanen, 1971). Literature focused on public expenditure management also introduced these issues early on through the analyses of performance budgeting, planning programs, zero-based budgeting, and so on.

[15] The work of Herrera and Pang (2005) is a good source for estimating efficiency of public expenditures.

sophisticated, but at least need to be mentioned in the decision-making process—or whether the decisions are based on other considerations. Another way to approach the same issue is to look at the degree of execution and how it impacts the efficiency of project managers. This perspective has determined that highly volatile disbursement of public funds clearly affects such efficiency. For example, a previous study of the budget process in Bolivia shows a high volatility of expenditures at the item, state, and ministry level for the period 1990–2002, which affected the ability of managers to execute their projects (Scartascini and Stein, 2003).

How well Latin American countries are able to **adapt** to shocks and how their reactions affect public spending has been evaluated in the literature through two approaches. In one approach, the measure used is the procyclicality of fiscal policy, which is a common concept in the literature with a standard methodology (Braun and di Gresia, 2003). In the second approach, the measure used is the rigidity in the budget. Yet so far no standards have been applied in this approach, as the existing analysis has not clearly identified the makeup of the rigid budget. For example, most analysts would include salaries as part of the rigid budget. This standard would define Argentina's budget as one of the more rigid budgets in Latin America (Echeverry, Bonilla, and Moya, 2006). However, as the evidence shows, stark definitions do not always present the complete picture. During the crisis at the beginning of the current decade (2000), Argentina cut nominal salaries in order to balance the budget.[16] Similarly, funds earmarked for investments have usually been categorized as part of the rigid budget, even though many countries have found different ways to circumvent the spirit of the law and reduce investments during crises. Consequently, each chapter herein has treated this issue according to the standards of the country of focus. Therefore, while the hardwiring of expenditures might be a relevant issue in Brazil and Colombia, as demonstrated in Chapters 3 and 4, it has not been very relevant in Bolivia. Moreover, hardwiring and measures of rigidity are different in Brazil and Colombia, because the issues affecting these two countries are also different.

The process of measuring **representativeness** also differs from one country study to the next, and it is assessed in the subsequent

---

[16] For more information, see http://www.clarin.com/diario/2000/05/29/e-00315.htm.

chapters according to the outcomes or the procedures. Representativeness tries to capture whether public expenditures are designed to favor the population at large or whether they favor only a subset of the population with better access to policymakers and bureaucrats. Some chapters in this volume examine fairness in terms of the distribution of resources across groups and localities. For example, the analysis of Argentina (Chapter 2) shows that the provinces of the president tend to be favored in the distribution of resources. Others, such as the study of Ecuador (Chapter 5), examine the role of malapportionment. Under this influence, those states with a larger share of representatives tend to receive larger budget allocations. Almost all chapters in this volume look at this issue in terms of processes and examine the role that Congress, as the most diverse representative body of people's preferences, has during each process. For example, does Congress change allocations in the approval process? Does the executive reverse these changes during execution?

SPECIFICS OF THE PROJECT

Building on the framework described in this introductory chapter, the subsequent chapters in this volume have the following characteristics:

a. They focus on **individual countries,** but within a broader project and through a common framework. Detailed country analyses on Argentina, Brazil, Colombia, Ecuador, Paraguay, Peru, Uruguay, and Venezuela provide comparative knowledge about the workings of policymaking and budget processes in Latin America, which allows for the formulation of better policy recommendations. Such processes in Chile and Bolivia are also analyzed herein based on studies presented in previous working papers. It is possible to make comparisons across countries and generate (albeit sometimes tentative) conclusions by examining these 10 countries at the same time.
b. The **institutional setup** of the budget process in each country is studied in great detail. Each chapter describes the formal budget process, the laws and regulations that affect the incentives, and the

rules that affect how each actor behaves in the process. In some cases, the description moves beyond the budget process to the general policymaking process and the laws that govern economic policy, such as changes to the constitution or the role of monetary policy (e.g., convertibility laws).

c. The authors of each of the chapters go to great lengths to describe the key actors, the actors' incentives and the institutional determinants of these incentives, and the way the game is played.
d. The authors focus on **actual practices**, looking beyond the written rules. There is a visible shift from the traditional characterization of the formal budget process to an in-depth analysis of how decisions are made.
e. The chapters present the incentives of actors from a general equilibrium perspective.
f. Throughout the analysis, the authors are aware of the key role that the budget process may play in the broader policymaking game as a crucial arena in which key political transactions take place.
g. The authors focus on fiscal sustainability, but also on other outcome dimensions such as efficiency, adaptability (procyclicality and budget rigidity), and the degree to which allocation reflects the preferences of the population (representativeness).
h. The authors use detailed budget data corresponding to each stage of the budget process to substantiate their claims regarding the interaction between the different players.
i. Certain chapters try to explain the dynamics of institutional change: for example, why some reforms take place and others do not, why some changes in formal rules may not alter actual behaviors, and why inefficient arrangements persist.

The concluding chapter further develops the idea that budgetary rules and institutions are embedded in a broader policymaking process. The conclusion reinforces the importance of taking a closer look at how these rules and institutions are used in the countries discussed in this volume in order to understand them better. There is also further exploration of the influential institutional relationships, particularly between Congress and the president, during the different stages of the budget process. Along with the effect of such relationships, the chapter also reexamines the effect of the fiscal responsibility laws discussed in various chapters and provides insight into why such laws generally fail to meet their goals. Finally, the chapter provides a thorough examination of the relationship between the policymaking process and the budget process in all of the countries discussed in this volume. The volume as a whole provides valuable lessons for a deeper understanding of such processes in other countries in Latin America and the Caribbean and around the world.

REFERENCES

Alesina, A., R. Hausmann, R. Hommes, and E. Stein. 1996. Budget Institutions and Fiscal Performance in Latin America. NBER Working Paper No. 5586. National Bureau of Economic Research, Cambridge, MA.

Alesina, A., and R. Perotti. 1995. The Political Economy of Budget Deficits. *IMF Staff Papers*, March 1–31. Washington, DC: International Monetary Fund (IMF).

———. 1996. Budget Deficits and Budget Institutions. NBER Working Paper No. 5556. National Bureau of Economic Research, Cambridge, MA.

Alt, J., and R. Lowry. 1994. Divided Government, Fiscal Institutions and Budget Deficits: Evidence from the States. *American Political Science Review* 88(4): 811–28.

Arrow, K. J., A. K. Sen, and K. Suzumura. 2002. *Handbook of Social Choice and Welfare*, Volume 1. Amsterdam: North-Holland.

Bawn, K., and F. Rosenbluth. 2006. Short versus Long Coalitions: Electoral Accountability and the Size of the Public Sector. *American Journal of Political Science* 50(2) April: 251–65.

Bohn, H, and R. P. Inman. 1996. Balanced-Budget Rules and Public Deficits: Evidence from the U.S. States. *Carnegie-Rochester Conference Series on Public Policy* 45: 13–76.

Braun, M., and L. di Gresia. 2003. Towards Effective Social Insurance in Latin America: The Importance of Countercyclical Fiscal Policy. RES Working Paper No. 487. Research Department, Inter-American Development Bank, Washington, DC.

Buchanan, J., and R. Wagner. 1977. *Democracy in Deficit*. New York: Academic Press.

Cheibub, J. 2006. Presidentialism, Electoral Identifiability, and Budget Balances in Democratic Systems. *American Political Science Review* 100: 353–68.

Drazen, A. 2002. Fiscal Rules from a Political Economy Perspective. University of Maryland. Unpublished.

Echeverry, J. C., J. A. Bonilla, and A. Moya. 2006. Institutional Rigidities and Budget Flexibility: Origin, Motivation and Effects on the Budget. Universidad de los Andes, School of Economics, Bogotá.

Eichengreen, B. 1992. The Political Economy of Fiscal Policy after EMU. Center for International and Development Economics Research (CIDER) Working Papers C92–004, University of California, Berkeley.

Filc, G., and C. Scartascini. 2007. Budgetary Institutions. In Eduardo Lora, ed., *The State of State Reform in Latin America*. Palo Alto, CA: Stanford University Press.

Filc, G., C. Scartascini, and E. Stein. 2005. Decentralization, Budget Processes and Feedback Effects. In Inter-American Development Bank, *The Politics of Policies*. Economic and Social Progress in Latin America: 2006 Report. Washington, DC: IDB/DRCLAS–Harvard University.

Grilli, V., D. Masciandaro, and G. Tabellini. 1991. Political and Monetary Institutions and Public Financial Policies in the Industrial Countries. *Economic Policy* 13: 341–92.

Hallerberg, M. 2003. Fiscal Rules and Fiscal Policy. In B. Guy Peters, and Jon Pierre, eds., *Handbook of Public Administration*, 393–401. London: Sage.

Hallerberg, M., and P. Marier. 2004. Executive Authority, the Personal Vote, and Budget Discipline in Latin American and Caribbean Countries. *American Journal of Political Science* 48(3): 571–87.

Hallerberg, M., R. Strauch, and J. von Hagen. 2009. *Forms of Fiscal Governance: Evidence from Europe*. Cambridge, MA: Cambridge University Press.

Herrera, S., and G. Pang. 2005. Efficiency of Public Spending in Developing Countries: An Efficiency Frontier Approach. World Bank Policy Research Working Paper No. 3645. World Bank, Washington, DC.

Hommes, R. 1996. Evolution and Rationality of Budget Institutions in Colombia. RES Working Paper No. 317. Research Department, Inter-American Development Bank, Washington, DC.

IDB. 2005. *The Politics of Policies*. Economic and Social Progress in Latin America: 2006 Report. Washington, DC: IDB/DRCLAS–Harvard University.

———. 2006. *Living with Debt: How to Limit the Risks of Sovereign Finance*. Economic and Social Progress in Latin America: 2007 Report. Washington, DC: IDB/DRCLAS–Harvard University.

Kontopoulos, Y., and R. Perotti. 1999. Government Fragmentation and Fiscal Policy Outcomes: Evidence from OECD Countries. In James

Poterba and Jurgen von Hagen, eds., *Fiscal Institutions and Fiscal Performance*, 81–102. Chicago: University of Chicago Press.

Lizzeri, A., and N. Persico. 2001. The Provision of Public Goods under Alternative Electoral Incentives. *American Economic Review* 91(1): 225–39.

Meltzer, A., and S. Richard. 1980. A Rational Theory of the Size of Government. *Journal of Political Economy* 89(5) October: 914–27.

———. 1981. Test of a Rational Theory of the Size of Government. *Public Choice* 41(3): 403–18.

Milesi-Ferretti, G., R. Perotti, and M. Rostagno. 2002. Electoral Systems and Public Spending. *Quarterly Journal of Economics* 117(2): 609–57.

Neto, A. O., and H. Borsani. 2004. Presidents and Cabinets: The Political Determinants of Fiscal Behavior in Latin America. *Studies in Comparative International Development* 39(1): 3–27.

Niskanen, W. 1971. *Bureaucracy and Representative Government.* Chicago: Aldine Atherton.

Ostrom, E. 1990. *Governing the Commons.* Cambridge: Cambridge University Press.

Peltzman, S. 1980. The Growth of Government. *Journal of Law & Economics* 23(2) October: 209–87.

Persson T., and G. Tabellini. 2000. *Political Economy: Explaining Economic Policy.* Cambridge: MIT Press.

———. 2003. *The Economic Effects of Constitutions.* Cambridge: MIT Press.

Poterba, J. M. 1997. Do Budget Rules Work? In A. Auerbach, ed., *Fiscal Policy: Lessons from Empirical Research.* Cambridge: MIT Press.

Scartascini, C., and M. Crain. 2002. The Size and Composition of Government Spending in Multi-party Systems. Working Papers in Economics. George Mason University, Fairfax, Virginia.

Scartascini, C., and E. Stein. 2003. The Bolivian Budget (1990–2002): A Year Long Bargaining Process. Inter-American Development Bank, Washington, DC. Unpublished.

Spiller, P., E. Stein, and M. Tommasi. 2003. Political Institutions, Policymaking Processes, and Policy Outcomes: An Intertemporal Transactions Framework. Design paper No. 1 (DPI). Inter-American Development Bank, Washington, DC.

Stein, E., E. Talvi, and A. Grisanti. 1998. Institutional Arrangements and Fiscal Performance: The Latin American Experience. NBER Working Paper No. 6358. Cambridge, MA: National Bureau of Economic Research.

Stein, E., and M. Tommasi. 2007. The Institutional Determinants of State Capabilities in Latin America. In F. Bourguignon and B. Pleskovic, eds., *Annual World Bank Conference on Development Economics, Regional: Beyond Transition*. Washington, DC: World Bank Publications.

Stigler, G. J. 1970. Director's Law of Public Income Redistribution. *Journal of Law & Economics* 13(1): 1–10.

Strøm, K. 2000. Delegation and Accountability in Parliamentary Democracies. *European Journal of Political Research* 37(3): 261–89.

Tommasi, M. 1998. Instituciones y resultados fiscales. *Desarrollo Económico* 38(149): 409–38.

Vargas, J. E. 1999. Las relaciones entre el ejecutivo y el legislativo. In M. Gandourand and L. B. Mejía, eds., *Hacia el rediseño del Estado*. Bogotá: Tercer Mundo/DNP.

von Hagen, J. 1992. Budgeting Procedures and Fiscal Performance in the European Communities. Economic Paper No. 96. Commission of the EC, Directorate-General for Economic and Financial Affairs, Brussels.

———. 2006. Fiscal Institutions. In B. Weingast and D. Wittman, eds., *The Oxford Handbook of Political Economy*. Oxford: Oxford University Press.

von Hagen, J., and I. Harden. 1995. Budget Processes and Commitment to Fiscal Discipline. *European Economic Review* 39(3–4) April: 771–79.

Yläoutinen, S. 2004. Fiscal Frameworks in the Central and Eastern European Countries. Discussion Paper No. 72. Economics Department, Ministry of Finance, Helsinki, Finland.

2

Who Decides on Public Expenditures? The Importance of the Informal Budget Process in Argentina

Emmanuel Abuelafia, Sergio Berensztein, Miguel Braun, and Luciano di Gresia

A POLITICAL ECONOMY ANALYSIS OF ARGENTINA'S BUDGET PROCESS

Despite recent improvements in fiscal solvency in Argentina between 2003 and 2007, public debt still stands above 60 percent of gross domestic product (GDP). Moreover, there are still concerns regarding medium-term sustainability because of the growing dependence of revenues on volatile export taxes and rapid growth in primary spending. Based on Argentina's history of fiscal profligacy—including two hyperinflations in 1989 and 1991—these concerns are not unfounded. Furthermore, there is increasing awareness of inefficiency and inequality in budget allocations.[1] Consolidating the sustainability, representativeness, and efficiency of Argentine fiscal outcomes remains a daunting challenge.[2]

---

[1] For example, news articles in major newspapers (e.g., cover story in *La Nación*, 24 April 2004) reflect doubts regarding the extent to which social spending actually reaches beneficiaries.

[2] *Sustainability* refers to intertemporal fiscal solvency; *efficiency* refers to the traditional measure of equating the marginal social benefit of public spending across state activities; and *representativeness* refers to the extent to which budgetary outcomes satisfy overall social preferences rather than particular group preferences.

Fiscal rules, and in particular the procedural rules that regulate the budget process, are increasingly considered a relevant part of reform efforts to improve fiscal outcomes (see, for instance, Kopits, 2004). However, it is not clear precisely which rules have to be changed, how the designated rules should be changed, and to what effect. To deepen the understanding of the role of budget institutions, as well as who determines budget outcomes, this chapter embarks on a political economy analysis of Argentina's budget process in the spirit of the Inter-American Development Bank (IDB) project Political Institutions, Policymaking Processes, and Policy Outcomes (see Spiller, Stein, and Tommasi, 2003, and Scartascini and Olivera, 2003). In particular, the chapter characterizes the institutional framework that regulates the preparation, approval, implementation, and control of the budget. Furthermore, the actors involved—both formally and informally—are identified in the process at each stage, and their incentives and interactions are analyzed. This knowledge should help determine the extent to which the current institutions of the budget process contribute to, or mitigate, Argentina's fiscal policy problems, and thus serve as a valuable input in the effort to improve its fiscal institutions and outcomes. For reasons of data availability, the analysis herein focuses mainly on the years between 1995 and 2006, but this period is also contrasted with previous experiences. The analysis is based not only on fiscal information, budget discussions, and legislation, but also on unstructured interviews with policymakers, legislators, and experts. These individuals were able to provide more detail on the informal rules of the budget process.[3]

The main finding of this chapter is that the executive, and in particular the president, has a de facto role that is much more powerful than what the laws and institutions of the budget process stipulate. However, it is important to note that the federal budget is not the main arena for political bargaining. During the last decade, negotiations—particularly with the provinces—have taken place outside the budget process (i.e., through the creation of fiduciary funds that are not included in the budget). The rigidity of the budget, together with other constraints such as the strength of some recent macroeconomic shocks—and to a lesser degree, fiscal rules, agreements with international financial institutions (IFIs), and the influence of other actors such as governors, legislators, and lobbies—have

[3] The interviewees were guaranteed anonymity, which allowed them to speak more freely.

limited the ability of the executive to modify the budget substantially and use it for political bargaining. Furthermore, compared with the 1983–1991 period of high inflation, in the past decade there have been dramatic improvements in the institutionalization of the budget process, in both political and administrative terms. These reforms accompanied a strong improvement in fiscal outcomes in the 1990s compared with the 1980s and have provided some of the tools necessary to limit the depth of the recent crisis and regain macroeconomic stability.

The chapter is organized into several sections. The section that follows this introduction discusses literature that concerns Argentine policymaking, in particular, those studies relevant to the budget process. The third section outlines the political and economic environment in which the budget process has evolved, with particular attention to fiscal policy reforms and outcomes. The fourth section presents an outline of the formal rules of the budget process. The fifth section introduces an analysis of the actual workings of the budget process, and the sixth section relates the results on these workings to fiscal policy outcomes. The final section concludes.

THE ANALYTICAL FRAMEWORK

Spiller and Tommasi (2003) provide an in-depth analysis of Argentina's policymaking process. They focus on explanations related to features of this process that determine policy outcomes. As this analysis points out, the Argentine political negotiation environment is far from ideal. Legislators have low tenure rates, a condition which generates few incentives to specialize or to acquire specific policy or legislative expertise. Governors and local party leaders are highly influential in regard to legislative careers. Therefore, many key political transactions take place at the level of provincial party leaders. Furthermore, there is a lack of an independent bureaucracy that could serve as an enforcement mechanism for intertemporal political agreements. Finally, the Argentine Supreme Court has not been an important enforcer of political agreements. This environment has led to deficient policies in Argentina in terms of instability, lack of coordination—between different levels of government and across ministries—and lack of cooperation among key actors. These aspects of policies are central in explaining Argentina's poor outcomes in terms of development, since policy instability leads to lack of credibility and economic volatility, which in turn lead to low investment and growth.

In their analysis, Spiller and Tommasi argue that the difficulty of striking long-term political deals in Argentina is caused by the institutional legacy of political and economic instability suffered between 1930 and 1983—a period in which 12 presidents were removed by force—and the institutional characteristics defined by the country's constitutional structure and its electoral rules.

Political instability has led to short planning horizons and myopic behavior by policymakers and interest groups. Furthermore, the short horizons of upper political leaders have led to a high rotation in the bureaucracy, which has left Argentina with weak cooperation and coordination mechanisms across agencies and government levels, along with a lack of a stable and professional civil service. In addition, presidents have tended to replace Supreme Court justices, leading to a weakened judiciary barely capable of limiting political decisions.

In turn, the specific characteristics of electoral rules, federalism, and the constitutional structure have conspired to weaken the arenas for intertemporal political transactions in Argentina. In particular, Congress has been rendered practically ineffective by the combination of the electoral system and strong presidential powers. As mentioned above, this environment gives provincial party elites—mainly provincial governors—ample influence in appointing and removing candidates for Congress. This leads to a high rotation of legislators, giving them low incentives to invest in a legislative career and thus low incentives to develop congressional capacity for policy analysis and oversight. Furthermore, the president has ample legislative initiative—as reflected, for example, by the regular use of decrees (Decretos de Necesidad y Urgencia) to make policy. The bottom line is that Congress is not the arena in which political deals are made. Rather, the president, provincial governors, and interest groups make these deals in informal arenas. However, deals made under these conditions are short-lived and unstable, because they lack the enforcement provided by formal political agreements, or by an independent bureaucracy capable of implementing such agreements or a judiciary able to enforce them.[4]

[4] For instance, Aninat et al. (2006) argue that in the case of Chile, the ability of veto players to block reforms in Congress implies that once a law is passed, it is unlikely that it will be reversed, providing stability to political decisions that pass through Congress.

The Political Economy of the Budget Process

Few studies have been undertaken on the political economy of the budget process in Argentina. Two exceptions are the analyses of Jones (2001) and Rodriguez and Bonvecchi (2004), which study the role of Congress in the budget process and arrive at radically different conclusions. On the one hand, Jones claims that Congress has had an important role in the budget process and that the smooth passage of budget proposals sent by the executive branch to Congress is not evidence of the lack of power of Congress in the process. Rather, he argues that the Peronist party is a disciplined party that had a congressional majority during most of the 1990s, that negotiations between legislators and the executive take place in the formulation stage of the budget process, and that the Peronist majority allows these deals to be enforced in Congress with swift passage. Jones shows, through the example of the Menem regime, that the percentage of federal transfers that go to a province is positively correlated with the percentage of the president's party legislative bloc that comes from that province. Jones claims that this is evidence of the power that (Peronist) legislators wield in the budget process.

On the other hand, Rodriguez and Bonvecchi (2004) study the role of Congress in the budget process and claim that it has been systematically weak over the past 20 years. They divide the period into three stages, defined by differences in the macroeconomic context and in the cohesiveness of the party system, and find that in periods of high macroeconomic instability (1984–1991 and 1996–2004) Congress played a merely validatory role in terms of the executive's decisions. In periods of economic expansion (1991–1995), Congress played a marginally expansive role, adding some items of pork to the executive proposal.

The analysis presented below reconciles these two points of view. Herein, it is argued that the evaluation of the role of Congress in the budget process depends on the universe of public expenditure that one analyzes. If one looks strictly at the federal budget process—the universe studied in this chapter—without including "coparticipation" (a tax-sharing system which is regulated by a specific law that needs to be approved by each provincial legislative body to be modified) and other transfers to provinces that are earmarked and therefore not voted on in each year's budget, then one would have to agree with Rodriguez and Bonvecchi (2004). The role of Congress is very limited, and in fact, most changes to the budget are made during the implementation phase, controlled by the executive, so agreements made in Congress are not necessarily sustainable. However, when the sum of all transfers to provinces is analyzed, it is indeed found that over-represented provinces in Congress receive greater transfers per capita. This reflects the political power of local party bosses—especially governors—who are capable of trading their votes in Congress in exchange for a larger share in the allocation of funds to provinces.[5] These negotiations do not occur in the arena of the federal budget process. In fact, most interviewees argued that governors are not significant actors in the federal budget process, despite being key actors in policymaking in general.

An important corollary is that the budget process is really the arena in which society reflects and implements its decisions to allocate the resources collected each year through the tax system. Here the term *reflects* as opposed to *decides* is emphasized, because many of the expenditures included in national budgets arise from past decisions and agreements by policymakers. For example, social security and debt payments reflect past decisions regarding the pension system and the accumulation of past fiscal deficits. Although in theory these and other decisions made in the past can be modified during the budget process, in practice many budget items are rigid. The next section contains an in-depth analysis of this issue.

FISCAL POLICY IN ARGENTINA: THE ROLE OF THE BUDGET PROCESS

Before describing how the budget process actually works in Argentina and who decides on public expenditures, this section begins with a discussion of *what* is actually decided in the process. First, it is important to understand that the national budget process in Argentina accounts for

[5] Spiller and Tommasi (2003) and Jones et al. (2001) show that the electoral system for Congress gives substantial power over who gets nominated to local party bosses and thus imposes loyalty and discipline on legislators, whose votes can be exchanged in negotiations between the provinces and the executive.

FIGURE 2.1 **The Argentine National Budget, 2004**
(revenues and expenditures in billions of Argentine pesos)

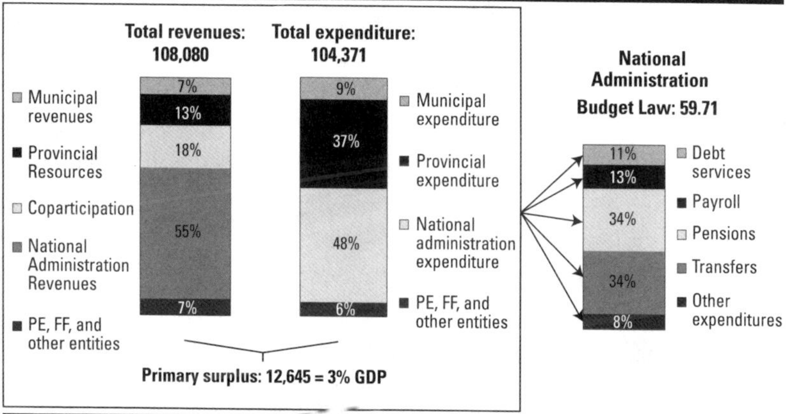

Source: Informe de Presupuesto, CIPPEC (2004).
Note: PE = public enterprises, FF = fiduciary funds.

only a portion of overall public spending. Argentina is a federal country, with a very centralized tax structure and a decentralized allocation of spending responsibilities. In 2003, the federal government collected 81 percent of total tax revenues but accounted for only 53 percent of total expenditures. The federal government automatically transferred a total of Arg$25,335 billion, or 5.85 percent of GDP, to the provinces by coparticipation and through other automatic transfers. As a result, the federal budget process accounted for only 48 percent of consolidated public spending in 2004. Figure 2.1 illustrates the percentage of total aggregate revenues and spending that actually passed through the federal budget process in 2004.

Fiscal Policy Reforms and Outcomes

The discussion now turns to a brief description of the main fiscal policy reforms and outcomes in the recent past. In 1989, following the hyperinflation, Carlos Menem was elected president, and the first part of his administration was characterized by various attempts to control inflation. The depth of the economic crisis had created an unusual opportunity for audacious, orthodox reforms in line with the international recommendations crystallized in the Washington Consensus. Indeed, an ambitious program of structural reforms was implemented during the first part of the 1990s that was supported by a large, ambiguous, and plural coalition (both political and electoral) that brought about a remarkable performance in terms of growth, increased productivity, and foreign direct investment. After a couple of unsuccessful stabilization attempts, Domingo Cavallo was appointed as finance minister in 1991, and in the same year he implemented a strict currency board regime known as the Convertibility Law. This regime implied that fiscal discipline was a necessary ingredient of the macroeconomic program, since the traditional reliance on inflationary finance of deficits was no longer a policy option. This led to several efforts to improve fiscal outcomes, such as a tax reform focused on increasing value-added tax (VAT) and income tax collection, a massive privatization program, a reform of the pension system to improve long-term fiscal solvency, several fiscal pacts with the provinces, and the implementation of an ambitious reform in the federal budget process known as the Law of Financial Administration (Ley de Administración Financiera, LAF).[6] This law increased the relative power of the finance ministry and the executive vis-à-vis spending ministries and Congress by centralizing the formulation and execution of the budget in the finance ministry and by increasing the quantity and quality of information available to the executive.

As a matter of fact, fiscal outcomes improved substantially during the 1990s, compared with Argentina's history of fiscal profligacy (see Figure 2.2). Thanks to strong economic growth, stable prices (which reversed the loss of revenues produced by the Olivera-Tanzi effect under high inflation) and revenues from a massive privatization program, the country ran a primary budget surplus for the first time in at least 30 years in 1992. Throughout the 1990s, the primary balance averaged 0.3 percent of GDP, compared with –3.1 percent in the 1980s. The overall budget balance was –2.3, against –7.8 percent in the 1980s.

Despite this dramatic improvement in long-run fiscal performance, fiscal outcomes worsened starting in 1994. The main culprits were the rapid growth of interest payments, the costly privatization of the pension system, and the increase in provincial spending.[7] Growing interest

[6] See Abuelafia, Braun, and Díaz Frers (2005) for further details about the LAF.

[7] See Cetrángolo and Jiménez (2003) for a detailed account of fiscal policy in the 1990s.

FIGURE 2.2 **Primary and Overall Budget Surplus, 1961–2007**
(percentage of GDP)

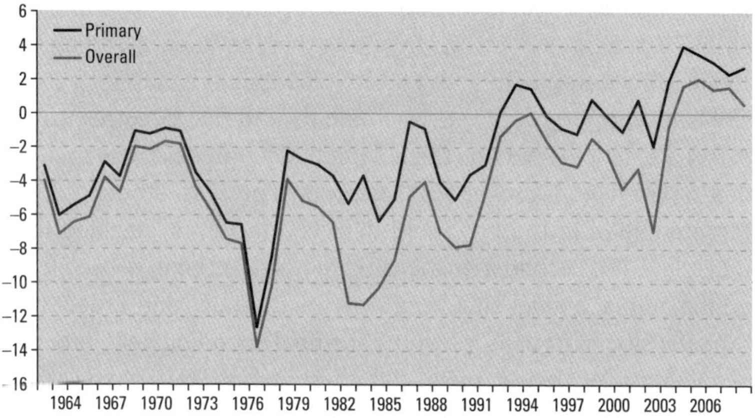

Source: Ministry of Economy.

payments account for the widening gap between the primary and overall budget balance observed in Figure 2.2 after 1995. The reform of the pension system generated a deficit that grew from about 1 percent of GDP in 1993 to an average of well over 3 percent of GDP in the period 1996–2001. This deficit arose because of the well-known transition costs involved in converting a pay-as-you-go pension system into a system of private accounts: the public system lost revenues to the newly created private pension administrators, but still had to pay for current pensioners who did not have retirement accounts. Provincial spending grew at a rate of over 5 percent per year in real terms between 1991 and 1999.

Some analysts argue that the maintenance of strong fiscal surpluses during the years of high growth in the 1990s could have averted the crisis, and that therefore, the fiscal stance was incompatible with a currency board in a small open economy subject to a volatile international context (Mussa, 2002; Fanelli and Heymann, 2002).Others argue that the magnitude of the shocks suffered by Argentina could not have been averted even with more prudent fiscal policy and that fiscal policy in place at the time was not that bad (Hausman and Velasco, 2002; Calvo, Izquierdo, and Talvi, 2002).

Although the goal of this chapter is not to resolve this dispute, a relevant ambiguity that arises from this discussion is the extent to which the budget process has enhanced or mitigated fiscal problems in Argentina. But first, a caveat: it has been shown herein that the federal budget process accounts for about half of total public spending in Argentina. Furthermore, it is worth noting that the three spending items identified by Cetrángolo and Jiménez (2003) as the culprits behind a significant proportion of the fiscal imbalances that occurred starting in 1994 are actually outside the federal budget process. The first item, interest payments, is exogenous to the budget process—these payments are determined in the bond and debt contracts, not decided in the budget law. The second item, pension reform, has been passed by law, and the annual budget simply reflects the revenues and expenditures of the pension system as it stands. The final spending item, provincial spending, is decided by provincial governments. This observation is consistent with the idea that the federal budget simply reflects the cash implications of decisions made in other arenas and could lead one to argue that the budget process is of limited importance to understanding fiscal outcomes in Argentina. Even so, important decisions regarding the allocation of resources are still made in the federal budget process, and political actors and lobbies aim to exert influence regarding these decisions. To explore this argument more formally, this section analyzes the degree of exogeneity of spending decisions in the federal budget process in Argentina and tries to address two questions. First: to what extent do governments actually decide on public expenditures? Second: are changes in spending simply exogenous or automatic responses to shocks?

How Much do Governments Decide on Public Expenditures?

To study this issue formally, a simple methodology is developed in this subsection that explores the relationship between changes in expenditure and observed changes in different economic variables in Argentina, such as GDP growth, employment, debt burden, and inflation.[8] The possibility of structural breaks prompted by the convertibility regime is also explored herein. Then, the model is applied to data for the 1980–2003

[8] See Blanchard (1990) and Alesina and Ardagna (1998) for a discussion of problems with determining the exogeneity of fiscal policy changes and a proposed methodology.

period and the residuals of the regressions (deviation from the trend) are considered as proxies of the "degree of discretionality" of different classifications of public expenditure.[9] These steps allow comparison of the results across different kinds of spending and different years.

A significant reduction in the discretionality of spending is found after 1991. The observed reduction is probably related to the privatization process and the reduction of inflation, which hardened the government budget constraint and thus limited the degree of feasible changes in spending. It can also be hypothesized that the reform of the federal budget process, brought about by the implementation of the LAF, contributed to a reduction in discretionality by improving the organization of public spending.

Regarding the discretionality observed in spending, this chapter finds that the degree in areas such as justice, defense, education, health, social services, and social security tends to be low, averaging close to 5 percent for the whole period. On the other hand, it finds a large degree of discretionality—above 20 percent and up to 100 percent for housing—of spending in housing and water and sewers and of investment spending (energy, fuel, mining, industry, and services).

The hypothesis that discretionality increases when tax revenues increase is also tested. If spending is perceived as rigid and incremental, then last year's budget in Argentina is a good proxy for what this year's budget will look like. Therefore, when tax revenues increase, the government has the possibility of allocating the additional funds at will, thus increasing the observed discretionality. This chapter in fact finds that a 1 percent increase in tax revenue in terms of GDP is associated with a 2.5 percent increase in the measure of discretionality.

The point of this discussion is to show that federal public spending has a high degree of rigidity and exogeneity, and that therefore when the topic of "who decides on public expenditures" is discussed in the context of the federal budget process, it refers to who decides on the allocation of the discretionary fraction of public spending that passes through the budget process. This is the precise meaning of what is mentioned in the second section: to a large degree, the budget is a

---

[9] See Abuelafia, Braun, and Díaz Frers (2005) for further details about the technique and results.

reflection of past decisions and agreements, rather than a reflection of the arena where these decisions are made.

Now that this point has been made, the subsequent section turns to an analysis of the federal budget process itself, and the discussion regarding the relevance of budget institutions for fiscal outcomes is revisited in the conclusion of the chapter.

THE FORMAL BUDGET PROCESS IN ARGENTINA

The budget process in Argentina consists of four stages that involve several activities, negotiations, and actors. The first stage entails the formulation of the executive's budget proposal, and the second involves the congressional discussion of the proposal and approval of the budget law. In the third stage, the proposal is implemented, and in the fourth, the execution of the budget is evaluated and controlled.

In a nutshell, during the formulation stage the president, the chief of cabinet, and the line ministries jointly decide the aggregate budgetary policy and define expenditure ceilings across ministries and agencies. The Ministry of Economy sets the budget priorities and defines the investment programs, prepares macroeconomic forecasts, and provides support to the executive in defining the expenditure ceiling. The National Budget Office (ONP), the ruling authority of the budget process, then evaluates the *anteproyectos* (preliminary budget proposals) prepared by the agencies and puts together the aggregate proposal. The executive submits to Congress the general guidelines of the budget (the only information it receives about the budget during this stage) in June.

In September, which begins the approval stage, the executive submits the proposal to Congress. Congress then evaluates the proposal through the Comisión de Presupuesto y Hacienda (budget committee) of both chambers and can summon members of the executive to discuss the issues it finds relevant. Congress is empowered to approve or reject the budget proposal, to introduce modifications, and to remove articles. If the executive uses its veto power, Congress can overrule the vetoes with a two-thirds majority. After Congress approves the budget, the executive can introduce line item vetoes.

During the next stage, the implementation stage, the executive distributes the expenditure authorizations among the line ministries—

which allocate the resources they receive among programs and formulate the *anteproyectos*—and introduces modifications. These modifications cannot alter the total expenditure and the debt level. In fact, during this stage Congress is the only institution that can modify total expenditure, the debt level, and the purpose and objective of expenditures.[10] Throughout this stage, the ONP administers the quota system (which regulates the pace of the budget's execution) and prepares the quarterly execution reports that are submitted by the executive to Congress. During the final stage, the evaluation and control stage, Congress—through the Government Accountability Office (Auditoria General de la Nación, AGN)—performs ex post controls regarding budget implementation and has to evaluate and approve the Cuenta de Inversión (the annual budget execution report elaborated by the executive).

THE ACTUAL WORKINGS OF THE BUDGET PROCESS

The actual workings of the budget process—which involve its informal rules, unwritten traditions, and informal actors—differ in practice from the formal process described in the previous section. The main finding of this chapter is that the executive plays a much more important role in practice vis-à-vis Congress than the role defined by the formal rules. In addition, several actors that are not mentioned in the formal process play a role. These actors include provincial governors, lobbies—both inside and outside the government—and international financial institutions.

In terms of arenas for decision making, the formal rules designate the approval stage in Congress as the arena in which budgetary bargains are discussed and sealed. Yet in practice most changes in the budget are made during the implementation phase, which makes it difficult to sustain agreements made in Congress.

This section revisits each stage of the budget process presented in the previous section. However, instead of focusing on the formal rules, it discusses the salient features of the actual workings of the budget process during the period 1995–2006 in Argentina.

---

[10] In 2006, Congress granted powers to the chief of cabinet to modify the budget allocation without congressional approval.

Formulation Stage

The Executive's Role

Members of the executive branch mainly conduct the formulation stage of the budget, and they follow the formal steps outlined in the previous section. The key actor is of course the president, but his or her actions are constrained by a combination of macroeconomic conditions, internal negotiations in his or her government coalition, the rigidity of the budget, legal constraints imposed by fiscal rules, agreements with international financial institutions, and the influence of powerful actors, such as provincial governors and other lobbies.

The first stage of the process involves the development of macroeconomic and revenue forecasts, which are theoretically designed to limit spending and contribute to fiscal sustainability. However, in practice these forecasts, which in Argentina are developed by the Secretariat for Economic Policy and the Treasury Secretariat, have a systematic strategic use. For example, the forecasts significantly overestimated the total revenues of the national government in Argentina between 1995 and 2001. This trend was reversed in 2002, when the total resources were underestimated by 8 percent. In 2003, revenues were again overestimated, but in this case it was not provoked by an error in the GDP growth forecast. Instead, the inflation rate was lower than expected. From 2004 to the end of 2006, revenues were once again significantly underestimated.

These Argentine forecasts are not presented with sensitivity or risk analysis, nor are they subject to public validation. In addition, they usually differ from market expectations, which tend to be closer to actual outcomes. This suggests that the government uses forecasts strategically. Since macroeconomic forecasts by the government affect the expectations of economic agents, a plausible explanation for this strategic behavior would take into account the differing goals of the government regarding both the budget and the influence of forecasts on private expectations.

During the period 1995–2001, and especially once the recession started in 1998, the government had incentives to try to influence expectations by announcing high growth forecasts. During the years in which the macroeconomic models of the Secretariat for Economic Policy predicted negative growth, political authorities insisted on presenting positive growth forecasts. Furthermore, given the growing debt burden in these years, the executive required high growth and revenue forecasts. This would allow the executive to present a budget to Congress without proposing spending cuts, which would lead to a smoother approval process. The theory was that these required cuts could easily be implemented later in the budget implementation stage. Hence, both political convenience and economic incentives promoted a systematic overestimation of growth and revenue forecasts in these years.

Following this economic crisis, however, this pattern was reversed, with the executive significantly underestimating revenues in 2004. In this case, the executive faced a high growth environment and therefore had less incentive to bolster growth via higher expectations. At the same time, given the extent of the real adjustment in spending that followed the devaluation—inflation caused an increase in nominal revenues, without a corresponding increase in the most relevant spending categories such as wages and pensions—the executive had no problem presenting a politically appealing budget, at least in nominal terms, to Congress. Finally, as the executive was in the middle of a debt renegotiation process, it faced further incentives to be prudent in its macroeconomic estimates. For all these reasons, in this case the strategy of systematic overestimation was seemingly replaced with one of underestimation of revenues. However, there is a constant: the strategic use of macroeconomic forecasts by the executive.

Once the executive develops its revenue forecasts, the president, together with the national cabinet, establishes the expenditure ceilings for each ministry. In years of high revenue growth, such as 2003 or 2004, the president has had more flexibility to push his or her agenda by allocating resources to preferred programs and provinces. In years of low growth, given that resources are probably overestimated, adjustments to the budget have occurred in the implementation phase.

While the budget is being prepared, the heads of each ministry, secretariat, and government program try to obtain the maximum amount of resources possible for their jurisdictions. In this stage, the chief of cabinet is a relevant actor because he or she is in charge of resolving the divergences that may arise among ministries regarding resource allocation. There are no formal rules about this issue, but the common solution is that the disputes among line ministries are resolved by satisfying demands at least partially. If an agreement cannot be reached, the president allocates the resources. The results of these negotiations are influenced by the relative strength of the ministries.

Constraints Faced by the Executive

Apart from the constraints of the macroeconomic conditions and internal negotiations, the president faces another limit to his or her ability to implement policy priorities via the budget process: the rigidity of expenditure in Argentina. For example, looking back on 2004, around 78 percent of spending included in the budget that year can be considered rigid. This figure includes wages, pension payments, specific transfers to provinces, debt payments, and other payments that theoretically cannot be changed without affecting acquired rights of individuals or without renegotiating federal agreements and debt contracts. This rigidity most likely constrained the president's ability to implement his desired policies because he could modify only the remaining 22 percent of federal expenditure.

During the formulation stage, the president is also constrained by legislation designed to secure fiscal discipline, and, at least until 2006, by agreements with the International Monetary Fund (IMF) that stipulate deficit limits. However, these constraints are often violated at the budget implementation stage. For instance, faced with a deteriorating budget balance and growing debt payments, the Argentine Congress approved a fiscal solvency law in September 1999. The law stipulated the adoption of pluriannual budgeting, the creation of a countercyclical fiscal fund, and the implementation of transparency measures. The law established that fiscal balance had to be reached no later than 2003 and it set nominal targets for nonfinancial public sector deficits between 1999 and 2002. In its first year, the law was broken, as the observed deficit was significantly higher than the target (3.1 percent versus 1.9 percent of GDP). The 2001 budget law modified the targets and extended the deadline for achieving the balanced budget to 2005. Again, the target was unfulfilled in 2001.

Finally, during this stage the executive must deal with the influence of lobbies and pressure groups, from both inside and outside the government. Spiller and Tommasi (2003) highlight the important impact that provincial political leaders have on Argentine national policy. They also point out that governors and local party bosses are highly influential in regard to legislative careers. They conclude that key political transactions are made at the level of provincial party leaders.

The Formulation Stage as Part of the Political Game

The Argentine budget process is part of a larger policymaking process that involves several other dimensions over which political actors bargain and compete. It involves negotiations between the national government and the provincial governors. For example, the executive might use the budget as a vote-buying mechanism by means of pork barrel investments in some provinces to guarantee the legislators' support for another issue. However, it is not clear that governors exert their influence in the budget formulation stage. Rather, agreements between the president and provincial governors appear at this stage as done deals and contribute to the rigidity of the budget process. For example, the decision by the national government to take over the deficit of provincial pension systems in 1997 became part of the budget, but was not strictly a decision made at the formulation phase. There is a continual negotiation between the president and provincial governors in informal arenas, and the budget process simply reflects some of the agreements reached. For instance, in 1999, the national government committed to financing an increasing percentage of the provincial pension system deficit. This policy was a result of the negotiation that took place during the sanction of the 1999 Fiscal Pact. Through this pact, fixed monthly transfers to the provinces were set, the national and subnational governments committed to approving a new tax-sharing law, and the provincial governments committed to passing both solvency and fiscal responsibility laws in their provinces.[11] As an extra incentive for the deal, besides the predictability of resources for the provinces, the federal government offered to finance the provincial pension systems' deficits, which otherwise would have become unsustainable in the long run.[12] With these commitments, the national government would keep a larger share of incremental revenues expected from both an economic

[11] As previously mentioned, these subnational laws were hardly fulfilled.

[12] Some provinces transferred their pension systems in 1994 (see Nicolini et al., 2002, for further details).

recovery and an increase in federal tax pressure as compensation for the absorption of the risk involved in the fixed amount (see Gonzalez, Rosenblatt, and Webb, 2002).

Other pressure groups influence the formulation stage—for example, trade unions, pensioners, and corporations—and can have a significant impact on the budget. For instance, towards the end of President Menem's term, teachers' unions established a permanent protest known as the *carpa blanca* (white tent) in front of Congress to demand a salary increase. As a result of this protest, a special fund was created—Fondo de Incentivo Docente—that provided an additional salary payment for teachers. At the beginning this extra payment was financed by an earmarked tax on motor vehicles, but later this vehicle tax was eliminated and the national treasury provided the funding. As a result of resource shortages, the government delayed the payment of this funding for some time, accumulating several periods of debt. The union lobbied and finally managed to introduce extra resources into the 2003 and 2004 budgets to cancel this debt.

Finally, there is some evidence on the discretionary use of funds by certain Argentine presidents through the allocation of investment funds to their home provinces. For example, La Rioja was the most favored province during the Menem presidency, while the Buenos Aires province gained 64 million (13 percent of the total budget) during Duhalde's brief presidency. Santa Cruz received Arg$236 million (15 percent of the total budget, despite representing close to 1 percent of the total population) under Kirchner. Each of these presidents was governor of his home province prior to his term. This suggests that the political goals of presidents in general include the provision of resources to their home provinces and the power to achieve this goal through the budget process.

Approval Stage

The Role of Congress

Formally, the constitution and laws provide Congress with a key role in the budget process in Argentina. However, in practice Congress has played a weak role, limited to marginal changes in budget decisions associated with pork barrel spending items tagged on by eager legislators, rather than the role as given by the constitution of discussing the executive proposal in depth and monitoring and evaluating budget implementation.

It is important to highlight some characteristics of the approval process in the period under study, 1995–2006. In the first place, and contrary to previous practice, the budget proposal was submitted within the legal dates in almost every year (the only exceptions were 1995 and 1997, in which the proposals were submitted six and two days after the established date, respectively). Secondly, all budgets except the one in 2002 (the year of the default and devaluation, which forced a sharp revision in the budget proposal in the first quarter) were approved by both chambers of Congress before the beginning of the corresponding fiscal year. The average time that elapsed in the budget approval stage during this period was 87 days. The least time was spent in 2002 (29 days) and the most in 2000 (104 days). The lower chamber used, on average, 84 percent of the total time to analyze, modify, and approve the corresponding budget. The Senate approved the budgets within an average of 14 days of receiving them.

In all proposals approved by Congress, the president vetoed some articles. The lowest number of vetoes was introduced in the 1997 budget, in which only one partial veto was introduced. The president used his veto power 18 times in the 2003 budget proposal—16 articles were completely vetoed and four were partially vetoed. Congress can override presidential vetoes by two-thirds of the total votes. During the period under study, Congress overrode the executive's vetoes on only three occasions, in regard to the 1998, 1999, and 2003 budget laws. These modifications were focused on the economic promotion scheme (tax breaks for investment in some provinces), small public works, and other minimal changes in expenditure.

Rodriguez and Bonvecchi (2004) argue that the veto of the economic promotion scheme was a standard political maneuver played as follows: the executive would introduce the proposed extension of the scheme. The legislators from the affected provinces could show to their constituents that they had succeeded in obtaining more pork, and then they could blame the executive for vetoing it. The veto overrides of 1998 and 1999 were exceptions, caused by the need of legislators to sustain cooperation among themselves and by the pressure of provinces not involved in the Peronist internal struggle to extract the maximum possible revenues. The small size and relevance of veto overriding incidences during the period is consistent with Congress's having a marginal role in the budget process.

It is also important to note that Congress lacks institutionalized technical ability to analyze the budget and question the executive's assumptions. There is no congressional budget office, and legislators have to rely on their usually small and nonexpert staff.

Modifications to the Budget by Congress

To what extent does Congress actually modify the budget? In four out of the nine years studied, these changes were lower than 0.5 percent of the budget in absolute value, and in two others, they were below 2 percent. Exceptions were 1997, 2002, and 2003. In 1997, the high percentage of change (6.1 percent) was due to the agreement between the national government and some provincial governments to take over the funding of the deficits of provincial pension schemes. This agreement was signed after the executive's proposal entered Congress and therefore had to be included in the approval stage. Clearly, this last case is consistent with the weak role of Congress and it is not really an exception. The changes in the 2002 budget (the highest in this period at 12.6 percent) reflected the inevitable adaptation of the proposal to the crisis. In 2003, the changes, which represented a decrease of 6 percent of the budget, were caused by the executive's attempt to include an unspecified item of spending of 3.7 million in order to gain flexibility to face the volatile economic context. This item was rejected following a public outcry from the opposition and independent analysis. The fact that this is the only case in which Congress significantly changed the budget provides another example of the weak role of Congress in the budget process.

It could be argued, following Jones (2001), that the fact that Congress does not make significant changes in the budget is not sufficient evidence of its weak role. Rather, it could be that Congress makes few changes because legislators negotiate with the executive in the implementation phase or that the executive tailors its proposal to fit the preferences of Congress so as to ensure the budget's approval. However, most interviewees rejected this claim, arguing that the preparation phase of the budget is mainly an internal matter in the executive and that legislators do not have much say at that stage. Furthermore, the next subsection shows that significant changes in the budget occur in the implementation phase. Therefore, agreements in Congress included at the approval stage do not appear to be credible or sustainable, since the executive has the power to unravel them at the implementation stage. This power is enhanced by the weakness of the oversight and control institutions.

Implementation Stage

Roles of the Executive and Congress in Practice

Formally, the implementation stage of the budget process is envisaged as one in which the executive simply implements the allocations approved by Congress in the most efficient manner possible. If any significant change has to be made to the size or allocation of the budget, Congress must approve it. However, in the past the executive has clearly exerted its political power at this stage and has increasingly put Congress in the back seat of the budget process.

There are two main ways in which the executive changes the budget. The first is through a change to the approved budget (*crédito vigente*) by using decrees (Decretos de Necesidad y Urgencia). In this case the executive uses—or rather, abuses—the power conceded by the LAF to increase the total amount of the budget in case of an emergency. In theory, whenever the executive promulgates this kind of decree it has to be submitted, with justification, to Congress. A bicameral committee is empowered to overrule these decrees; however, the committee was not constituted until November 2006 and therefore prior to this, the executive could modify the budget unchecked.

During the 1995–2003 period, the executive systematically modified the corresponding budget law, increasing the total amount in almost all years. The exceptions were 2001 and 2002, in which the executive actually decreased the budget. The decrease in the 2001 budget was due to the zero-deficit rule—an emergency rule that called for government expenditures to be less than or equal to revenues each month—and a 13 percent reduction in nominal wages. In 2002, the reduction in the budget was mainly for debt interest payments (see Figure 2.3).

FIGURE 2.3 Changes between the Bill, Budget Law, and Executed Budget *(weighted by discretionality index)*

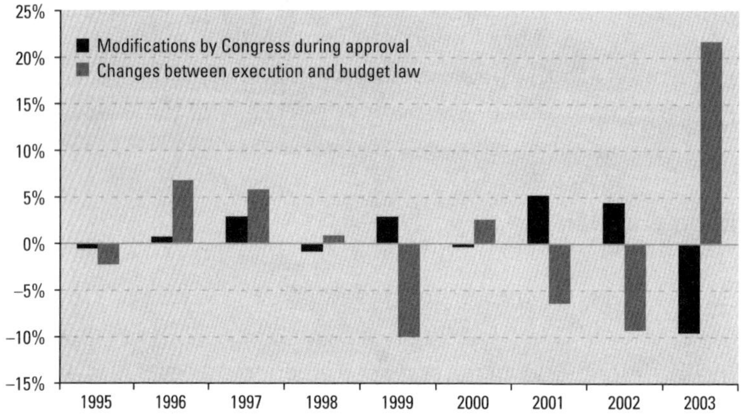

Source: Authors' elaboration.

The second way in which the executive changes the budget allocation is through the discretional administration of the quota system. In theory, the quota system is simply an administrative tool by which the budget is implemented. In practice, it has been used in years of overestimation of resources as a de facto way for the executive to decide on budget allocations. By choosing which agencies and ministries receive their full quota and which receive less, the Treasury Secretariat can decide the actual allocation of the budget. This allocation has often differed substantially from the allocation approved by Congress. As mentioned, revenue forecasts were in general too optimistic in the period 1995–2001. This led to insufficient revenues to cover planned expenditures, which made it necessary for the executive to make an adjustment. An across-the-board adjustment was out of the question, because of the rigidity of several budget items. Therefore, the executive was left with the option of implementing selective cuts, related to minimizing political costs.

In theory, Congress is the only branch of government entitled to modify total expenditures, the total authorized debt level, and the economic classification of expenditures and their objective and function. In practice, the combination of overestimation of revenues in the formulation stage with the discretionary use of the quota system has led to the erosion of the actual influence of Congress on budgetary decisions and left the executive with the ability to decide changes in budget allocations unilaterally. From the analysis of the degree of underexecution of expenditure in different years, it is clear that, as argued by Baldrich (2003), with the crisis in 2001 this became a strategy to limit spending and avoid the economic collapse that ensued. The preponderance of the executive is also evident whenever the difference between the approved budget and the executed budget is considered.

The analysis of the role of the executive and Congress in regard to changes in discretionary spending shows that when the actual possibility of making changes is taken into account, the relative power of the executive is even more evident. The changes in absolute value at the implementation stage are systematically larger than at the approval stage. The bottom line is that when an analysis is made of who decides on the public expenditures that are actually considered in the federal budget process, the answer is that clearly the executive has a preponderant role.

The Effect of Rigid Spending in the Implementation Stage

Returning to the issue of the rigidity of spending discussed in regard to the formulation stage, it is important to note that the rigidity of certain budget items is also related to ease of execution. The degree of underexecution is not homogeneously distributed among the different budget components. Rather, the degree of execution of consumption and durable goods is systematically lower than that for other budget components, and it is higher for payroll expenses, transfers, and debt services (at least before default).

Thus, expenditures that are classified as rigid also appear to be those more likely to be executed. This probably reflects in part the rigidity itself—it is legally difficult to pay lower salaries and pensions, for instance—and in part the relative technical difficulty of executing some items of expenditure, such as investment projects and consumption goods that require complex purchasing processes, such as auctions. This result coincides with the findings herein that there is a learning process in the budget's execution. It has been found that higher rotation of ministries—and of the so-called parallel bureaucracy—undermines the degree of execution of the budget. Among the other variables that affect the execution are the source of funding and the percentage of consumption and durable goods and payrolls.[13]

Other Relevant Actors

In terms of the relevant actors besides the president and Congress at the implementation stage, the Treasury Secretariat, via the ONP, is in charge of setting expenditure quotas for the line ministries and agencies. As was mentioned above, the government, in case of fiscal tightening, uses this system strategically. The budget offices of the agencies receive expenditure limits each quarter and have to distribute them, following the guidelines given by the head of the ministry, among different programs and activities. Baldrich (2003) indicates that the fiscal tightening process in Argentina is highly decentralized; although the Treasury Secretariat sets the expenditure limits, the final decision on what expenditures to cut is taken at the ministry level by the ministry's head.

The roles of the ministers and other agency heads are also very important at this stage. They manage the quotas within their agencies; as such, they protect their budget from cuts and exert pressure to obtain resources for their jurisdictions. A classic question regarding bureaucracy is its capacity to influence policy vis-à-vis elected officials.[14] Spiller and Tommasi (2003) argue that the high rotation of the bureaucracy in Argentina limits its power, and therefore its capacity, to act as enforcer of intertemporal political agreements. They point out that the lack of bureaucratic power leads to unstable and lower-quality policies. This chapter finds evidence consistent with this hypothesis: more experienced ministers can protect and increase their budget more efficiently and can execute a higher percentage of their budgets.

The high rotation of the bureaucracy leads to problems in the execution and efficiency of the budget. An interesting exception to this hindrance, however, is the fact that the bureaucracy that is responsible for most of the budget process in Argentina—the Treasury Secretariat—has shown remarkable stability relative to other areas of government

---

[13] See Abuelafia, Braun, and Díaz Frers (2005) for further details.

[14] For a classic study, see Niskanen (1971).

and furthermore is considered to have a high degree of professionalism. The personnel from the Argentine Ministry of Economy are more experienced and more highly educated and are in higher echelons in their career compared to other employees in the National Civil Service Career System (Sistema Nacional de Profesión Administrativa, SINAPA).

Interviewees both within and outside the ministry argued that this is because of the complexity of managing the budget system. In other line ministries, political appointees can bring in their loyal followers and allocate jobs and funds to them; yet if this were done at the Treasury Secretariat, the budget system would grind to a halt. Furthermore, political appointees to this department tend to be highly qualified and therefore value the expertise of the established bureaucracy.

According to some interviewees, the IMF has been another relevant actor at this stage of the budget process in some periods. The agreements signed by the Argentine government with the IMF have usually established quarterly fiscal deficit targets. Consequently, these targets have affected the rhythm of the budget execution, as the government has sometimes postponed some spending from one quarter to another to fulfill its commitment.

In summary, Congress clearly has a weak role during the implementation stage, and its modifications introduced at this stage are almost minimal. Congress delegates—in the budget law itself in some cases—or the executive entitles itself to the powers that the LAF stipulates for Congress to modify the budget law. The chief of cabinet has to submit the quarterly execution report to Congress. When this happens, Congress can ask for explanations regarding changes and underexecuted expenditures. These are just questions that do not have any legal consequences.

In addition to legal delegation of powers, the executive has also increased its power by creating special funds to implement its policy goals while avoiding the obligation to transfer extra tax resources to provinces automatically via the coparticipation scheme. During the last 10 years, the executive—in the majority of the cases—has created 15 different fiduciary funds and has excluded six agencies from the national budget. The funds have been created through different legal instruments (decrees, laws, and resolutions). Fiduciary funds and excluded agencies accounted for 9 percent of the federal budget in 2005. These funds have financial autarky, legal entity and own assets, can formulate their own budgets, and have to submit the budgets to the ONP for evaluation. The executive is entitled to approve their budgets without congressional intervention. There have also been instances of removal of programs from the budget by initiative of bureaucrats (AFIP) or provinces and lobbies (Fondo del Tabaco). These instances demonstrate the advantages for specific programs of escaping the budget process and obtaining earmarked funding, so as to avoid oversight and executive discretion.

Evaluation and Control

A corollary of the weakness of Congress is that oversight by congressional audit and control institutions is weak. This section analyzes the role of the Accounting Office of the State (Sindicatura General de la Nación, SIGEN) and the AGN, the two public entities empowered by the LAF with oversight and control responsibilities in the budget process. The SIGEN is the internal control institution of the executive and responds to the president. The AGN is the external auditor and formally responds to Congress. Berensztein, Ortiz, and Peña (2000) argue that AGN audits are sparse, usually untimely, do not go above and beyond legal compliance, and have not been used as effective tools to improve budget efficiency or punish corrupt practices.

The main problem affecting the way control mechanisms work relates to their being highly politicized; that is, they are subject to political interference and manipulation by powerful actors who are able to limit and/or distort the functioning of the agencies and personnel involved in the process. Both the AGN and the SIGEN are influenced by those behaviors, yet the former is somewhat more politicized than the latter. This has to do with their respective institutional settings.

A representative of the opposition chairs the AGN; thus it meets the existing formal requirement. Yet rather than providing an independent and fair evaluation and control of public expenditures, the AGN report is used as an additional resource at the bargaining table. Thus, only certain events, agencies, or officers are subject to auditing procedures. Also, the severity of these procedures depends on politically driven strategies and may fade away. In sum, if a particular agency, program, or officer is audited and irregularities are identified, the AGN report may be used as a bargaining chip before it becomes public.

The SIGEN is arguably organized and staffed more effectively than the AGN. The SIGEN's main advantage stems from its capacity to control constantly each jurisdiction of the state, which permits internal auditors to have a better grasp and knowledge of the respective operations. However, the agencies that are audited are often reluctant to provide the requested information in due time and manner. Also, there is a trend not to audit certain issues depending on their political significance and/or according to the electoral cycle. Finally, the auditing committee must report to the president, which means that the president has discretionary powers to manage a specific case.

Another important issue to be considered is the fact that auditing controls are carried out ex post, while no preventive device exists to provide for more rigorous, random inspections of areas suspected of corruption or other misconduct. Furthermore, an additional topic refers to the moment in time when auditing reports are presented. There is broad evidence that both the SIGEN and the AGN run behind schedule, sometimes postponing deadlines for years. As such, considering the habitual high turnover in public administration, individuals eventually responsible for potential wrongdoing or questionable decisions may no longer hold office once the audit is complete.[15]

The bottom line is that oversight and control mechanisms are very weak in Argentina. They generate some formality in compliance with regulations, but they do not serve as enforcers of efficiency and honesty in public administration.

THE CONTRIBUTION OF THE BUDGET PROCESS TO IMPROVEMENTS IN FISCAL SOLVENCY, EFFICIENCY IN PUBLIC SPENDING, AND REPRESENTATIVENESS OF ALLOCATIONS

It is not straightforward to link the institutions of the budget process to fiscal policy outcomes, since there are many factors that influence these outcomes, and as illustrated earlier, the federal budget process accounts for only a part of fiscal policy in Argentina. However,

---

[15] For example, the AGN presented the 1994 auditing report of PAMI (the social program for retired citizens and pensioners in Argentina) in August 1999.

the reform of the budget process in the early 1990s was probably a contributing factor to the improvement witnessed in fiscal solvency. The reason is that the postreform process is very hierarchical: the president is clearly the key player in the budget process, and he or she has more incentives for overall fiscal discipline than Congress and other political actors.

Regarding the contribution of the budget process to efficiency in public spending, although it is hard to obtain evidence, clearly a high level of rotation in the Argentine bureaucracy contributes to the under-execution of the budget, which can be taken as a proxy for inefficiency. The current political economy of the budget process—by which there are no incentives in the line ministries to generate a professional bureaucracy to increase the efficiency of spending and in which Congress has low incentives to monitor and control spending—is not conducive to efficiency in public spending. Furthermore, the fact that the executive has so much unchecked power in the process leads to political abuse of public resources, in which political gain is a more important criterion than efficiency and representativeness.

The evidence presented in this chapter on the distribution of funds to the president's province is consistent with the existence of unchecked executive power. Another issue that affects the representativeness of budgetary allocations is the level of overrepresentation in Congress. This means that public resources are not necessarily allocated to the poorest regions, or those most in need of public funding, but rather to those regions with the possibility of extracting resources from the common pool. Based on the calculations for this chapter, the amount of tax payments and resources allocated to finance public goods varies extensively among provinces, even when the comparisons are made between provinces with similar economic characteristics.

This result is explained in part by the fact that small provinces are highly overrepresented in Congress. Porto and Sanguinetti (1993) argue that this explains, in part, the inequality in the distribution of coparticipation funds across provinces. They point out that there is a negative correlation between the population per representative and the net fiscal benefit (Figure 2.4). This implies that provinces that are overrepresented (have less population per representative) receive a larger fiscal benefit. Similar results were obtained from a simple regression analysis.

FIGURE 2.4 **Population per Representative (Underrepresentation) as an Explanation for the Distribution of the Net Fiscal Benefit per Province**

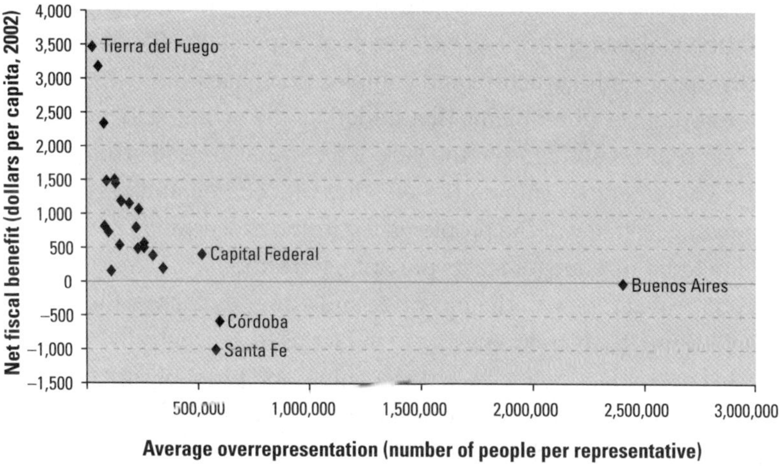

Source: Authors' elaboration

CONCLUSIONS

This chapter has presented the actual workings of the budget process in Argentina. Overall, the picture that emerges is that the president is the leading actor in the budget process. He or she seeks to maximize his or her objectives, which include obtaining reelection, maintaining high levels of support from public opinion, and helping his or her home province. To achieve these objectives, in terms of the budget process, the president needs to sustain a sufficient degree of fiscal solvency—probably below the optimal level, but above the level desired by other actors, such as provincial governors—to provide a set of national public goods, as well as pork for his or her province and political coalitions. The president also needs to overcome a series of constraints, which include the rigidity of the budget, fiscal rules, and agreements with international financial institutions. He or she has to deal with macroeconomic shocks—which require changes in the level and composition of spending—and with pressure from other actors, such as provincial governors, legislators, and lobbies. Budgetary outcomes are a result of this game.

Rigidity, high ministerial rotation, and executive discretionality help explain why budget allocations are inefficient and, in many cases, particularistic—as opposed to representative. Social conditions across provinces can change, but the rigidity in budget allocations makes it difficult for leaders to respond. Furthermore, high levels of ministerial rotation makes it difficult to execute public spending efficiently, especially that for infrastructure and complex purchases.

Another set of problems that underlies the actual workings of the budget process stems from the lack of a consensual and strong political commitment to enforce the existing procedures and regulations. For instance, many of the problems regarding executive discretion can be limited if revenue forecasts are not used strategically. Yet there are no political actors with the incentive and power to change the current equilibrium, in which forecasts are in fact used strategically.

In fact, budget politics is not the only—and probably not the most important—policy area in which the rule of law is not applied. As described by Spiller and Tommasi (2003), other major policy issues are also characterized by the constant manipulation, modification, and erosion of legal procedures according to the short-term preferences of influential political and social actors.

In the context of such an ambiguous environment, there is a high probability that the most important rules and regulations can be changed, limited, or even ignored. Noncooperative behavior prevails, as actors develop strategies that assume short-term horizons and that discount the eventual consequences of an ex post facto regulatory change. As the literature on collective action suggests, this kind of strategic interaction entails the creation of intricate vicious circles that are very difficult to eliminate.

There is, however, a natural temptation to suggest possible changes in the existing budget process in order to make it more transparent, effective, and accountable. Indeed, any institutional mechanism can be improved after the elaboration of proper diagnosis and reasonable proposals. Moreover, the most logical strategy seems to be to synchronize with international standards in terms of capacity building and institutional strengthening. Yet in the absence of a previous substantial effort to promote a democratic compromise in regard to the need to enforce the rule of law and reverse the negative incentives for institutional development documented by Spiller and Tommasi (2003), almost any policy recommendation may seem futile.

REFERENCES

Abuelafia, E., M. Braun, and L. Díaz Frers. 2005. Coparticipación Federal: una mirada más allá del debate de corto plazo. Documento de Políticas Públicas N°3, Center for the Implementation of Public Policies Promoting Equity and Growth (CIPPEC), Buenos Aires, Argentina.

Alesina, A., and S. Ardagna. 1998. Tales of Fiscal Adjustment. *Economic Policy* 27: 489–545.

Aninat, C., J. Landregan, P. Navia, and J. Vial. 2006. Political Institutions, Policymaking Processes, and Policy Outcomes in Chile. Research Network Working Paper R-521. Inter-American Development Bank, Washington, DC.

Baldrich, J. 2003. The Political Economy of Short Run Fiscal Policy under Fund Supported Agreements: Some Evidences from Argentina. Buenos Aires, Argentina. Unpublished.

Berensztein, S., L. Ortiz, and M. Peña. 2000. Transparencia, instituciones y reforma: la economia politica del proceso de ejecucion y ajuste presupuestario. *Revista Internacional de Presupuesto Publico Año 27(44)* November–December: 61–94.

Blanchard, O. 1990. Suggestions for a New Set of Fiscal Indicators. Economics and Statistics Department Working Paper No. 79. Organisation for Economic Co-operation and Development (OECD), Paris.

Calvo, G., G. Izquierdo, and E. Talvi. 2002. Sudden Stops, The Real Exchange Rate and Fiscal Sustainability: Argentina's Lessons. Research Department, Inter-American Development Bank, Washington, DC. Unpublished.

Cetrángolo, O., and J. P. Jiménez. 2003. Política fiscal en Argentina durante el régimen de convertibilidad. Economic Commission for Latin America and the Caribbean (ECLAC), Santiago, Chile. Unpublished.

Fanelli, J., and D. Heymann. 2002. *Monetary Dilemmas: Argentina in MERCOSUR*. Serie Estudios y Perspectivas. Santiago: Economic Commission for Latin America and the Caribbean (ECLAC).

Gonzalez, C., D. Rosenblatt, and S. Webb. 2002. Stabilizing Intergovernmental Transfers in Latin America: A Complement to National/

Subnational Fiscal Rules? World Bank Policy Research Paper No. 2869. World Bank, Washington, DC.

Hausman, R., and A. Velasco. 2002. Hard Money's Soft Underbelly: Understanding the Argentine Crisis. Kennedy School of Government, Harvard University, Cambridge. Unpublished.

Jones, M. 2001. Political Institutions and Public Policy in Argentina: An Overview of the Formation and Execution of the National Budget. In S. Haggard and M. D. McCubbins, eds., *Presidents, Parliaments, and Policy.* Cambridge, England: Cambridge University Press.

Jones, M., S. Saiegh, P. Spiller, and M. Tommasi. 2001. Amateur Legislators–Professional Politicians: The Consequences of Party-Centered Electoral Rules in a Federal System. *American Journal of Political Science* 46(3) July: 656–69.

Kopits, G. 2004. *Rules-Based Fiscal Policy in Emerging Markets: Background, Analysis and Prospects.* Washington, DC: Palgrave Macmillan.

Mussa, M. 2002. *Argentina and the Fund: From Triumph to Tragedy.* Policy Analyses in International Economics 67. Washington, DC.: Peterson Institute for International Economics.

Nicolini, J. P., J. Posadas, J. Sanguinetti, P. Sanguinetti, and M. Tommasi. 2002. Decentralization, Fiscal Discipline in Sub-national Governments, and the Bail Out Problem: The Case of Argentina. Research Network Working Paper No. R-467. Inter-American Development Bank, Washington, DC.

Niskanen, W. 1971. *Bureaucracy and Representative Government.* Chicago: Aldine-Atherton.

Porto, A., and P. Sanguinetti. 1993. Descentralizacion fiscal en America Latina: el caso Argentino. Serie Politica Fiscal No 45. Economic Commission for Latin America and the Caribbean (ECLAC)/GTZ, Santiago, Chile.

Rodriguez, J., and A. Bonvecchi. 2004. *El papel del poder legislativo en el proceso presupuestario: la experiencia Argentina.* Serie macroeconomia para el desarrollo no. 32. Santiago: Economic Commission for Latin America and the Caribbean (ECLAC).

Scartasini, C., and M. Olivera. 2003. Political Institutions, Policymaking Process and Political Outcomes: A Guide to Theoretical Models and Possible Empirics. Design Paper 2. Inter-American Development Bank, Washington, DC.

Spiller, P., E. Stein, and M. Tommasi. 2003. Political Institutions, Policy-making Processes and Policy Outcomes: An Intertemporal Transactions Framework. Design Paper 1. Inter-American Development Bank, Washington, DC.

Spiller, P., and M. Tommasi. 2003. The Institutional Foundations of Public Policy: A Transactions Approach with Application to Argentina. *Journal of Law, Economics, and Organization* 19(2) October: 281–306.

3

Presidential Power, Fiscal Responsibility Laws, and the Allocation of Spending: The Case of Brazil

Lee Alston, Marcus Melo, Bernardo Mueller, and Carlos Pereira

BRAZIL'S RECENT BUDGETARY HISTORY

This chapter analyzes the budgetary process in Brazil to determine who decides on public expenditures, and concentrates on the period between 1988, when the current Brazilian constitution was adopted, and 2008. The focus is not so much on the actual fiscal outcomes that emerge from the budgetary process during this period, but rather on the policymaking process that generates those outcomes. This analysis involves looking not only at the budgetary rules and institutions, but also at the political institutions that determine the players involved and their motivations, incentives, and power. In essence: who can initiate proposals that affect the budget and spending, who can vote, who can veto, and what is the sequence in which these actions take place? The political institutions set the formal and informal rules under which these players interact, that is, the policymaking game. The policy space also influences the game and the outcomes. The acts of crafting, approving, executing, and controlling a budget incite specific types of intertemporal political transactions among the various players that set the stage for the budgetary policymaking game. The final outcomes from this game will vary over time, as the result of a shift in players and setting as well as unexpected economic and political shocks. However, the outcomes will tend to have certain common characteristics.

Political institutions in Brazil provide the president with a wide and powerful array of instruments with which to pursue his or her policy preferences, such as decree and veto power as well as the ability to dispense pork to members of Congress. Most importantly, political incentives to induce economic growth and stability influence the president's preferences over budgetary outcomes. In addition, global financial markets, which are extremely sensitive to countries' policy choices, provide further incentives for macroeconomic discipline. Furthermore, despite the high levels of presidential powers, these are not absolute. There are a series of constraints that effectively restrict what the president can do.[1] Among these checks are the judiciary, the constitution, public prosecutors, and a free and active press. The result is that a political system with a strong president in place—who is subject to incentives to pursue "good" economic policy within a supportive institutional framework—yields a policymaking process that has several merits, among them the capacity to adapt to shocks and the tendency to move toward sound reform, even if at a gradual pace. This is not to say that policy outcomes have been outstanding in Brazil. Clearly, economic growth and several other indicators have left much to be desired in the period under study in this chapter (1988–2008). However, over this period much has been accomplished in terms of reform, despite several internal and external shocks. This includes not only more obvious achievements, such as the end of inflation, economic liberalization, privatizations, and regulation, but also a less visible process whereby many unsound fundamental constitutional provisions have been gradually changed over the years, such as the recentralization of the federalist structure, which has been crucial for allowing the president to pursue fiscal discipline. The upshot is a gradual—if bumpy—process through which reform and institutional strengthening mature and generate the basis for positive economic outcomes in the future.

Fiscal Performance in Brazil

Brazil's fiscal history over previous decades places the country within the group of underperformers and points to the existence of funda-

[1] These assertions are elaborated in Alston et al. (2006); this is a project in which the same theoretical framework as the one discussed herein is applied to the general policymaking process in Brazil.

mental problems. Figure 3.1 shows the net debt of the public sector as a percentage of GDP from 1991 to 2008. Not only has the level of debt been very high throughout this whole period, but for a long period, the tendency appeared to indicate an unsustainable path, as the average level of net debt for the period since 1999 has increased substantially compared to the average prior to that year. These data certainly do not seem compatible with the claim about the merits of the Brazilian policymaking process, which this chapter extends to the budgetary process, even if one considers the slight improvement in the past four years.

However, by simply looking at policy outcomes, such as the data in Figure 3.1, one will miss much of the underlying context through which policymaking has evolved over the period since 1988. The early period until 1994 was a convoluted time, marred by high inflation and the impeachment of President Collor in 1992. With the end of inflation in the first term of the Cardoso government (1995–1998), fiscal policy became even more lax, and the public sector's debt started to grow at alarming rates (see Figure 3.1). This behavior was clearly unsustainable, and an overvalued exchange rate and fiscal profligacy led to several speculative attacks against the currency. After the crises erupted in Mexico, Asia, and Russia, all bets were that Brazil would be the next country to succumb. During this period, the Brazilian Congress passed

FIGURE 3.1 Net Debt of the Public Sector
(percent of GDP)

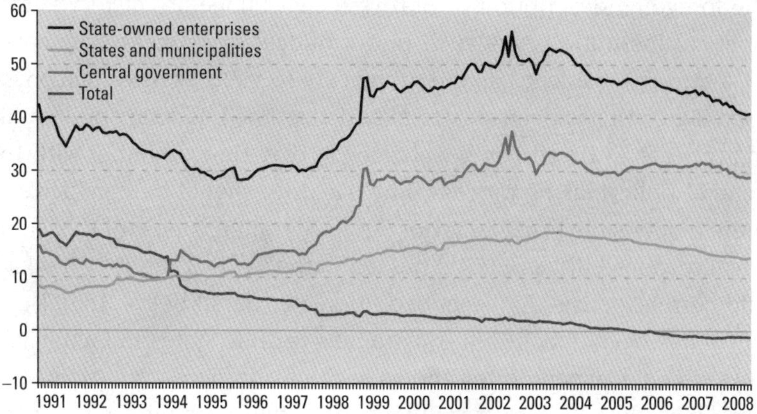

Source: Banco Central do Brasil, *Boletim de Finanças Públicas*.

several crucial structural reforms, and with the end of inflation and increased incomes for much of the population, President Cardoso experienced high levels of popularity, allowing him to clinch reelection easily in 1998. Once the election was won and the devaluation allowed to occur in January 1999, the government was faced with a very severe credibility problem in which the only way to avoid a prolonged and destructive crisis would be to signal to the markets the government's intent and ability to regain fiscal control. Given the country's image as an underperformer in this area, this was not an easy task, and most prognoses were pessimistic.

Nevertheless, now that it was absolutely crucial that fiscal discipline be adopted, the government met the challenge. Starting in 1999 and lasting through 2008, the government has consistently set and met extremely tough primary surplus targets. It is important to stress the immense effort that meeting these targets has required of the government. It has involved systematically denying expenditures that have been approved in the budgetary process and that have important constituencies. It is remarkable that the Brazilian government has been not only willing, but also able, to go through with the unpleasant politics involved in achieving these surpluses. This feat is consistent with the framework discussed herein, in which the president is the dominant player who faces virtuous incentives. It has been possible for the president to overcome the natural resistance to expenditure cuts and to ensure the primary surpluses only because of his or her immense control over the budgetary process, in particular in the execution phase. The point of the foregoing description of Brazil's recent budgetary history is that political institutions are such that a budgetary process dominated by a strong president has the propensity to yield positive outcomes, even if growth has been slow to materialize. The budgetary policymaking process in Brazil has been evolving over time, together with the general policymaking process, in a way that should be conducive to more responsible fiscal behavior. An important example of this is the fiscal responsibility law (FRL) passed in the wake of the 1999 banking and currency crisis. As described in greater detail below, the FRL in Brazil has been effective in constraining federal, state, and municipal governments' expenditures and as such has decisively contributed to fiscal discipline. This is yet another remarkable accomplishment, as the simple passage of a law is generally insufficient to change deep-rooted fiscal behavior. In order to understand why the FRL in Brazil has proven to be effectively binding (in its still brief existence), it is necessary to consider once again the political institutions, in particular, the dominant role of the president and why it is in his or her best interest that the law be enforced.

The main findings of this chapter can be summarized in the following four points:

1. The most fundamental characteristic of the Brazilian political system is a strong presidential power, which emerges from political institutions that provide the executive branch with an extensive set of instruments to pursue its preferences. This characteristic applies as well to the budgetary process. Therefore the executive is able to control that process closely and ensure that budgetary allocations are made—most of the time—closely in line with its preferences.
2. The executive's preponderance over the budgetary process is achieved at a relatively low cost. This is so because political institutions, including those specific to the budgetary process, provide the president with several effective means to guide his proposal through Congress. The ability to execute selectively amendments to the budget by members of Congress, for example, is a key power that generously endows the president with a political currency that is used to purchase support.
3. Given that points 1 and 2 above posit that the president is generally able to get most of what he or she wants, the questions are: what does the president want and what are his or her motivations? It can be argued that in Brazil, the president has political incentives to pursue responsible fiscal and monetary policy conducive to growth and stability. Because the budgetary process should be instrumental to achieving those goals, the president's behavior within this procedure should be consistent with those objectives.[2]
4. Despite the high level of presidential powers, the president's powers are not absolute. Political institutions provide several checks that

[2] Although these imputed motivations fit well with the presidents' behavior since 1995 (Cardoso and Lula), the match with previous presidents is not so clear. It is worth mentioning, however, that, even though they were not approved at the time, President Collor proposed several constitutional reforms that would eventually be adopted in subsequent policy reform.

limit the his or her control. On one hand, these constraints help to prevent opportunism and to facilitate the provision of credible commitments, but on the other, they prevent adaptation to shocks. When the costs created by these restrictions are very large, the constraints will be gradually relaxed in a manner consistent with hypotheses 1, 2, and 3 above, that is, favoring the executive and being conducive to responsible macroeconomic policy.

The next section analyzes how political institutions in Brazil map into the policymaking process behind budgetary choices. The subsequent section describes the preparation, approval, execution, and control stages of the budgetary process in light of the analysis herein of the working of the policymaking process. Special attention is then given to the FRL and the role of subnational governments in the budgetary process. This is followed by a section that analyzes why the level of budget rigidity is so high in Brazil and what impact this characteristic has on the overall budgetary policy. Finally, this chapter concludes by stressing the intense process of reform that the Brazilian budgetary process has undergone since the 1988 constitution. This process has been led by strong presidential powers in a manner conducive to fiscal responsibility and budgetary equilibrium.

THE POLICYMAKING PROCESS FOR THE BUDGETARY PROCESS IN BRAZIL

This section focuses on the political institutions that determine which actors are involved in the budgetary process and how political institutions affect the incentives and constraints of political actors as well as their ability to enter into and sustain intertemporal political transactions. Strong powers have generally allowed the president to initiate, pursue, and gain approval for much of his or her policy agenda. These powers are checked, however, by two sets of safeguards. The first check involves the electoral connection. This connection is such that the president has incentives to pursue sensible macroeconomic policies, as the electorate holds the president responsible for outcomes related to basic issues, such as a strong economy, economic growth, and stabilization. Given the strong presidential powers, failure in these areas cannot be credibly blamed on other political actors, such as Congress or the judiciary. The second check involves other actors. Although the separation of powers is clearly biased towards the president, several other political actors with different motivations are able to check the president's actions in different ways. Thus, if an incompetent or ill-intentioned president were to come into power, strong presidentialism would not mean a blank check to pursue misguided policy.

The rules of the budgetary process in Brazil are such that the executive runs very few risks of seeing its proposal disfigured by Congress. Not only can the executive veto any undesirable changes that Congress may inflict on its proposal, but the executive can also use its institutional instruments and informational advantages to guide the process safely through Congress. If that were not enough, the budgetary institutions further safeguard the executive's preferences by putting the most important parts of the budget out of the reach of members of Congress, since they are allowed to amend only an astonishingly small part of the entire package. Additionally, the Brazilian budget law approved by Congress is not mandatory; rather, it merely authorizes the executive to execute the budget based on the availability of resources collected during a specific fiscal year. That is, although the budget decision-making process within Congress is very open and transparent, there is a great level of discretion for the executive during the appropriation phase of the budget, which, of course, raises doubts about its transparency and accountability.[3]

Despite this high level of executive control, Congress systematically proposes and approves a large number of amendments (collective and individual) to the annual budget. Such amendments, however, are limited to items in the investment category, which are typically only a small part of the entire budget. For example, as shown in Table 3.1, the fraction of the total budget allocated to investments from 1996 to 2004 was consistently very small—never above 3 percent. Another interesting aspect demonstrated by this table is that Congress tried to increase the original amount allocated by the executive to investments in the budget

[3] The Latin American Index of Budget Transparency (2003) places Brazil as one of the countries with the highest positive response rates of transparency, affirming that "the legislature is a privileged actor with authority to modify and approve the budget proposal crafted and sent by the executive" (available at www.internationalbudget.org/themes/BudTrans/LA03.htm).

TABLE 3.1 **Difference in Expenditure among the Budget Bill (PLO), the Budget Law (LOA), and What, In Fact, Was Appropriated, 1996–2004**
(R$ millions)

Specification	Personal	Interest rate on debt	Local and state transfers	Investments: amount (%)	Capital investments	Debt amortization	Total
1996							
PLO	41,346.5	22,262.2	111,097.2	8,122.6 (2.64)	11,267.0	114,134.0	308,229.5
LOA	39,685.3	22,262.2	104,633.2	8,832.2 (2.94)	10,927.3	114,134.0	300,474.1
Appropriated	40,900.9	19,492.0	92,392.7	5,706.4 (1.98)	13,290.7	116,785.3	288,568.0
1997							
PLO	42,576.8	25,252.8	113,654.3	7,747.4 (1.83)	10,779.2	223,806.1	423,816.6
LOA	45,060.8	25,252.8	113,015.3	9,901.2 (2.31)	11,519.1	223,806.1	428,555.3
Appropriated	44,530.0	21,033.2	105,764.2	7,537.9 (2.22)	13,290.7	147,040.0	339,196.0
1998							
PLO	48,172.9	37,162.3	120,440.1	8,353.7 (1.92)	21,834.1	199,534.1	435,497.2
LOA	48,175.6	37,162.3	119,141.5	11,110.0 (2.54)	21,122.5	200,187.4	436,899.3
Appropriated	47,946.5	30,812.5	120,384.8	8,284.6 (1.66)	71,343.9	221,150.9	499,923.2

Specification	Personal	Interest rate on debt	Local and state transfers	Investments: amount (%)	Capital investments	Debt amortization	Total
1999							
PLO	52,170.6	50,323.0	125,154.1	4,934.0 (0.91)	14,473.0	295,098.9	542,153.6
LOA	50,570.1	50,178.2	120,876.8	7,887.6 (1.46)	14,169.9	295,243.8	538,926.2
Appropriated	51,571.0	45,355.6	131,408.8	6,955.3 (1.18)	56,348.8	296,423.3	588,062.9
2000							
PLO	52,116.4	78,123.0	142,063.3	6,756.9 (0.67)	15,872.6	707,897.7	1,002,829.9
LOA	52,086.8	78,123.0	143,565.0	12,448.8 (1.24)	11,572.1	709,072.8	1,006,868.5
Appropriated	58,240.6	38,834.8	152,925.5	10,099.1 (1.64)	11,420.8	344,861.6	616,382.5
2001							
PLO	59,569.6	67,801.5	183,442.8	12,129.8 (1.30)	14,574.2	594,495.2	932,013.1
LOA	59,483.7	70,299.5	174,649.5	18,268.9 (1.93)	14,962.9	607,537.0	945,201.5
Appropriated	65,449.4	52,816.4	175,412.8	14,564.9 (2.41)	20,446 1	274,681.4	603,371.0

(*continued on next page*)

TABLE 3.1 Difference in Expenditure among the Budget Bill (PLO), the Budget Law (LOA), and What, In Fact, Was Appropriated, 1996–2004 *(R$ millions)*

Specification	Personal	Interest rate on debt	Local and state transfers	Investments: amount (%)	Capital investments	Debt amortization	Total
2002							
PLO	—	—	—	—	—	—	—
LOA	68,497.8	58,452.2	204,354.5	17,649.5 (2.71)	16,864.7	277,697.9	650,409.6
Appropriated	75,029.0	55,260.7	208,782.9	10,126.8 (1.50)	20,936.2	304,792.3	674,928.0
2003							
PLO	76,892.6	93,644.1	213,302.2	7,350.8 (0.73)	23,054.4	582,315.1	1,009,532.2
LOA	77,046.2	93,644.1	223,972.4	14,180.2 (1.37)	24,376.3	582,315.1	1,036,056.1
Appropriated	78,974.7	65,706.8	239,237.6	6,452.1 (0.74)	23,440.7	462,644.6	876,456.6
2004							
PLO	84,291.1	117,829.6	263,291.3	7,823.8 (0.54)	32,752.8	926,097.6	1,457,686.7
LOA	84,120.0	117,769.8	273,628.6	12,370.0 (0.84)	33,249.4	925,989.9	1,469,087.4
Appropriated	89,431.6	74,373.4	275,905.8	10,866.0 (1.20)	21,580.7	436,020.3	908,177.7

Source: Elaborated with data from Sistema Integrado de Acompanhamento Financeiro (SIAFI).
Note: Data for the budget bill for 2002 are unavailable.

bill, but the amount in fact appropriated was smaller than the budget law approved by Congress in most years in this period. This indicates that the executive has the prerogative to protect its preferences continuously by strategically adjusting legislators' attempts to modify the original proposal. As a result, as shown in Figure 3.2, the changes made by Congress in the budget bill sent by the executive are in fact extremely small. This figure illustrates—for the total budget—how much Congress modified the original executive proposal each year between 1996 and 2004, as well as how much of this modified bill was actually appropriated by the executive. These data show that the norm is for the executive to leave unappropriated a significant fraction of the budget approved by Congress. The exceptions are 1998, which was the year Fernando Cardoso voted for an alteration in the constitution to allow reelection of the president, and 1999, which was the year of the devaluation crisis.

Even though the budgetary resources added by Congress are small relative to the whole budget expenditure, it may seem surprising that the executive, given the instruments at its disposal, would allow the original proposal to be moved from its preferred position at all. Because, as a result of the separation of purpose inherent in the political institutions,

FIGURE 3.2 Changes Made by Congress to Original Executive Proposal and Proportion of the Bill Modified by Congress Actually Appropriated by the Executive

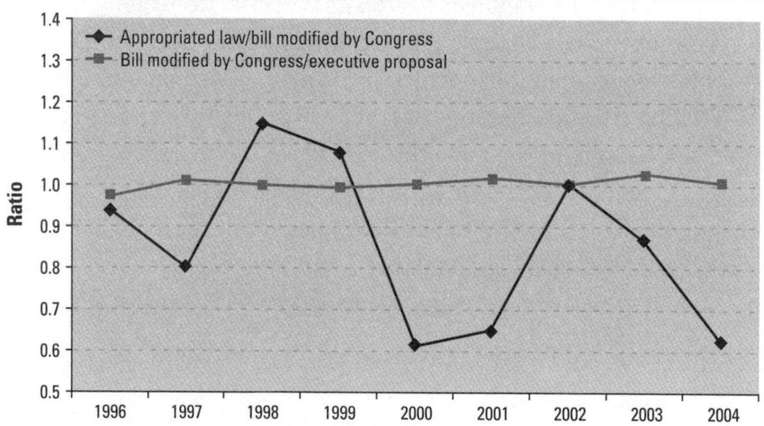

Source: Elaborated with data from Sistema Integrado de Acompanhamento Financeiro (SIAFI).
Note: Value for 2002 set at 1.00 because of lack of data for that year.

the president pursues broad national public goods, whereas other actors that also have a say in producing legislation, particularly Congress and—to a lesser degree—governors, have more narrow constituencies, there is potential conflict. However, this conflict is diffused by legislative rules that result in trades of support for patronage between Congress and the president (Alston and Mueller, 2006). The president is able to use his powers to control the legislative agenda and to create a stable supporting coalition that enables policy reform.[4] Any other coalition that is not coordinated by the president would be inherently unstable and occasional, as it would not have any enforcement mechanism to ensure compliance and prevent defections. In addition, the president possesses considerable discretion over patronage (such as jobs in the public bureaucracy, appropriation of individual budget amendments, voluntary transfers to states and municipalities, etc.), which, together with the career incentives of the members of Congress, leads to a well-institutionalized exchange of policy support for patronage. Although these exchanges are often seen as being less than legitimate by the press and much of society, they form the basis of executive-legislative relations in Brazil and lead to high levels of governability that allow important reforms to get accomplished. Furthermore, it can also be argued that this achievement comes at relatively low costs to the executive, as political institutions facilitate the trades, and the patronage that is dispensed is a very small part of the budget (Pereira and Mueller, 2004).

This explains why the executive not only does not use its institutional and informational advantages to stop its proposal from being changed, but even encourages amendments by systematically overestimating the level of revenues that it expects to be available. Members of Congress are not fooled by this strategy, but they are willing to go along with this game since it provides means through which the majority coalition is able to coordinate to secure its own political benefits. The parties and the individual members of the coalition benefit by receiving budgetary resources that, though small relative to the entire budget, significantly increase their probability of electoral success and political survival.

---

[4] This is necessary because Brazilian electoral rules (open-list proportional system) induce a multiparty system in which the president's party alone has typically held around 20 percent of seats in Congress.

A consequence of the president's prioritization of stability and fiscal discipline is that the pursuit of all other policies remains contingent on there being space on the legislative agenda as well as availability of budgetary resources. These residual policies, in turn, are affected by both economic and political shocks; this implies that many of them will be characterized by high volatility and, in some cases, be reversed. Whenever the economic and political conditions are favorable, these policies are given priority and are implemented. When negative shocks occur, residual policies are usually suspended or put on hold to help secure the first-category policies. Residual policies thus have a tendency to oscillate unpredictably. Also, because such policies only produce results in the medium and long term, politicians have more leeway to pursue their own visions than they do when they are dealing with the first-category policies, where mistakes are more quickly perceived and punished by internal and foreign markets.

There are cases in which the volatility of residual policies can be particularly damaging. In these instances, political actors often try to hardwire the policies through the budget. At some "constitutional moment," politicians establish impediments to changing these policies by tying the hands of future political actors. This results in rigid policies. Such rigidity is an advantage when it constrains opportunistic behavior, but it comes with the cost of reducing the ability to adapt to unforeseen future contingencies. The magnitude and nature of the rigidities in the budget will be analyzed in the next section.

The remainder of the chapter includes a description and analysis of the Brazilian budgetary procedures. The discussion focuses on two key issues related to the budgetary policymaking process. The first is the relationship between the legislature and the president briefly described above. The second is the fiscal responsibility law, which is a key component of the fiscal process.

THE BRAZILIAN BUDGETARY RULES AND COMPONENTS

This section describes how the governmental budget is formulated in Brazil, focusing on how budgetary rules constrain and shape the relative power of Congress and the executive. Historically, the role of Congress in Brazil's budgetary process has alternated between cases in which it has effectively participated and defined where and how public resources were allocated and cases in which it has not wielded any direct influence. Currently, even when legislators have an effective role, it is mostly limited to amending the budget bill so as to target their main electoral strongholds with local policies.

The Brazilian constitution of 1988 brought about a set of new, complex rules to regulate the budgetary decision-making process. Three main instruments are responsible for regulating, planning, and allocating federal resources: the Multiannual Plan (Plano Plurianual, PPA), the Law of Budgetary Guidelines (Lei de Diretrizes Orçamentárias, LDO), and the Annual Budgetary Law (Lei Orçamentária Annual, LOA). These three instruments are hierarchically interconnected at different stages: the PPA, which serves as a framework for planning expenditures and government action, is formulated by the executive four months before the end of the first year of a government's term and defines the main strategic targets of the federal government in the long run. The plan must be analyzed, amended, and approved by Congress by the last month of the first year of its mandate and is valid until the end of the first year of the next elected government.

The LDO is renewed annually and has to be sent by the executive to Congress no later than the first quarter of the second year of the government's term. Congress has to endorse this law by June of the same year. The LDO should include (a) the goals and priorities of the federal government; (b) guidelines for changes in tax laws; (c) the parameters for personnel spending and recruitment, which should include details on pay raises and the minimum wage rate; and (d) the policies and objectives set for the official federal financial institutions. Despite the short period of time allowed for its discussion (two months), the LDO provides ample opportunity for the legislature to influence the budgetary process. The fact that Congress is legally required to vote on the LDO before it adjourns for its midyear recess is an important constraint. The LDO becomes the major institutional device for guiding the formulation of pubic policies, because it defines the priorities that have to be considered in the formulation of the LOA in the next fiscal year.

The executive uses the targets and guidelines defined by the PPA and the LDO to formulate the Annual Budget Proposal (Proposta de Lei Orçamentária, PLO), which estimates the total revenue and expenditures for the next fiscal year. In other words, the PLO details specific programs and activities that must be in accord with the two previous instruments. The president has to send the PLO to Congress by August 30 of the same year, and Congress has until December 15 to make and approve amendments. The Joint Budget Committee (Senate and Chamber of Deputies) initiates this process, and then the PLO passes through Congress as a whole. It is then sent back to the executive to be enacted as a law with or without vetoes.[5]

Crafting the Budget Proposal in the Executive Branch: Preparation Stage

The executive branch, or more specifically, the Secretary of Budget (SOF) of the Ministry for Planning, Budget, and Management (MP), has the responsibility for coordinating and crafting the Annual Budget Proposal, The SOF is the agenda setter and must estimate the total revenue and expenditures for each ministry (staff, social security contributions, debts, etc.), for Congress, and the judicial branch. Subsequently, it defines parameters for all other expenditures, including operational and investment spending. After collecting the necessary information, the SOF specifies expenditure restrictions for each program that each federal public institution proposes to develop. With those budget constraints, the ministries and agencies send their proposals back to the SOF, which has the responsibility of reshaping them into a single proposal, the PLO, and sending the proposal to Congress.

It is relevant to note that at this stage some legislators, especially the top-ranked ones, take advantage of their political networks inside ministries and public agencies to include their demands and projects in the executive's proposal. In other words, these legislators can avoid a significant step of negotiation inside Congress, since their demands are already included in the PLO. It is at this stage that the trickiest negotiations occur within the executive branch itself, with each part trying to enlarge its own budget and the treasury trying to hold back their demands.

---

[5] In Brazil, the executive can veto the budget proposal approved by Congress in parts or as a whole.

As previously mentioned, the executive has to send the budget bill to Congress by August 30. Prior to this deadline, much negotiation takes place among the executive branch, legislators, and interest groups. The goal of these actors is to convince the executive to include projects of their interest within the budget bill before sending it to Congress. This accomplishment, of course, would improve their chances of having a project ultimately approved, because approval would not require an amendment.

The budgetary game, however, does not end after the PLO has been approved by Congress and enacted by the president. The budget can still be changed after these stages through the additional credit mechanism, which allows new amendments that reallocate resources. This possibility makes the budgetary decision-making process effectively endless, turning it into a sequential game in which the executive and Congress interact on more than one occasion. As shown in the next section, the executive plays this game from a very favorable position compared to Congress, as it benefits from asymmetric information and institutional mechanisms that allow it considerable discretionary powers. Resources to be allocated as additional credits come mainly from cancellations of previous spending in the LOA, excess tax collection, and loans. Note that the executive has an informational advantage regarding the availability of these resources.

Decision Making in Congress: Approval Stage

The involvement of legislators in the Brazilian budgetary cycle occurs predominantly in the Joint Budget Committee (Comissão Mista de Planos, Orçamentos Públicos e Fiscalização, CMPOF). Rocha (1997: 108) compares the number of amendments approved by the CMPOF and by the floor of the House and Senate and points out that Congress does not substantially modify the report approved by the committee. According to Rocha, the CMPOF is the main decision-making locus regarding the budget within Congress. It is the largest committee of the Brazilian Congress, with 84 effective members, 63 of which are deputies and 21 of which are senators, and 28 substitutes. The composition of the committee is proportional to the number of seats that each political party holds in Congress; therefore the larger parties have greater representation within the committee. It is a prerogative of party leaders to appoint committee members as well as to determine the president of the committee and its three vice presidents, leaving them well-placed to control the budgetary process as well as to reward and punish party members.

The CMPOF is composed of thematic standing subcommittees with a maximum of seven legislators. Each subcommittee has a sectoral rapporteur whose responsibility is to compile a partial report with the amendments approved by its members. The CMPOF's general rapporteur then consolidates these pieces. The positions of sectoral and general rapporteurs are highly influential, and appointments are made to such positions by the president of the committee, subject to the restriction that the appointments must follow party proportionality.

When a bill reaches the CMPOF, the general rapporteur submits a preliminary statement based on negotiation among party leaders. One of the most important aspects of this preliminary report is the definition of parameters and deadlines for legislators to submit collective and individual amendments. This explains the fierce competition among legislators to become members of the CMPOF, and especially to be appointed to high hierarchical positions in the committee, such as rapporteur or subrapporteur. These positions allow the legislators to propose specific resource reallocations, since the process of approving amendments is centralized on the rapporteurs' positions. Furthermore, only committee members are allowed to headline legislators' amendments during the voting process on the committee floor.[6]

Although legislators have the right to amend bills that are exclusively introduced by the president, they can do so only if those amendments are compatible with the PPA as well as with the LDO. Moreover, Congress may not authorize expenditures that exceed budgetary revenues. The rules regarding making amendments to the PLO have varied considerably in the past years. However, since 1995 individual legislators, standing committees, regional blocs, and state blocs have been able to propose amendments.

---

[6] The competition among legislators to take part in the CMPOF has led to frequent increases in the number of its seats. In 1988 there were 60 effective members (45 deputies and 15 senators), and now there are 84 members (63 deputies and 21 senators). According to Serra (1994), the increase of the number of seats within the CMPOF has been the way party leaders have found to cope with different legislators' pressures, as, from the legislators' perspective, a mere presence on the committee will significantly boost the chances that their proposed amendments will be approved.

Until 1993, there were no limits regarding the number of amendments that each legislator could make to the PLO.[7] Currently, there is a limit of 20 amendments per member of Congress and a ceiling of R$3.5 million. Similarly, there is a limit of five collective amendments per standing committee, five per regional bloc, and 10 per state bloc. However, even with a limited number and monetary value of amendments, legislators do not have any guarantee that their amendments will be approved by the committee; thus, they still have to negotiate with rapporteurs and party leaders to have their demands approved in the LOA, as many amendments are simply set aside.

Budget Execution under Executive Discretion

All the steps and complex negotiations to approve amendments inside Congress do not ensure that a project, once approved and enacted by the president, will be delivered. The executive is responsible for the execution of the budget law, which includes the legislators' demands. Although legislators have the right to propose individual and collective amendments to the annual budget, the executive determines which amendments will be executed, which makes the budget contingent on the amount of resources in the national treasury. The great majority of legislators make use of their prerogative to amend the budget to push through projects targeted at their main electoral base of support. That is, the process is used to realize pork barrel politics and maximize the future electoral and political careers of the legislators. Therefore, it is plausible to expect that the executive will take advantage of this power to constrain legislators' behavior, especially on individual amendments when the executive can identify the author and the target of the amendment, rewarding and punishing them accordingly (Pereira, 2000; Pereira and Mueller, 2004).

The absence of synchronization between tax collection and expenditure has allowed the executive to act strategically by making the execution of budgetary amendments contingent on the availability of resources. In other words, the Brazilian budget is not mandatory, but merely authoritative. As a result, the executive has had extreme flexibility

[7] In 1989, the total number of amendments was approximately 11,000; in 1990, 13,000; in 1991, 71,000; in 1992, 76,000; in 1993, 13,000; in 1994, 23,000 (Rocha, 1997).

and discretion when negotiating with legislators and does not apply a homogeneous criterion when deciding which amendments to execute. Evidence demonstrates that the president rewards those legislators who most vote for his or her interests by executing their budgetary amendments and, at the same time, punishes those who vote less for his or her preferences, simply by not executing their individual amendments (Pereira and Mueller, 2004; Alston and Mueller, 2006).

In addition, it is also the case that, ceteris paribus, the greater the amount of an individual legislator's amendments executed by the president, the higher the probability of that legislator's reelection (Pereira, 2000; Pereira and Rennó, 2001). In other words, with this institutional design in place, it is not surprising to observe legislators who consistently give support to the executive's initiatives, aware of the effect that it might have on their individual demands being met by the president. On the other hand, legislators who do not frequently follow the executive's preferences in Congress have less chances of delivering local policies to their constituents. It is important to recognize, however, that in the case of collective amendments, this rewarding/punishing mechanism, which characterizes the gains from trade between the executive and members of Congress in Brazil, is difficult to implement. This is true especially because the executive branch cannot fully identify who is benefiting from the execution, which is based on legislative performance, nor can it identify who can claim credit for the appropriation, since these amendments have no individual author and are wide-ranging in scope.[8]

Control Stage

Compared to the preparation, approval, and execution stages, there is relatively little literature on the control stage of the Brazilian budgetary process. Although it is less visible, the control stage is nevertheless an important component in the overall process, as it contributes to shaping the incentives of the agents in those previous stages.

Over the past 15 years, the institutional capacity of Congress dedicated specifically to monitoring and evaluating budget issues has improved dramatically. Both the House and the Senate recruit staff

---

[8] This explains why top government officials and party leaders from the governing coalition systematically criticize collective amendments and have proposed eliminating them.

for these specialized assignments through highly competitive public examinations and also offer attractive salaries. In the House, there are 41 consultants dedicated to budget issues and in the Senate there are 28. Corresponding levels of equipment and access to information match the high levels of human and financial resources. Nevertheless, despite the existence of a suitable structure to monitor and control budgetary procedures, the incentives for the political agents involved to use the structure for that purpose are missing. The constitution establishes that Congress is responsible for oversight and control of all acts of the executive, including the budget. However, as noted above, Congress does not fully exert this control, as it has in a sense delegated this control back to the executive. This behavior is consistent with the incentives faced by Congress. The executive is the dominant player and is able to coordinate and maintain a governing coalition by—among other things—distributing patronage through individual and collective amendments to the budget. In this game the supporting coalition is very much interested in the elaboration of the budget, so as to ensure the size and shape of that patronage, but has no real incentive to dedicate resources to ex post control of the process. Given that a majority of Congress is not motivated to pursue those functions, it is not surprising that the control stage remains in the background, despite the existence of the Federal Audit Court (Tribunal de Contas da União, TCU). This organization possesses the means, in terms of enabling legislation as well as resources, to perform the monitoring and control functions required by best practices. However, its formal link to the legislative branch has meant that, in the end, its actual performance has not had as big an impact on the budgetary process as could be expected.

In Brazil, the TCU monitors the accounts of administrators and others responsible for federal resources. As such, the TCU has the potential to have an important effect on the policymaking process. It could, for example, constrain the way the president executes the budget, as one of its functions is to monitor legislative budgetary authorizations. Also, with the new FRL of 2000, the TCU has started making individualized reports of the accounts not only of the president, but of the Senate, the House, the Supreme Court, other federal courts and the head of the Public Prosecutor's office (Ministério Público). What role the TCU actually plays in Brazil, however, depends on its structure and process, as well as on the motivations of its members and the restrictions imposed by other political players. The most important institutional feature that affects the TCU's performance is the fact that, despite its quasi-judicial structure—and unlike European audit courts—it has very limited sanctioning powers. These powers remain restricted to the judicial branch, which has to act following TCU's recommendations and to decide on appeals to fines imposed by the TCU. The only real power enjoyed by the TCU is the negative one of having the unilateral prerogative to cancel ongoing bids and public works on suspicion of irregularities, which amounts to a great potential to affect the preferences of the executive branch.

Perhaps the greatest potential limitation for the TCU has been the appointment procedure for selecting the nine ministers who decide each case in a joint session by majority vote. The rules are designed so that the board is highly politicized and reflects the composition of power in Congress, thus extending the power of the president's coalition to the control stage. The fact that current board members are tenured until they are required to retire at age 70 mitigates politicization, but has not precluded it (Melo, 2007; Melo, Pereira, and Figueiredo, forthcoming). Thus, despite a large, motivated, and well-trained staff that strives to go beyond simply checking accounts so as to play a more proactive role, the TCU's impact has been limited.

THE FISCAL RESPONSIBILITY LAW AND SUBNATIONAL GOVERNMENTS

This section turns to the role of subnational governments in the budgetary process, which brings up the issue of the FRL. It is arguable that this law does in fact constrain the behavior of the state governments, contributing greatly to achieving and maintaining fiscal sustainability. This is a strong claim and requires an explanation of how and why the law was passed, why it works, and whether it is sustainable.

Problems with the subnational fiscal game were already endemic in Brazil even before the 1988 constitution, which granted an expansion of states' autonomy. Between 1987 and 1996, four initiatives to control subnational debts were attempted. In 1996, the states' debt exploded as a result of the extremely high interest rates adopted under the Real

Plan (Plano Real, an economic stabilization plan put into action in early 1994). Two features explain the high levels of debt and the failure of the existing subnational fiscal system. First, the institutional rules were extremely permissive in terms of debt rollover. In certain cases, Senate resolutions authorized the states to roll over up to 100 percent of the debt service (interest plus principal). Because of the high real interest rates, this led to the rapid growth in debt due to the capitalization of interest, even with no new borrowing. Second, the federal government had a record of bailing out insolvent state and local governments.

The fast growth of the state debt in this period, especially the debt in securities, forced the federal government to exchange state bonds for federal bonds to make the debt rollover viable, as the states were not able to finance their debts in the market. To quote Goldfajn and Guardia (2003: 16), "these procedures artificially reduced the sub-national governments' cost of borrowing, created an incentive for indebtedness, and introduced a dangerous moral hazard into Brazil's fiscal federalism." The federal government's behavior should not have been interpreted as a direct response to the states' pressure. Rather, it reflected a concern for the collapse of state governments, which was partly externally produced. In other words, some of the increase in states' indebtedness was caused by federal monetary policy. The incentive structure that the states as institutional actors faced, however, produced suboptimal results.

These rules were changed only in late 1997, and particularly in 1998, when the Fiscal Stabilization Program of the second Cardoso administration was announced. The program involved a comprehensive debt refinancing agreement with states and local governments, as well as a radical fiscal adjustment aimed at increasing the primary surplus of the consolidated public sector. The agreement set targets for revenue and expenditures, required the reduction of the share of payroll in net revenues, and encouraged states to privatize public utilities and state banks, among other measures.

This fiscal adjustment program produced very significant results. While in 1997 there was a primary deficit, the consolidated public sector has since shown primary surpluses in excess of 3.5 percent of GDP. The primary balance for the states changed from a deficit of 0.31 percent to a surplus of 0.5 percent of GDP. These surpluses have been generated partly by high increases in the tax burden, but the most significant aspect is the change in fiscal institutions that the central government managed to produce. The federal government's program has had a significant fiscal cost, but it has also produced a restructuring of Brazilian federalism, thereby eliminating the loci of fiscal uncertainty and reassuring the central government's power over fiscal affairs. This was a precondition for the management of the fiscal problem.

The FRL, enacted in 2000, is the main piece of legislation in the area of budget and fiscal control. Its adoption represents the apex of a relatively successful set of measures to constrain fiscal behavior and control the state governments' indebtedness.[9] The FRL illustrates the executive's ability to implement its policy preferences in the political game discussed in previous sections of this chapter. Furthermore, it reflects a learning process on the basis of a repeated game between the federal government and the states. Unlike other similar laws promulgated in Latin America, the FRL in Brazil is applicable to the federal as well as the state and municipal governments. Moreover, unlike its counterparts in other countries of the region (e.g., Argentina), this single federal law sets parameters for all levels of government and thus represents a top-down approach to fiscal rules and budgetary control (Webb, 2004). The FRL provides ex ante and ex post controls on both borrowers and lenders. It specifies in great detail the budgetary and fiscal rules governing public sector indebtedness, credit operations, and public accounts reporting. The law prohibits the federal government from financing subnational governments, therefore eliminating the possibility of bailouts as well as changes in the financial clauses of the existing debt-restructuring agreement.

Since the inception of the FRL, the fiscal performance of the subnational governments has improved. Between 2002 and 2006, the states' primary surplus grew by 22.2 percent, climbing to 0.70 percent of GDP in 2006 from 0.58 percent in 2002. As a percentage of GDP, the states' nominal deficit (which includes interest payments) fell from 2.96 to 0.59 in the same period. According to the most recent data available, the overwhelming majority of states were meeting the targets stipulated by Resolution 40 for the ratio of net debt to total net revenue. Only three states—São Paulo, Rio Grande do Sul, and Alagoas—were

[9] At the end of 2003, the states were producing a surplus of 9 percent of their net revenue, and their production represented 1 percent of GDP in Brazil (Afonso, 2004).

above the stipulated ceiling, whereas two states—Minas Gerais and Rio de Janeiro—were close to noncompliance. These impressive results should be taken with some caution, considering that there has been some "creative accounting" by the states, thereby masking real trends. Such trends, nevertheless are still very positive (Afonso, Meirelles, and Castro, 2007).

Although it can be argued that the executive has the upper hand in executive-legislative relations, particularly in fiscal and budgetary matters, the interests of subnational executives are relevant for explaining the highly successful implementation of the FRL. In order to understand the interest of governors in the law, one has to consider governors as rational actors seeking political survival, who thus have an interest in fiscal expansion. However, in the context of highly indebted and fiscally vulnerable states, governors also have an interest in shifting the blame for austerity measures to other actors. This calculation is, however, affected by the future electoral chances of governors. For example, a governor in a highly polarized state who faces close elections would have an interest in "stacking the deck" of the future governor and curbing his or her "fiscal powers." In cases in which the incumbent is in his or her second term of office—and therefore barred from competing in the next election—he or she would also have an interest in the FRL. This interest would be stronger in case of polarization. But the incumbent would also benefit from the law, because he or she would have an excuse to say no to demands from his or her own constituency—particularly demands concerning pay hikes. In 2000, when the law was in the formulation and implementation stages, most governors were leading states that were in a situation of great fiscal vulnerability, and most of them would not be able to run for office again (in 1998, 4 governors were reelected and would not be allowed to run for a third time). These circumstances help explain the high levels of support by most governors for the FRL. However, their support was not sufficient—or maybe not even necessary—as suggested by the approval of many initiatives that directly impinged on subnational interests. Nonetheless, their deep interest helps explain the smooth and successful implementation of the FRL.

The FRL helped produce a major change in the approach to fiscal issues. Among other things, as the law required major procedural changes in budgetary matters, it generated new stakeholders in fiscal issues, such as the TCU and other watchdogs. The fiscal record of the three tiers of government has been impressive, with increasing primary surpluses produced at the state and national levels. The deficit of the consolidated public sector changed from 0.3 percent of GDP in 1997 to a continuous surplus since 1999. More importantly, most states have significantly improved their primary fiscal results, meeting the targets regarding ratio of net debt to total net revenue. Similarly, there have been marked reductions in the share of personnel expenditures, which had previously been a major source of imbalance. Notably, although the FRL provision states that the Brazilian federal government should have a ceiling for the ratio of net consolidated debt to total net revenue (2.45 in 2004), the Senate has not imposed a ceiling. This underscores the fact that the FRL is primarily an instrument of the federal government to control subnational spending. This is consistent with the interpretation in this chapter about the preponderance of the executive in the budgetary and fiscal game.

Is this performance of the FRL sustainable in Brazil? As Braun and Tommasi (2002) point out, fiscal rules require self-enforcement by the players (states) or an external enforcer with the power to ensure compliance. It is arguable that Brazil approximates a self-enforcement case: the executive has the enforcement technology, and the FRL has been an effective commitment device. This argument contrasts with that of Webb (2004), who takes the external enforcement view. He argues that the passage and sustainability of the FRL was made possible primarily because of the cooperation of key large states (such as São Paulo) and their governors. However, the old view of the Brazilian political system as a federal structure in which governors wield vast powers is currently inaccurate. The circumstances that produced the former status quo that favored the states were unprecedented and extraordinary: a constituent assembly in which the federal executive played a minor role; the political conjuncture of transition to democratic rule, in which fiscal decentralization and increased social spending were important banners; and the specific sequence through which the political transition (democratic elections) occurred first at the state level (1982) and subsequently at the national level (1996), converting the governors to key political figures in the transition.

The president had the capacity to impose his or her fiscal preferences because of (a) the ability to exchange development bank advancements for fiscal reforms, including privatization of state banks and utilities; (b) the agenda powers and other legislative prerogatives to implement his or her agenda; and (c) the approval of the reelection amendment, which not only strengthened the president vis-à-vis governors but also helped extend the time horizons of governors (21 governors ran for reelection in 1998), thus introducing some element of self-enforcement in the fiscal game. Without the reelection amendment, incumbent governors would have an incentive to exacerbate the common pool problem by leaving the fiscal problem to future governors. In addition, because of the devastating impact of hyperinflation in the mid-1990s, the president's policies were viewed favorably by much of the public, which became strongly inflation averse. It can be argued that the sustainability of the current fiscal situation is therefore not dependent on the state's cooperation. Although the FRL could be reversed, there is some rigidity in the procedures, as a majority of three-fifths in two rounds of votes in the two chambers is required for a change in the law.

THE RIGIDITY OF THE BUDGETARY PROCESS IN BRAZIL

One of the most striking features of the Brazilian budgetary process is the rigidity that has been built in through earmarking of tax revenues and hardwiring of expenditures. Although all countries have such rigidities, the Brazilian case is particularly severe. This characteristic is of central importance to the analysis herein, because these rigidities are a means through which intertemporal political transactions are sealed. Figure 3.3 shows the evolution over time of the composition of tax revenues in Brazil classified in terms of whether or not they are earmarked, and if so, how. The 1988 constitution led to a marked increase in the proportion of revenues that were earmarked and a corresponding decrease in the proportion of revenue that could be freely used. Major examples of earmarking in the 1988 constitution are (a) a requirement that at least 18 percent of all taxes be spent on development and maintenance of education (Article 212); (b) a requirement that a series of social contributions be earmarked for social security (Article 195); and (c) automatic transfers to states and municipalities. Several other instances of revenue earmarking have followed since the enactment of the new constitution. The use of "contributions," specific earmarked

FIGURE 3.3 Evolution of Earmarking of Budgetary Revenues
(percentage of GDP)

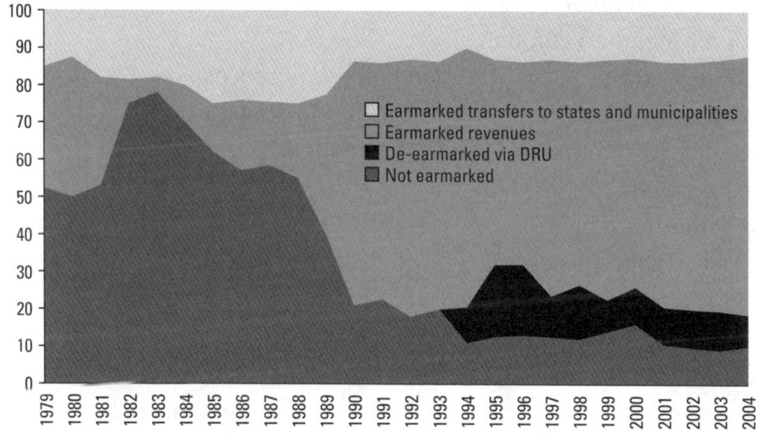

Source: Secretaria de Orçamento Federal (2003).

taxes sheltered from disbursement to state and local governments, has been a favored means of raising and earmarking revenue as opposed to taxes. The creation of these contributions, generally associated with social expenditures, has been a major instrument in the government's fiscal adjustment strategy. As a consequence, the amount of revenues raised through contributions has increased markedly in the past decade, almost reaching the same level as revenue derived from taxes.

Soon after the 1988 constitution, it seemed that revenue rigidity had wrapped a straitjacket around the Brazilian government, as it imposed constraints on the pursuit of its policymaking preferences. In reaction to these constraints, in 1993 the government created a fund called the Social Emergency Fund (Fundo Social de Emergência, FSE), which received resources that were deearmarked from 20 percent of all taxes and contributions received by the union. The idea was to create a temporary source of flexibility to allow the government to address the problem of inflation, until fiscal reforms that could provide a definitive solution were put into place. However, when the FSE expired, a similar fund, the Fund for Fiscal Stabilization (Fundo de Estabilização Fiscal, FEF), was substituted, which in turn gave way to the DRU (Delinked Budgetary Resources) in 1999. The existence of the DRU meant that in 2003, 19.7 percent of total revenues were not earmarked, whereas without the DRU the figure would have been 12.9 percent (Secretaria de Orçamento Federal, 2003). Thus the DRU does provide some flexibility, but only a limited amount.

The rigidities in the Brazilian budgetary process can be classified in two categories. The first type is associated with expenditures that have a dynamic that is largely independent of the political process. These include, for example, social expenditures whose expansions are determined by exogenous factors. The largest components of the budget fall into this category: social security, personnel expenditures, and payment of interest rates. The second type of rigidities is produced by active strategic interaction among the various political actors involved in the budgetary process. Hardwiring in this case is the result of purposeful action. Rigidities of this type are constrained by those of the first type described above and also produce unintended perverse effects over time.

The political transactions around the hardwiring game in the last decade can be seen as a reaction against the state of affairs produced by the 1988 constitution. The constitution produced short-term fiscal impacts and introduced a number of fiscal rigidities. First, it mandated a new distribution of the public revenue that augmented the share of state and municipal governments in tax revenue. In addition, the subnational governments saw their tax base expanded. Second, the constitution set the minimum value of pensions at the level of the minimum salary, guaranteed the real values of social security pensions over time—explicitly prohibiting the inflationary erosion of any pecuniary benefits—and also equalized the level of urban and rural pensions. In addition, it expanded the range of welfare benefits to rural workers, which in the past were a fraction of those of urban workers. Third, with the stated goal of professionalizing the public bureaucracy, the constitution upgraded public employees' social security contracts.

This pattern of rigidity is a direct consequence of the "Christmas tree–like" nature of the 1988 constitution, in which a gamut of different groups managed to insert their own provisions and insulate them from future policymakers. In addition, many of these items were justified as the need to repay the "social debt" to groups that had been marginalized during the previous decades, such as rural workers, those who had no access to health services, and retirees who had had their pensions systematically eroded by inflation (Velloso, 2004: 27). In addition to the favorable nature of the benefits in the social security system, one might be tempted to interpret the hardwiring of the other regular benefits, such as pensions in the civil service, as desirable from the point of view of representativeness, as they impede opportunistic raiding of those resources by politicians. However, this argument becomes less compelling when one considers that of all the beneficiaries of the social security system, there are several privileged groups who receive the bulk of the benefits at the expense of the majority. The hardwiring of these expenditures protects these benefits from changes that could make the system more representative.

There are generally two types of rationales for budgetary rigidities: hardwiring as precommitment device and hardwiring as spin-off of opportunistic interaction. In the Brazilian case, there is evidence that confirms both uses of hardwiring. In certain cases, hardwiring appears as a result of meta-preferences by the actors for a certain outcome. This is exemplified in the hardwiring for education and health care. This is also the case when actors use hardwiring to protect themselves from pressures in blame-shifting strategies (exemplified by the FRL, which was used by actors as an excuse to say no to special demands from their own constituencies). But most of the instances of hardwiring are of the second type identified above. The extensive hardwiring of subnational fiscal practices has been the product of mutual opportunism between subnational and federal governments. A history of opportunism by the federal executive, which used its institutional prerogatives to impose losses on the subnational governments, led to countervailing measures by subnational actors that expanded the fiscal and budgetary powers of subnational governments in contexts in which they were able to react. As discussed above, the 1988 constitution was one of these exceptional moments. The history of post-1988 constitutional reforms can be read as a series of countermeasures taken by the executive—to deconstitutionalize issues—to reestablish its preponderance in the Brazilian federalism (Melo, 2004). The political dynamics of constitution making and constitutional reforms are very different. In the former process, the interests involved have managed to introduce provisions that typically have generated diffuse costs and concentrated benefits. Because of the history of opportunistic behavior of authoritarian governments in the past, the constitutional text is one of the longest and most detailed of existing constitutions. It includes detailed hardwiring to protect pensions, subnational finances, and public sector employees. The end result of this process has been a very distorted tax system (but still capable of extracting 37 percent of GDP) and, at the same time, severe and chronic fiscal problems. In contrast to these "Christmas tree dynamics," constitutional reforms have entailed the opposite, thus generating intense resistance from organized interests. However, despite the procedural hurdles involved, because of the preponderance of the executive in the polity, there have been extensive constitutional changes—4.1 amendments per year on average from 1989 to 2002 (Melo, 2002, 2004). These changes have been made at a relatively low economic cost (Pereira and Mueller, 2004), but have certainly concentrated the political energies of the country to the detriment of other issues.

The prima facie attempt to introduce rigidity in the budget for the purposes of poverty alleviation can thus be understood as part of logrolls between the executive and legislative branches: the executive maintains fiscal stability by increasing taxes, and in return Congress receives some poverty alleviation programs sheltered from discretionary executive budget cuts. This is consistent with the political game discussed in Alston et al. (2006). The executive prefers to hardwire subnational spending and at the same time to expand the scope of discretion at the national level. The gains from trade between Congress and the executive are that the latter is primarily interested in raising taxes and the former seeks to expand social expenditures and funding for pork. To allow the executive to extract resources from society—a move that has significant political costs for legislators' constituencies—Congress increasingly demands that some of the resources be hardwired to the social sectors. Many of these resources are also in the interest of the federal executive—they are meta-preferences, in the sense used above—and therefore the political market is "cleared" in this exchange.

CONCLUDING REMARKS

The overall picture of the Brazilian budgetary process that has been conveyed in this chapter is one in which political institutions create forces that push towards budgetary equilibrium. The key features of the political institutions that are responsible for yielding this outcome are strong presidential powers and incentives for the president to use these for attaining stability and fiscal sustainability. It is important to stress, however, the path-dependent nature of how the Brazilian budgetary process has reached the point where it now stands, as this evolution over time is crucial for understanding why several current aspects of the process—such as the high levels of rigidity of budgetary allocations—have emerged and persist. The starting point of the analysis herein is the enactment of Brazilian constitution in 1988, which created a highly decentralized and rigid budgetary process with few incentives and many obstacles for fiscal sustainability and budgetary equilibrium. The evolution of this budgetary process from that point to the current situation has been a sequence of gradual but persistent changes in which strong presidential power has been crucial for altering these incentives and obstacles, recentralizing power, and molding the budgetary game. In this process, subnational units have been losing power and have been forced to check the profligate ways by which the previous set of rules were stimulated. The president's control of the legislative agenda and his ability to use discretion to execute budget amendments have been key features in the political institutions behind these outcomes. Similarly, the FRL has been successful in contributing towards fiscal sustainability, because it is, in essence, an instrument of the executive for constraining the behavior of subnational units.

This does not mean that presidents have full rein, and their preferred allocations are not always included in the budget. Although presidents have promoted substantial alterations in the budgetary process since the 1988 constitution, several elements persist which they have been unable to change. In particular, the extreme rigidity of the budget has frequently constrained the executive from pursuing policies that it would have liked to have had implemented. These rigidities were designed for the purpose of constraining the president and continue to have that effect despite the president's power. It is true that these restrictions have been relaxed somewhat through the creation of special funds that have provided the executive with some flexibility over previously earmarked revenues and expenditures; nevertheless a great proportion of the budget remains hardwired, severely limiting the president's choices. The process through which presidents try to change these rules by means of their institutional powers is clearly an ongoing game. As those rigidities become increasingly constraining—which they are bound to do given their organic nature—further attempts by the executive to make the budget more flexible are expected. As with the previous reforms, the expectation is that most future changes will be conducive to budgetary equilibrium and fiscal responsibility, an outcome due not only to the electoral incentives of the president, but also to the existence of several political actors that actively check the opportunistic use of the strong presidential powers. In particular, an independent and politically active judiciary, similarly independent and active public prosecutors, and a free press have in the past been veto points that have crucially constrained presidential behavior in budgetary and other matters.

REFERENCES

Afonso, A. 2004. Fiscal Sustainability: The Unpleasant European Case. Paper presented at the Money Macro and Finance (MMF) Research Group Conference, Washington, DC.

Afonso, J. R., B. Meirelles, and K. Castro. 2007. Os indicadores fiscais tradicionais e a realidade das finanças estaduais no Brasil. Technical Note, Federal Senate, Brasília.

Alston, L. J., M. A. Melo, B. Mueller, and C. Pereira. 2006. Political Institutions, Policymaking Processes and Policy Outcomes in Brazil. Working Paper No. R-509. Latin American Research Network, Inter-American Development Bank, Washington, DC.

Alston, L. J., and B. Mueller. 2006. Pork for Policy: Executive and Legislative Exchange in Brazil. *Journal of Law Economics and Organization* 22(1) April: 87–114.

Braun, M., and M. Tommasi. 2002. Fiscal Rules for Subnational Governments: Some Organizing Principles and Latin American Experiences. Economics Working Paper No. 0410004. Archive at Washington University in Saint Louis (WUSTL).

Goldfajn, I., and E. R. Guardia. 2003. Fiscal Rules and Debt Sustainability in Brazil. Banco Central do Brasil Technical Notes, No. 39. Banco Central do Brasil, Brasília.

Latin American Index of Budget Transparency. 2003. The International Budget Project. Washington, DC. Available at: http://www.internationalbudget.org/themes/BudTrans/LA03.htm.

Melo, M. A. 2002. Reformas constitucionais no Brasil: instituições políticas e processo decisório. Rio de Janeiro, Revan.

———. 2004. Social policy and the Transformation of Brazilian Federalism. Paper presented at the 25th International Congress of the Latin American Studies ASA Meeting, October 5–7, Las Vegas.

———. 2007. O controle externo na América Latina. Working Paper. Instituto Fernando Henrique Cardoso, São Paulo.

Melo, M. A., C. Pereira, and C. M. Figueiredo. Forthcoming. Political and Institutional Checks on Corruption: Explaining the Performance of Brazilian Audit Institutions. *Comparative Political Studies* 42(9).

Pereira, C. 2000. What Are the Conditions for the Presidential Success in the Legislative Arena? The Brazilian Electoral Connection. Doctoral dissertation, New School University, New York.

Pereira, C., and B. Mueller. 2004. The Cost of Governing: Strategic Behavior of the President and Legislators in Brazil's Budgetary Process. *Comparative Political Studies* 37(7) September: 781–815.

Pereira, C., and L. Rennó. 2003. Successful Re-election Strategies in Brazil: The Electoral Impact of Distinct Institutional Incentives. *Electoral Studies* 22: 425–48.

Rocha, P. 1997. Congresso nacional e orçamento público: o processo decisório da fase legislativa do ciclo orçamentário ampliado. Master's thesis, University of Brasília, Brazil.

Secretaria de Orçamento Federal. 2003. Vinculações de Receita dos Orçamentos Fiscal e da Seguridade Social e o Poder Discricionário de Alocação de Recursos do Governo Federal—Vol. 1, No. 1, p. 6. Secretaria de Orçamento Federal, Brasilia.

Serra, J. 1994. *Orçamento no Brasil: raízes da crise.* São Paulo: Atual Press.

Velloso, R. 2004. Ajuste do gasto público e retomada do crescimento. Federation of Industries of the State of Rio de Janeiro (FIRJAN), Rio de Janeiro.

Webb, S. 2004. Fiscal Responsibility Laws for Sub-national Discipline: The Latin American Experience. Policy Research Working Paper Series 3309. World Bank, Washington, DC.

4

Changes in Fiscal Outcomes in Colombia: The Role of the Budget Process

Mauricio Cárdenas, Carolina Mejía, and Mauricio Olivera

GENERAL TRENDS IN FISCAL OUTCOMES AND THE BUDGET PROCESS

In their comparative analyses of budgetary institutions, Stein, Talvi, and Grisanti (1999) and Alesina and Perotti (1999) conclude that the formal rules of the Colombian budget process have been exemplary, superior even to those of Chile and Mexico. Nonetheless, a more recent study by Filc and Scartascini (2004) concludes that Colombian budgetary institutions have fallen behind relative to those of other Latin American countries, because limited progress has been made in defining more clearly the roles and prerogatives of the actors involved in budget negotiations, and transparency rules have not improved.

At the same time, fiscal outcomes in terms of adaptability, efficiency, and sustainability have tended to deteriorate. This chapter explores, from a political economy perspective, the causes of these recent trends, emphasizing the role of both formal and informal budget rules. Formulating, approving, and executing a budget are, by definition, *political* processes that involve a host of actors with heterogeneous interests and incentives. The results of these processes depend on a nexus of formal rules and real practices, which determine the incentives and restrictions that every player brings to the budgetary decision-making arena.

This chapter examines how the budgetary process in Colombia operated between 1970 and 2006 and how fiscal outputs during that time frame were related to the country's fundamental political institutions. The analysis focuses on the national government's budget, which corresponds to the central government and decentralized entities that provide public services at the national level.[1] This level of aggregation excludes local governments, social security, and state-owned industrial and commercial companies, which are nonetheless relevant components of the Colombian public finances.

Given that formal budget rules and actual practices of the key players in the budget process have evolved over time, it is useful to identify (a) when changes in fiscal policy results took place and (b) whether those changes are attributable to institutional reforms of the budgetary process. The most important institutional changes stem from the 1991 Colombian constitution, which reformulated the rules of the political game at the highest level, introducing new decisive players with their own incentives and redefining the restrictions that govern how the negotiations occur.

Drawing on the framework developed in a recent study by the IDB (2005), it can be argued that the initial drafting, subsequent discussion, final approval, and execution of the budget are most likely to have desirable outcomes when the key political actors interact continuously and attain agreements that are easy to enforce. More simply, if actors cooperate among themselves, budgetary outcomes are more likely to be sustainable, efficient, representative, and adaptable.

For example, if the legislature can increase and change the amount and composition of government spending without restriction, and is comprised of members with high turnover, the resulting national budget is unlikely to contribute to sustainable public finances. If the budget is executed by a nonprofessional bureaucracy or with little coordination among the different sectors of the executive, it is likely that public expenditures will not be efficient. If there is a lack of trust in the relationship among the key actors, or if the actors do not interact for repeated periods of time, they will very likely resort to rigid rules that diminish the adaptability of fiscal policy.

This chapter is divided into seven sections. The subsequent section examines the formal and informal rules of the budget process in Colombia, underscoring the changes resulting from the 1991 constitution. It

[1] The data before 1990 exclude the decentralized entities.

lays out the background by providing some historical context, describing the main changes made to the budget statute in 1989, and identifying the main stages of the budget process (planning, programming, discussion and approval, implementation, and control and monitoring). The third section discusses the key players involved in the process, with the purpose of identifying their main incentives and constraints. The fourth section deals with the inflexibilities of the budget, which are perhaps the most relevant characteristics of the budget process in Colombia. This section not only provides a measure of those inflexibilities, but also traces their origin to changes in the fundamental political institutions that govern the budget process.

The fifth section provides some empirical evidence on the different stages of the budget process. The general purpose is to measure the changes (in the total amount as well as in the composition of the budget) introduced in each stage. The main conclusion of this section is that approval of supplemental budgets has been more costly in fiscal terms since the adoption of the 1991 constitution (meaning that there is a greater difference between what the executive proposes and what Congress approves). This has not been the case in the discussion and approval of the initial budget (where the executive prevails). The sixth section analyzes the budget outcomes and suggests that post-1991 gains in terms of representativeness have come at a cost in terms of sustainability. The chapter ends with a section of conclusions and policy recommendations.

FORMAL AND INFORMAL RULES THAT REGULATE THE COLOMBIAN BUDGET PROCESS

This section discusses the rules that govern the interaction among the main actors involved in different stages of the budget process in Colombia. A discussion of the formal rules, which impose restrictions and distribute powers, is the starting point for understanding the budgetary results. However, informal rules are equally important and the analysis must be complemented with a description of the actual budgetary practices. Formal rules are associated with constitutional provisions and statutory budget laws that shape the policymaking process. This section will discuss both types of provisions.

Background

Budgetary institutions or rules that regulate budget formulation by the executive, approval by Congress, and subsequent implementation are contained in the 1989 Organic Budgetary Statute (OBS) and the 1991 constitution.[2] In Colombia, since the mid-nineteenth century, the Ministry of Finance (MF) has played a leading role in the different stages of the budgetary process. For example, the 1886 constitution delegated budgetary authority to the MF and limited the role of Congress to the annual approval of the budget. Subsequent legislation empowered the MF even more, relative to other cabinet members, and imposed strict deadlines for congressional approval of the budget (in 1912). Further modifications banned Congress from increasing the budget without the approval of the executive (in 1923). Budgetary institutions were also strengthened by the creation of the Directorate of Budget in the MF (in 1950) and the National Planning Department (DNP), a technocratic cabinet-level entity, which in 1973 was given the role of preparing the investment budget.

1989 *Budgetary Reform*

Analysts agree that the 1989 reform to the budgetary statute was critical. Under the previous rules, the MF directly controlled monthly expenditures of other ministries, requiring the MF to preauthorize contractual commitments by the executing entities, and "spending agreements" through which the MF approved the amount ministries could disburse. These mechanisms gave the MF power to enforce budgetary restraint, but sacrificed efficiency in the use of public resources, since ministries could not plan and implement policies effectively, given that they had no certainty regarding the flow of resources actually available to them.

The 1989 statutory reform addressed the problem by providing ministries with greater autonomy to schedule their expenses. Government agencies set an annual funding ceiling and thus gained the flexibility to

[2] Organic laws (also called statutes) rank higher in the hierarchy than ordinary laws because they regulate the workings of a sector or a government agency or a legislative process (such as the annual budget law and its modifications).

plan and implement expenditure programs. However, the MF still has some control over the monthly cash flow according to the availability of resources. On the institutional side, the reform created a depository of investment projects at DNP—called the Banco de Programas y Proyectos de Inversión (BPIN)—as well as the Council for Fiscal Policy (CONFIS), formed by the economic cabinet and presided over by the minister of finance. BPIN registers investment projects and their technical evaluations and is in charge of certifying financial viability and suitability in light of the National Development Plan (which will be explained in detail later in this section). Similarly, CONFIS was created to generate additional analysis in the planning and implementation stages of the budget and to establish a better balance of responsibilities between the MF and DNP (Alarcón, 2004). In practice, the real power of CONFIS lies in its ability to create forward budget allocations (a mechanism that will be explained in detail below), without the control of Congress or any other entity within the executive branch. To summarize, the MF lost its power to determine the composition of expenditure (no control of the line items), but retained the power to regulate the monthly cash flow. A formal process of registry and evaluation of investment projects was adopted; however, a loophole in the statute allowed the congressional approval of projects without prior cost-benefit analysis and a new institution—CONFIS—was created to formalize the decision-making process within the executive.

It is widely believed that this procedural budgetary reform was a key step toward improving the quality and efficiency of public spending in Colombia, as Alarcón (2004) and Hommes (1996) mention. However, the reform also created a bicameral congressional commission as the competent authority to decide on the approval of loans to the government (bond issuances are excluded). As will be discussed below, this commission has been the focus of significant controversy, mainly because it strengthens the role of Congress in budgetary matters well beyond its role in the enactment of the annual budget law.

Another aspect of the formal rules that is questionable is related to the fact that the budget statute requires investment projects to be registered in the BPIN before their implementation, but not necessarily before congressional approval. In practice, this has allowed Congress to approve projects that have not been evaluated in terms of their financial and economic viability. Thus, over the years, BPIN registry and approval has become a mere formality, weakening the importance of the DNP.

1991 *Colombian Constitution*

After various reform attempts, a referendum passed in 1990 to convene a constitutional assembly that would write a new constitution. The resulting 1991 constitution reformed the policymaking game in many dimensions of direct relevance for the budget. The new constitution allocated public resources directly to certain activities (like education and health), defined new rules for fiscal transfers to municipalities and departments, and attempted to prioritize social expenditures (but failed to do so because the law later defined social expenditures in a very wide way that made this provision innocuous). On the political front, the reform reduced the costs of political participation and provided the system with more checks and balances, mostly through the creation of an independent central bank and a new and powerful constitutional court.

Recent Changes: The 2003 Fiscal Responsibility Law

Following the examples of other countries in the Latin American and Caribbean region, the executive presented and Congress enacted a fiscal responsibility law (FRL) in 2003. The law's origins can be traced to the discussions held between the Colombian government and the International Monetary Fund (IMF) that resulted in the extended agreement of 1999. The main thrust of the FRL is the Medium-Term Fiscal Framework (MTFF), which the executive must present annually to Congress (and, respectively, the departments and municipalities to their assemblies and councils). This document must contain (a) a financial plan for the following year; (b) a multiannual macroeconomic program; (c) cyclically adjusted primary surplus targets for the nonfinancial public sector for the next 10 years, as well as public debt level goals and an analysis of their sustainability; (d) a report of the previous period's macroeconomic and fiscal results; (e) an assessment of the main quasi-fiscal activities of the public sector, including the estimated cost of the laws passed in the previous fiscal term and the cost of tax exemptions and deductions; and (f) a list of contingent liabilities of the government.

To incorporate the provisions of the FRL into the budget statute, the executive submitted a bill in 2003. Although the bill was filed in June 2005, the executive issued a decree (so far upheld by the courts) introducing a more transparent budget classification system that is consistent with international standards. This system reduced the space for creative accounting and established the government's obligation to develop a Medium-Term Expenditure Framework (MTEF), which must include four-year spending projections and ceilings classified by sector and expenditure components (operational, debt, and investment). Although the MTFF has improved the level of the debate on public finances, it is still questionable whether it improves fiscal outcomes, since there are no sanctions associated with the lack of compliance.

Budget Process Stages

National Development Plan

The 1991 constitution introduced the National Development Plan as a new stage in the Colombian budget process. This plan, which the DNP must submit to Congress—six months after the president's inauguration—contains medium-term objectives by sectors and the strategies to achieve them. The development plan should also include a Multiyear Investment Plan (MIP) for each administration's four-year term and its projected funding. The MIP should also define and describe all investment programs and subprograms, their objectives, and the indicators needed for their evaluation. It must also be consistent with the government's economic growth and inflation goals. To ensure representativeness, the development plan has to be discussed with the National Planning Council before submission to Congress. Once the plan has been submitted, Congress has three months to discuss and enact it into law.

In practice, public investment figures fall significantly below what is stated in the MIP. For example, during the last two development plans whose period of execution has concluded (1999–2002 and 2003–2006), investment was 12.2 and 6.3 percent lower than planned, respectively. The largest differences between actual and planned investment are in the infrastructure and social sectors, contrary to what happens with the presidency and the interior ministry, which are responsible for coping with relatively unforeseen situations, through, for example, natural disaster management and giving attention to the displaced population.

Preparation of the Annual Budget

The annual budget must be prepared in accordance with the development plan's priorities. In the preparation stage each line item agency must express its appropriation needs (consistent with the MTEF and the development plan). The drafts are discussed with the MF and the DNP in the sectoral meetings. However, the final preparation of the draft budget bill is centralized in the MF and the DNP. Finally, the MF consolidates the budget and submits it to Congress.

According to the budget statute, the preparation includes three documents: the Financial Plan, the Annual Operating Plan for Investment (prepared by DNP), and the draft budget—based on the first two documents—which is submitted to Congress. The Financial Plan is prepared by the MF and must include the projected annual revenues, expenditures, deficit, and funding sources. It must be consistent with the macroeconomic objectives and take into account budgetary restrictions and sustainable public finances. Initially CONFIS and the Council on Economic and Social Policy (CONPES), presided over by the president, must approve these documents. After both councils approve it, the MF submits the draft budget to Congress.

Congressional Discussion and Approval

This stage begins each year during the first week of April when the executive power submits a draft budget to Congress for the following calendar year (which is also the fiscal year). This is a mere formality, because the real action begins during the first 10 days of the legislative year (which starts on July 20), when the final draft of the bill has to be submitted to Congress. The bill is debated in joint sessions of the Economic and Budget Committees (known as the Third and Fourth Committees, respectively) of both the Senate and the House (there are a total of four committees that make up the "Economic Committees"), although votes are taken separately for each committee. The first round of deliberations should end by September 15, when the four committees must decide on the total amount of the budget. The second set of deliberations among these committees is limited to budget composition issues and should end before September 25. The final (and plenary) debate has to be carried out between October 1 and 20 (together or separately for the Senate and House) and is limited to changes in the composition of the budget.

Congress does not have the power to increase the total budget. During the legislative discussion, changes to the total amount must be endorsed by the executive and incorporated into documents called Letters of Modification. An important element of this stage is that if Congress does not approve the proposed budget draft submitted by the executive, the proposal becomes law. If the executive does not submit a proposal, the previous year's budget becomes law. This strengthens the position of the executive relative to the legislature during the budget process.

Implementation

Three mechanisms can be used to amend the budget during its implementation. First, the executive may reduce or defer budgetary appropriations by decree under the following conditions: revenues run below their projected flows, macroeconomic consistency demands such actions, or executing agencies are falling behind in terms of actual outlays. These reductions and/or deferrals take the form of a presidential decree and require the approval of the entire cabinet. The second type of modification is the budgetary transfer, which permits an entity with an economically justified reason to shift resources from one item in its budget to another. When items have the same account classification (in the case of operating expenses and debt) and program (in the case of investments), transfers can be made by decree. Otherwise, Congress must authorize such transfers in a law. Finally, additions to the budget require a supplemental bill, which must also be approved by Congress. However, during a declared state of emergency (this is discussed in more detail in the next section), the government must only inform Congress of needed budget additions.

Control, Monitoring, and Evaluation

Congress exercises political control and oversight, while the general comptroller (elected by Congress) is in charge of fiscal control. The budget statute assigns financial monitoring responsibilities to the MF and monitoring and evaluation of the achievement of physical targets to the DNP through a program called SINERGIA (Sistema Nacional de Evaluación de Resultados de la Gestión Pública). This program is responsible for informing the president about budget execution (of all line item agencies) and submits reports to Congress every six months. It often relies on independent impact evaluation studies.

The Role of Congress: Formal versus Informal Practices

In general terms, the formal rules that govern the budget process in Colombia seem to be in line with international best practices. Nevertheless, it could be argued that fiscal results in Colombia compare unfavorably with those of other countries, such as Brazil and Peru, with similar budgetary institutions (including the existence of FRLs). This apparent contradiction can be explained by analyzing how the budget preparation, approval, and implementation stages actually occur, that is, the real practices. In many cases, the budget process in Colombia reflects customs and practices that are somehow different from the formal rules.

For example, Congress plays a greater role than the one inferred at first sight, because it has power in other policy areas (e.g., the approval of other bills) in which the executive requires its support. The possibility of exerting that power gives Congress greater leverage over the amount and the composition of expenditures. Although convincing evidence is difficult to find, there are few doubts that budget allocations to regional investment projects promoted by legislators are the main tool for governments to ensure support for their legislative initiatives. However, the degree of transparency for such allocations has varied according to the political moment.

Between 1968 and 1991, these allocations operated through a relatively formalized system with strong legal support (in fact, the system was adopted by the constitutional reform of 1968). During that period, "parliamentary slush funds" (*auxilios parlamentarios*) was included in the budget as line items in the form of scholarships for individuals selected by legislators or as contributions to foundations and other nonprofit organizations controlled by parliamentarians or their relatives. This was politically accepted and relatively visible, although no hard data show how much was assigned to each member of Congress for one use or another. Although the parliamentary slush funds were legal, no regulations existed. Informal and anecdotal evidence suggests that the ministers of finance had the greatest influence in determining the size of this line item and the allocation across legislators (presumably on the grounds of their ranking and influence). Naturally, the most influential members of committees—their chairpersons and the sponsors or rapporteurs of the budget bill—received better treatment.

Although the overall size of the slush funds was never a fiscal problem between 1968 and 1991, some scandals in the use of phantom foundations that served to enrich parliamentarians stoked outrage at a time when public opinion strongly rejected the political class, in general, and Congress, in particular. The assembly that drafted the 1991 constitution, which expressly prohibited the use of parliamentary slush funds, captured this feeling. At the time, this political achievement was widely reported and emphasized by the media and unquestionably raised public sympathy toward the constitutional assembly.

Nevertheless, parliamentary slush funds have not disappeared in the budget process, surviving in less formal and transparent ways. Rather than budget items being assigned for the direct benefit of a congressional member or members, resources are channeled through specific regional investment projects. In a strict sense, the use of political influence to manage these budget items is unconstitutional, but control agencies tolerate it as long as parliamentarians do not try to influence the selection of contractors, which obviously violates public procurement norms.

The allocation of the aforementioned budget items essentially occurs through two mechanisms. The first system operates through the approval of specific investment projects within the budgets of national-level agencies. Generally, these agencies are specialized "funds" that operate as instruments to control investment projects in a particular sector (local roads, energy, water and sanitation, etc.). Normally, the use of these agencies as vehicles to appropriate funds attracts the attention of public opinion and the judicial authorities. It is commonplace in presidential campaigns in Colombia to accuse the incumbent government of misusing these funds. Hence, one of the first decisions a new government takes is to abolish some or several of them. In any case, the resources channeled through these agencies rarely exceed more than 2 percent of the entire budget, which suggests that the cost of building congressional coalitions in this manner is relatively low. The selection of the officials who administer the funds is of enormous importance to members of Congress, who intend to exert future influence on them.

Inclusion of specific items in the budget occurs during discussions in the Economic Committees (the plenary rubber-stamps what is approved in these committees). This clearly increases the influence of the members of the Economic Committees, who often act as intermediaries between the executive and other parliamentarians who want their projects included. In some cases, the MF opposes the inclusion of specifically designated projects to avoid whetting the appetite of legislators. Once the law is approved—but before the president sanctions it—the MF has the opportunity to add detail to broad line items (at the level of program or subprogram) in a decree that closes the approval stage of the budget. In some cases, the executive makes a commitment to parliamentarians to add investment projects not included in the law to the decree. This commitment demonstrates the nature of the game, which requires a certain expertise, and benefits the long-serving parliamentarians.

It is worth noting that the inclusion of specific items is not confined to the discussion of the annual budget law. Negotiations are even more intense and significant during the approval of a supplementary budget, since the total amount is not predetermined and can be modified at any time during congressional debate. As an example, during the budgetary addition approved in 2001, the government asked for an increase of the investment budget by an amount equivalent to 22.9 percent of what had been approved in the annual budget law. Congress approved a 24.3 percent increase. Much of the difference came from additional items requested by legislators that were assigned to agencies in charge of housing subsidies, local roads, and rural development.

The second mechanism for allocation of favored budget items works through global appropriations for infrastructure, health, and education. During budget negotiation, interested legislators (with the support of the respective minister) request resources for general purposes, such as hospital and school funding or airport construction in rural areas. These resources are assigned to very broad budget items, without specifying the details of projects to be implemented. After the budget is ratified, the corresponding minister exercises the authority (sometimes the approval of the DNP is required) to assign the resources as needed, strengthening his or her importance in the budgetary process beyond that stated in the formal rules.

KEY PLAYERS

The analysis of formal and informal rules would be incomplete without a detailed description of the role of the different actors in the Colombian budget process. Therefore, this section examines the main incentives of and constraints on the actors, which will be shown herein as decisive in terms of fiscal outcomes.

President

Although the presidency is granted more powers in Colombia than in nearly all other countries in Latin America (surpassed only by Chile and Brazil), the 1991 constitution limited presidential power in several ways (see Payne et al., 2002). One example is the use of emergency powers, which allows the promulgation of decree-laws without the immediate approval of Congress. Contrary to what was the case prior to 1991, decisions adopted under a state of emergency relating to economic or internal affairs must now be ratified by a regular session of the Congress.

Furthermore, if the president vetoes a law, Congress can override the veto with a simple majority, whereas before 1991 a two-thirds majority was needed. Nevertheless, presidents have managed without exception to assemble majority coalitions in Congress. Traditionally the president uses the appointment powers to decide on the administration and control of budgetary items as a means to ensure congressional support of other presidential initiatives.

Cabinet

The ministers are key actors in planning, developing, approving and—especially—implementing the budget. With the exception of the minister of finance and the director of the DNP, the other members of the cabinet are responsible for spending and therefore press for additional line items, often with the support of members of Congress. With some notable exceptions, the ministers with spending authority have a political background and pursue (or have pursued) political careers. Until recently, the main characteristic of cabinet members was their frequent turnover (since 1970, the average term in office for ministers has been a year and a half). Ministerial survival depends on the minister's level of political support; legislators thus have some influence over the cabinet beyond what the formal rules predict, particularly in budgetary matters.

The Colombian tradition has been to nominate technocrats to top positions in the MF and the DNP.[3] For example, 11 out of 21 ministers of finance between 1970 and 2005, and virtually all the heads of DNP, can be considered technocrats in the sense that they have been professional economists and have previous professional experience in organizations like the Central Bank, Fedesarrollo (La Fundación para la Educación Superior y el Desarrollo), and Universidad de los Andes. Generally, technocrats have shown no aspirations for elected office. Although ministers of finance do not remain in office much longer than other ministers, their technical background gives them greater autonomy before Congress, especially on budget matters. The same is true for budget directors, who usually have moved on to higher positions in the hierarchy of the economic cabinet.

Congress

The Colombian Congress has two chambers: the Senate and the House of Representatives. The 1991 constitution reduced both the number of senators, from 113 to 102, and the number of representatives, from 199 to 165. Each of the 32 departments has the right to at least two representatives, and certain minorities (indigenous groups, Afro-Colombians,

---

[3] Technocrats made their appearance in Colombia following the creation of the DNP, which became a stronghold within the civil service. At the end of the 1960s, the creation of the CONPES (Consejo Nacional de Política Económica y Social), as a vehicle for formulating policies based on documents prepared by the DNP, further strengthened its role. In many cases, the implementation of these policies will also be delegated to the technocrats, over the mandate of the ministers. By the 1970s, the finance ministers began to be chosen within this group.

and Colombians living abroad) have a number of seats. The reform also introduced national election for the Senate (before 1991 senators were elected by departmental districts).

Despite the reduction of congressional seats, long-standing electoral rules (reaffirmed in the 1991 constitution) allowed (until 2003 when a reform changed this) several factions of the same party to present different lists. The result was an increase in the number of lists (to maximize the participation of each party in Congress) and the proliferation of factions within parties, which in most cases elected only a sole parliamentarian. This explains why the most salient characteristic of the Colombian Congress is its excessive fragmentation, which, as will be seen shortly, has directly affected the budgetary process. The rules for the election of representatives were reformed in 2003, with the objective of eliminating the fragmentation and strengthening the political parties.[4] This was reflected in the congressional elections of 2006, in which the number of lists for the Senate (House) fell from 321 (906) to 20 (412), relative to the 2002 elections.

Congressional rules require high degrees of specialization because legislators belong to only one committee during their four-year terms. The economic committees are four of the most coveted committees in the Colombian Congress. Joining these committees (especially the Third Committee) is not easy for a congressional member lacking seniority. The composition of the committees reflects a complex partisan and regional equilibrium, especially between the Caribbean coast and the interior. Also, low turnover rates imply that the probability of a new legislator entering the committees is relatively low. For example, in the March 2006 congressional elections, all members of the Senate's Third Committee were reelected and remained on the committee. Tenure in the Fourth Committee of the Senate is shorter, although it is evident that a core group of senators tends to be in control for long periods of time. Turnover in the economic committees of the House of Representatives is higher, but mainly because some members pursue political careers that take them to the Senate or to governorships.

Another very coveted assignment is to the above-mentioned committee that oversees public borrowing—the Interparliamentary Commit-

---

[4] The reform allows parties to register only one list. A threshold of 2 percent for the Senate and 50 percent of the quotient for the House is required for a party to gain representation.

tee of Public Credit—which is formed by six members of the economic committees (three from the Senate and three from the House). Although legal controversy surrounds the constitutionality of this committee, eliminating it has proven politically impossible. Members of the committee approve every loan operation, which gives them great influence over the executive, especially on budget matters.

Although Colombian political parties are among the weakest and least cohesive of political parties in Latin America, they exert some influence on congressional operations. This becomes particularly clear when one analyzes the internal rules of Congress, especially the assignment of members to committees, strategic functions (sponsors or rapporteurs for legislative proposals), and positions in the hierarchy (committee chairs). The committee chairs assign one or more sponsors to each legislative proposal, giving them substantial negotiating power, especially in regard to key bills such as the budget. Needless to say, the hierarchal position of a legislator and leverage in terms of bureaucratic posts or access to funds for regional investment projects go hand in hand.

Sponsors play very important roles in the approval of the annual budgetary legislation. They represent the different groups within the Congress and ensure smooth discussion and approval of the budget. The number of sponsors has augmented significantly since the mid-1990s, increasing political transaction costs between the executive and Congress.

Constitutional Court

The Constitutional Court (CC), established by the 1991 constitution, is a key player in the budget process. Its influence comes either through the constitutionality review process or in decisions related to the defense of individual and collective rights. Many of the rulings of the CC have budget implications. To comply with those rulings, the executive power has to resort to budgetary transfers and, sometimes, to the issuance of forward allocations. Often, the executive is forced to present supplemental budgets in order to avoid judicial risks vis-à-vis the court.

The way the CC has dealt with the issue of internal displacement problems—to the acclaim of many human rights groups in Colombia and abroad—is illustrative of this trend. In 2004, the CC determined that to vindicate the rights of families that have been forced to leave their dwellings as a result of the country's internal conflict, the national government had to develop a schedule of activities and expenditures, as well as a medium-term action plan with periodic review and specific goals. There are many other examples of rulings that have had enormous influence on many budget matters, such as public sector wages and pensions. In the case of constitutional review, the key aspect is that even if the executive reaches an agreement with Congress, it needs the approval of the CC. For example, the CC has ruled the budget unconstitutional in periods when the executive and Congress have approved increases in wages that fall short of accrued inflation.

The fact that many budgetary decisions have a constitutional rank explains why fiscal reforms usually take the form of constitutional amendments. An extreme example in terms of mechanisms for reforming the constitution is the 2003 referendum, which convened voters to decide mostly on issues related to public sector wages, pensions, and various other government expenditures. The proposals advanced by the executive in the referendum were rejected. Since then, reforms have taken the form of constitutional amendments approved by Congress.

INFLEXIBILITIES

The IMF (2004: 70) considers Colombia to be the country in the region with the largest percentage of earmarked spending.[5] Earmarking can be seen as a tool to solve the coordination problem among diverse agents, or as a mechanism to protect certain areas of public spending that require stability, buffering these agents from the ups and downs of political and electoral cycles. For example, investment in education and health requires long-term commitments to secure the desired results. The same is true of some public infrastructure projects.

While those arguments are sound, it is also true that budgetary inflexibilities can become problematic when they limit the use of fiscal policy for stabilization purposes. Also, rigidities are often the result of capture by special interest groups, which runs against the goals of representativeness and efficiency of public spending. The general per-

[5] Earmarked spending accounts for 81 percent in Colombia compared with 80 percent in Brazil, 60 percent in Argentina, 45 percent in Costa Rica, and 1 percent in Peru.

ception is that the proliferation of inflexibilities in Colombia has gone too far, to the point that the costs outweigh the benefits.

The 1991 constitution elevated budget rigidities in Colombia to new heights. According to Penfold (1999), representatives to the constitutional assembly generally were elected because of the traditional political machinery of the regions, which made them more beholden to regional rather than national political leaders. The influence of the constitutional reforms in Europe and other Latin American countries in the 1970s and 1980s, the presence of new political groups (such as the left-leaning M-19), and distrust that Congress would subsequently overturn decisions of the constitutional assembly explain the high level of detail and specificity in the new constitution, which moved away from being a guiding political document to establishing operational norms in specific policy areas.

The 1991 constitution introduced several inflexibilities that are worth mentioning. One article states that public social spending has priority over any other allowance in the sense that it cannot be reduced in percentage terms (relative to overall expenditures) from one year to the next. However, as noted in a 2007 report from the Comisión Independiente del Gasto Público (2007), the definition of social expenditure in the budget statute is so wide as to make this constitutional provision entirely ineffective. The constitution also mandated an increase in fiscal transfers to the municipalities from 14 percent of government revenues in 1993 to a minimum of 22 percent in 2002. Two constitutional amendments (2001 and 2007) tried to contain the increase in fiscal transfers, but succeeded only partially. Also, the constitution prohibited earmarked taxation, except for social investment, thus opening a substantial loophole. As such, taxes tied to specific "social" purposes have proliferated since 1991 (e.g., construction of sports infrastructure with revenues from a surcharge value-added tax applied to mobile telephones). According to estimates by the MF, 79 percent of the inflexibilities in the 2003 budget originated after 1991.

Why have inflexibilities mushroomed since 1991? The explanation is connected with changes in political institutions that have increased competition, rotation, and fragmentation in Congress (Cárdenas, Junguito, and Pachón, 2005). Such scenarios favor the adoption of rules that tend to be inflexible. Political actors want agreements to be immune from future renegotiations that will surely involve other and more diverse political actors. Following Echeverry, Fergusson, and Querubín (2004), the problem of inflexibilities can be analyzed by applying the theory of the "tragedy of the commons," which refers to the excessive appropriation of resources from a common pool. Each group that introduces inflexibilities reaps a benefit but passes on the fiscal cost (expressed in terms not only of sustainability but also of efficiency) to the society as a whole.

Another important source of inflexibility has emerged directly from the use by the executive branch of forward allocations (*vigencias futuras*), which are a mechanism for commiting expenditure in the medium term, especially for investment. The granting of these allocations rests solely in the executive's power and, more specifically, under the authority of CONFIS. Strictly speaking, forward allocations constitute inflexibilities in the budget, since they are shown as effective appropriations that are above the will of Congress or other norms. On the positive side, forward allocations are an ideal mechanism for completion of infrastructure investment projects. They provide stability, but at the expense of representativeness and adaptability.

During the period 1995–1999, forward allocations equaled 18.3 percent of the investment budget, while during the period 2000–2005, the figure jumped to 63.9 percent. Obviously, this substantially curtails budgetary adaptability. Based on an analysis of forward allocations by sector, it has been found that the increase has gone to transport infrastructure, followed by security and defense, basic sanitation, and communications.

EMPIRICAL EVIDENCE ON BUDGETARY OUTCOMES

This section presents some evidence on the changes in the budget during each one of the stages identified in the previous sections: from bill proposal to annual budget law (stage 1), from the budget law to definitive appropriation (stage 2)—which reflects the additions or cuts that usually happen throughout the fiscal year—and from final appropriation to implementation or execution (stage 3). Differences in stage 1 are the result of negotiations between the executive and Congress to enact the law. Changes in stage 2 result from modifications led by the executive, some of which Congress must approve. Finally, differences between the definitive appropriation and final implementation (stage 3) measure the operational capacity of the different public entities.

Using a variety of sources, it was possible to compile data from 1970 to 2005 on the changes in each of the three stages, disaggregated by functional expenditure type (i.e., operational, investment, and debt service).[6] With the exception of 1975 and 1991, normally the total budget amount approved has been higher than the initial proposal. On average, the total amount of the budget has increased 0.41 percent of GDP (or 2.17 percent of the total budget in the executive proposal). By expenditure type, the investment budget experiences the largest changes.[7] The fact that the correlation between the changes in investment and the changes in debt service is negative and significant suggests that Congress (with a nod from the government) transfers resources from debt to other items in the approval stage.

However, the largest changes appear in stage 2 of the budgetary process (i.e., between budget law enactment and the definitive appropriation). An important part of these changes comes from supplemental budgets, which have been a constant in the budget process (more than one addition is often made during the same fiscal term). However, this stage also includes other modifications like transfers, cuts and deferrals (which can reduce the total amount). During the period 1970–2005, resources equivalent to 2.2 percent of GDP were added on average in each fiscal year. In this stage, Congress has the upper hand: governments try to avoid presenting additions, because they are aware that passing them through Congress is very costly. If changes are categorized by expenditure type, debt is the only category whose change has generally been negative. This suggests a deliberate strategy of overestimating this item in the budget to provide certain capacity to accommodate subsequent pressures for additional expenditures. It is not common for governments to cut operational and investment budgets (a well-known exception was 1998, when the international financial crisis forced the Colombian government to cut expenditures).

---

[6] Data for the period 1970–1988 come from *Budgetary Facts 1970–1988*, published by the Directorate of Budget of the MF; for the period 1989–1994, the data come from the *Annual Reports of the Comptroller-General's Office*; and for the period 1994–2005, the sources are the MF (public credit) and DNP.

[7] According to data from Castiblanco (2005) for the period 1995–2003, the number of investment projects from the bill proposal and the budget law increased on average 210 percent. The increase was particularly pronounced for the period 1995–1999, when the figure was 313 percent. This shows that investment projects are an instrument used by the executive to negotiate with the legislature.

Regarding stage 3, the difference between the amount that is finally appropriated and what is implemented or executed is a measure of administrative and managerial capacity in using budgetary resources. From 1970 to 2005, it is possible to observe two periods of low implementation of the budget: at the end of the 1970s/beginning of the 1980s and in the second half of the 1990s. The data suggest an increase in the efficiency of investment implementation after the changes introduced by Law 38 of 1989, which were oriented toward providing more flexibility to the executing agencies and less control to the MF.

Using the methodology set forth in the first two chapters of this volume, it is possible to denote a significant recomposition among the three expenditure types in each of the three stages. A widespread phenomenon in the three stages is that the recomposition between different types of expenditure was lower in the nineties and even more notorious for stage 2 (from budget law to the final appropriation). This is the stage in which formal rules provide Congress with greater bargaining power.

Changes to the Budget Process Outcomes Associated with the 1991 Constitution

As already explained, the 1991 constitution gave Congress a more active role in fiscal policy formulation by limiting the power of the executive to legislate by decree and by making it easier to override a presidential veto. The creation of the CC further strengthened the system of checks and balances.

The constitution of 1991 also abolished parliamentary slush funds, which has, according to Echeverry, Fergusson, and Querubín (2004: 51), "generated a greater 'budget appetite' in Congress, which, along with the executive power, must now resort to less transparent mechanisms to ensure that its interests are reflected in the budget."

Thus, there are good reasons to believe that the 1991 constitution meant major changes in budget process outcomes. This section seeks to establish the effect, if any, of constitutional changes regarding the amount and composition of the budget in each of the three stages of the budget process described above. It also examines the relationship between those changes and the macroeconomic variables that may impact budget process decisions, such as the business cycle (measured as the percentage deviation of GDP compared to its trend) and the rate of real devaluation (which can increase the cost of debt).

For this purpose, the following equation can be used, where the dependent variable is the change in the total budget amount (during each one of the three stages):

$$\Delta\ total\ amount_{i,k,t} = \beta_0 + \beta_1 DPost1991 + \beta_2 EcoCycle_t + \beta_3 \Delta RER_t + \beta_4 DPost1991 * EcoCycle_t + \beta_5 DPost1991 * \Delta RER_t + \varepsilon\Delta_t.$$

More concretely, Δ *total amount*$_{i,k,t}$ is the change to the budget in stage i (i =1,2,3) (as a percentage of GDP) for expenditure type k (operational, debt service, and investment) in year t; *DPost*1991 is a dummy variable with a value of 1 for every year after 1991; *EcoCycle* is the measure of the business cycle (deviation from trend in logs), and ΔRER is the percentage change in the real exchange rate; ε is the error term.

Table 4.1 presents the results of changes in the budget in each of the three stages, both for the total amount and for each functional item. In stage 1, a positive deviation of 1 percent of the GDP deviation from trend is associated with an increase of 0.12 percent of GDP in investment, compared to what was submitted by the executive in the bill. This indicates that the investment included during discussion of the budget law in Congress has been procyclical.

In stage 2, which measures the result of budget modifications made from the initial budget proposal to the final budget appropriation, the dichotomous variable *DPost*1991 has a significant and negative effect for the total budget as well as for the amount spent in operation and investment. This means that the use of budgetary additions by the executive has had a downward slope, which could indicate increased costs of passing the budget through Congress as a result of the 1991 constitution. The economic cycle also shows an effect on the budget at this stage. Before 1991, the net changes to the budget had been procyclical (for the total, debt, and investment), while afterward they became countercyclical (though the effect disappears for the amount of debt and appears in operations). Likewise, the rate of real devaluation affects the actual result of the modifications to the budget during the second stage. Again, the effect changes if the variable interacts with the dichotomous variable *DPost*1991. Thus, a real devaluation of 1 percent before 1991 resulted in an increase of 0.10 percent in the total budget. Since 1991, real depreciations have been associated with reductions in expenditures. The reason may be related to the tax effect of the exchange

TABLE 4.1 Econometric Results: Determinants of Budget Changes, 1970–2005

Dependent variable	*DPost1991*	Economic cycle	Δ*RER*	Interaction *DPost1991* and economic cycle	Interaction *DPost1991* and Δ*RER*
Stage I: from bill proposal to annual budget law					
Change in total amount	0.103 (0.172)	0.002 (0.036)	0.008 (0.010)	0.076 (0.059)	0.022 (0.019)
Change in operational expenditure	0.154 (0.124)	0.008 (0.016)	−0.001 (0.004)	−0.004 (0.036)	−0.005 (0.009)
Change in debt service	0.045 (0.079)	0.039 (0.030)	0.001 (0.004)	−0.042 (0.034)	0.012 (0.008)
Change in investment expenditure	−0.099 (0.097)	−0.045 (0.043)	−0.005 (0.010)	0.122 (0.054)	0.015 (0.014)
Stage II: from budget law to definitive appropriation					
Change in total amount	−1.394 (0.331)	0.197 (0.101)	0.100 (0.031)	−0.470 (0.140)	−0.119 (0.042)
Change in operational expenditure	−0.354 (0.173)	−0.007 (0.065)	0.043 (0.019)	−0.148 (0.079)	−0.057 (0.025)
Change in debt service	−0.167 (0.132)	0.035 (0.016)	0.002 (0.009)	−0.038 (0.051)	0.007 (0.020)
Change in investment expenditure	−0.870 (0.162)	0.171 (0.070)	0.055 (0.021)	−0.285 (0.079)	−0.070 (0.023)
Stage III: from final appropriation to implementation or execution					
Change in total amount	−0.092 (0.197)	−0.112 (0.093)	−0.016 (0.022)	0.081 (0.108)	−0.009 (0.027)
Change in operational expenditure	−0.139 (0.071)	−0.024 (0.027)	−0.005 (0.006)	−0.015 (0.037)	−0.008 (0.009)
Change in debt service	−0.102 (0.044)	−0.009 (0.008)	−0.004 (0.003)	0.010 (0.016)	0.003 (0.006)
Change in investment expenditure	0.137 (0.125)	−0.078 (0.066)	−0.007 (0.016)	0.086 (0.072)	−0.003 (0.018)

Source: Authors' calculations.
Note: OLS estimation, robust standard errors in parentheses. Controls: dummy for first year of each administration, dummy for last year of each administration, and dummy for 1992 in Stage II regressions. Number of observations: 36.

rate. Pre-1991, devaluation produced additional revenues (because of the importance of exports in the public sector), while this effect has been reduced since then because of the weight of public debt denominated in dollars. Finally, the empirical evidence shows that in stage 3, the institutional changes of 1991 had only small effects.

In summary, results of the econometric exercises do not show strong evidence in favor of a structural break of the budget process in the wake of the 1991 constitution, at least for changes in the amount and composition of the budget in its different stages. To corroborate the absence of a structural change, Chow tests have been used for each of the dependent variables in the reported regression.[8] Only one series (change in total spending in operations during stage 1) has shown a structural change since 1991.

BUDGETARY OUTCOMES

This section describes the main results of the Colombian budget process in terms of four important dimensions of fiscal policy (explained in detail in the introductory chapter of this volume): sustainability, adaptability, efficiency, and representativeness.

Sustainability

In a long-run perspective, Colombian public finances have tended to be sustainable in the sense of being characterized by low deficits, relatively low debt (as a percentage of GDP) and, most importantly, absence of defaults (at least in the postwar period). For example, during the "lost decade" of the 1980s, while the rest of the region had large fiscal deficits, Colombia kept fiscal deficits below 4 percent of GDP and did not default on its obligations. This situation changed, however, during the 1990s. While most countries in the region adjusted their public finances successfully, the opposite happened in Colombia, where the national government's deficit sharply increased between 1995 and 1999 (in 1999, it exceeded 7 percent of GDP). Even though Colombia's fiscal situation

[8] The Chow test is a statistical and econometric test of whether the coefficients in two linear regressions on different data samples are equal.

has been improving since 2000, the national government's deficit still exceeded 3.3 percent of GDP in 2007 (see Figure 4.1).

Adaptability

Adaptability refers to the capacity to adjust the course of fiscal policy when facing economic shocks. In order for public finances to play a stabilizing role, the budget process must allow savings generation in boom years and expenditure increases in recessionary periods. A simple exercise estimation for the 1980–2005 period of the correlation between detrended GDP and public expenditures shows that the coefficient is relatively low (0.065), suggesting that fiscal policy has been neutral vis-à-vis the business cycle.

However, a more robust exercise—based on the "fiscal impulse" methodology—defines "discretionary" fiscal policy as the change in the cyclical component of the primary deficit. If the primary deficit increases over its trend level, it is understood that fiscal policy is deliberately expansionary. If this occurs when the GDP is below its potential or trend level, then fiscal policy is countercyclical. The results of this exercise illustrate how a primary deficit increase is characteristic in years when

FIGURE 4.1 **National Government: Debt and Total and Primary Fiscal Balance** *(percent of GDP)*

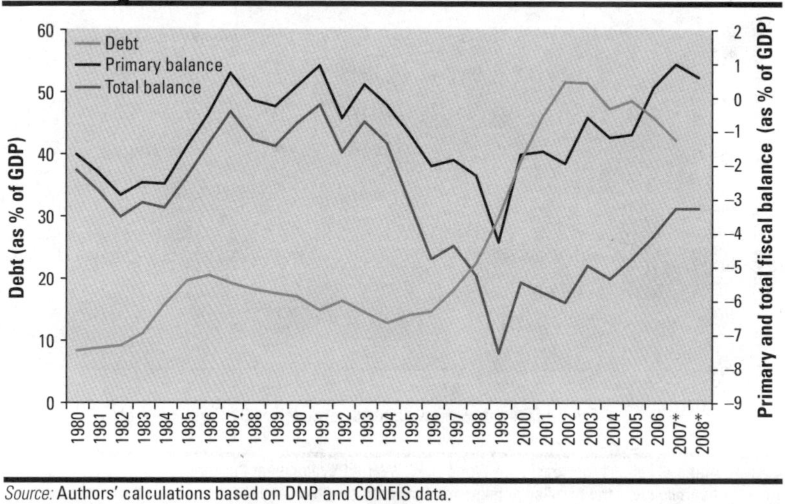

Source: Authors' calculations based on DNP and CONFIS data.
Note: Asterisks indicate that statistics for 2007 and 2008 are estimates.

GDP growth is above trend, while a primary surplus results when GDP is below its potential. This exercise provides evidence of the presence of a largely procyclical policy. Nevertheless, policy has been countercyclical at times, such as in 1999 and during the first half of the 1980s.

Efficiency

Measuring the efficiency of public spending is not an easy task. In a recent study, Herrera and Pang (2005) distinguish between two types of efficiency of fiscal policy. Technical efficiency refers to the optimum use of resources (inputs) to achieve expected results, while an effective allocation refers to the optimal distribution of resource spending (inputs) among different alternatives depending on their marginal productivity.

In the specific case of education, expenditures in Colombia—in both primary and secondary education—seem high in terms of actual enrollment rates, relative to other countries in the Latin American and Caribbean region. Figure 4.2 shows that among Latin American countries, Colombia is one of the countries that spend more, but its outcome in terms of enrollment rate is lower than expected. A similar

FIGURE 4.2 Net Secondary Enrollment and Public Expenditures in Education, Average, 1998–2002

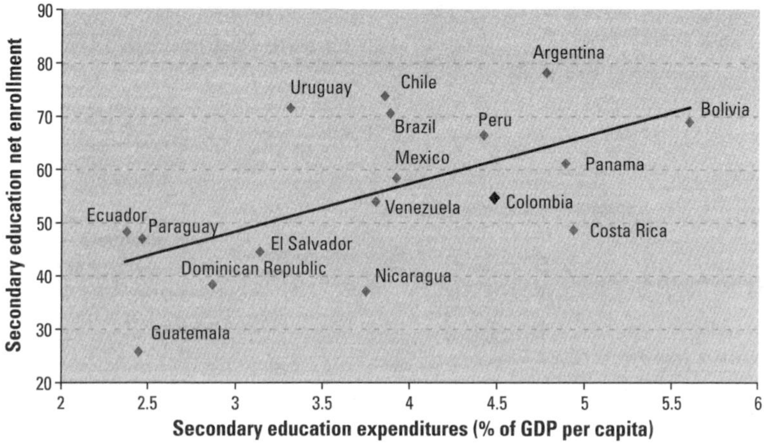

Sources: Authors' calculations based on World Bank, World Development Indicators.
Note: Net enrollment is the enrolled population of children of school age expressed as a percentage of the entire population of children of the corresponding age.

FIGURE 4.3 **DPT Immunization Rates and Public Expenditures in Health, Average, 1998–2002**

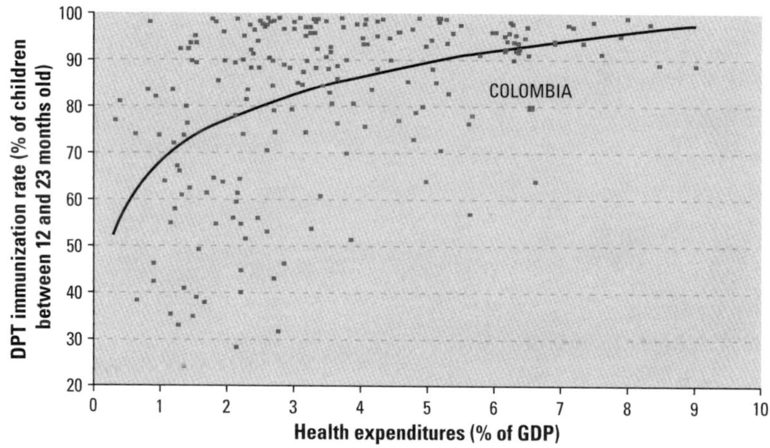

Source: Authors' calculations based on World Bank, World Development Indicators.

pattern emerges in the case of health: Colombia seems to spend more on health than other countries around the world with similar health outcomes, such as vaccinations (Figure 4.3).

Representativeness

There is no single definition for the representativeness of public expenditures. Conceptually, the planning process for public resource allocation can be a starting point for evaluating the budget's degree of representativeness. This plan must outline the promises the new administration made during the presidential campaign and define the policies and the resources to fulfill the stated goals within the context of fiscal and macroeconomic sustainability. The law differentiates between the planning authorities that participate in drafting the National Development Plan (the executive branch) and the authorities involved in the discussion process for its approval (including the National Planning Council and the Congress[9]). These two stages bring

[9] The president appoints the members of the National Planning Council in accordance with the following composition: the council must include members from four of the different municipali-

an incentive to the different political, economic, and civil society sectors to participate, giving public policies more representativeness. In this sense, the achievement of development plan goals can be one measure of representativeness. Also, as mentioned above, the role of the CC is important in budget matters and should be considered an important element of representativeness. However, the extensive use of earmarked taxes and other budget rigidities, such as forward allocations, where few actors intervene, often has a cost in terms of this dimension.

In sum, the budgetary process in Colombia today is more inclusive and representative than before the 1991 constitution. However, the results in terms of adaptability, efficiency, and sustainability leave much room for improvement.

CONCLUSIONS

This chapter shows that the political institutions play a large role in explaining some key features of the Colombian budget process. This process is known to be based on a complex and overlapping system of inflexible fiscal rules that determine funds allocated to various purposes, including sectors (such as education and health), expenditure types (such as public sector wages), and earmarks. Although a good theoretical model is lacking, it is commonly believed that these rigidities are an equilibrium outcome in a game with a large number of players that do not interact repeatedly and thus have difficulties in reaching cooperative outcomes.

In spite of this, the minister of finance still has the upper hand in most budgetary decisions. For example, the resources added by Congress during the approval stage are moderate (on average, 0.41 percent of GDP or 3.11 percent of the budget). Moreover, it is not true that the "cost" for budget approval has increased since the constitution of 1991, which in theory strengthened legislative power vis-à-vis executive power, took effect.

---

ties, nine of the different departments, one of the indigenous territories, four of the different economic sectors, five from civil society, two in the education sector, one from the environment sector, and five from ethnic minority groups.

In reality, most of the modifications occur in a later stage: between budget law enactment and the final appropriation. This shows that investment projects suggested by legislators are included more frequently in the process of passing budgetary additions than in the initial budget approval stage. Nevertheless, the amount of budgetary additions has decreased since 1991, suggesting that the new constitution has made enacting such legislation a harder process. In some sense, this suggests that there are more rigidities today than there were before 1991, but that there is less scope for negotiations over the flexible component.

The political reform of 2003 has strengthened the party system and will probably improve the quality of discussion on budget matters in Congress, as well as the overall budget outcomes. However, some important reforms are still needed, in particular, a set of measures that include (a) a reform to the Organic Budgetary Statute that will narrow the specific areas where inflexibilities and earmarking would be accepted; (b) strict restrictions on the amount of forward allocations, which should be allowed only in the case of projects that have been debated and approved in the context of the National Development Plan. The latter will ensure that the inflexibilities set by each administration are, at the very least, justified by the objectives and strategies included in the plan. The amount of forward allocations also should not exceed limits in the multiannual investment budget that accompanies the development plan, and the maximum duration of the allocations should not exceed eight years. Such limits not only would reduce the inflexibilities but also would improve the links between the planning, drafting, and implementation stages of the budget. Also, this provision would ameliorate the problems of representativeness associated with these forward allocations. These reforms will increase the degree of adaptability of fiscal policy.

Several reforms should be implemented regarding the formal rules. First, the Interparliamentary Committee of Public Credit should be eliminated. In terms of debt management, the role of Congress should end with the debate and approval of the budget and the corresponding amount of net borrowing in the annual budget law. The decisions made on the type of borrowing (domestic versus external) as well as particular contractual terms should not be subject to congressional interference. This reform would give more transparency to the entire process.

Second, it is essential to reform the Organic Budgetary Statute to demand the registration of investment projects in the BPIN (to carry out an economic analysis of project viability suitability) before Congress approves such projects. This is rather obvious but does not occur today. Legislators add proposals which have not been scrutinized and which have not passed the minimum standards for ensuring economic viability.

Third, CC rulings involving additional expenditures should explicitly take into account their impact on the budget. This can be achieved by requiring a technical memorandum, drafted by experts, to be attached to the evidentiary materials discussed by the justices. At the very least, justices should be aware of the costs of their decisions. This will probably not change the rulings, but will create a better understanding of the complex trade-offs that are involved in the budgetary decisions.

With regard to reforming informal practices, the evidence collected in this chapter suggests that the process of approval of supplemental budget laws is very costly from a fiscal viewpoint. Congress at this stage has great leverage to increase what the government proposes. Therefore, it is advisable to improve budgetary planning and programming in order to avoid the need for later add-ons.

REFERENCES

Alarcón, L. F. 2004. La defensa de la Ley 38 de 1989. In *Debates de Coyuntura Económica No. 55.* Bogotá: Fundación para la Educación Superior y el Desarrollo (Fedesarrollo).

Alesina, A., and R. Perotti. 1999. Budget Deficits and Budget Institutions. In James M. Poterba and Jürgen von Hagen, eds., *Fiscal Institutions and Fiscal Performance.* Chicago and London: University of Chicago Press.

Cárdenas, M., R. Junguito, and M. Pachón. 2005. Political Institutions and Policy Outcomes in Colombia: The Effects of the 1991 Constitution. Fedesarrollo Working Paper No. 28. La Fundación para la Educación Superior y el Desarrollo (Fedesarrollo), Bogotá.

Castiblanco, R. 2005. Incidencia de las negociaciones entre la rama legislativa y ejecutiva y/o de las externalidades en el presupuesto de inversión de la nación e inercia presupuestal en Colombia 1995–2003. Department of Economics, Universidad del Rosario, Bogotá, Colombia.

Comisión Independiente del Gasto Público. 2007. *Reporte.* La Fundación para la Educación Superior y el Desarrollo (Fedesarrollo), Bogotá, Colombia. Available at http://www.fedesarrollo.org/includes/scripts/open.asp?ruta=/images/dynamic/articles/537/informe.pdf

Echeverry, J. C., L. Fergusson, and P. Querubín. 2004. La batalla política por el presupuesto de la nación: inflexibilidades o supervivencia fiscal. Working Paper No. CEDE 2004–01. Centro de Estudios sobre Desarrollo Económico (CEDE), Department of Economics, Universidad de Los Andes, Bogotá.

Filc, G., and C. Scartascini. 2004. Budget Institutions and Fiscal Outcomes: Ten Years of Inquiry on Fiscal Matters at the Research Department. Office of Oversight and Evaluation, Inter-American Development Bank, Washington, DC.

Herrera, S., and G. Pang. 2005. Efficiency of Public Spending in Developing Countries: An Efficiency Frontier Approach. World Bank Series on Policy Research No. 3645. World Bank, Washington, DC.

Hommes, R. 1996. Evolution and Rationality of Budget Institutions in Colombia. RES Working Paper No. 317. Inter-American Development Bank, Washington, DC.

IDB (Inter-American Development Bank). 2005. *The Politics of Policies.* Economic and Social Progress in Latin America: 2006 Report. Washington, DC: Inter-American Development Bank.

IMF (International Monetary Fund). 2004. Stabilization and Reforms in Latin America: A Macroeconomic Perspective of the Experience since the 1990s. Western Hemisphere Department, IMF, Washington, DC. Unpublished.

Payne, J. M., D. Zovatto, F. Carrillo, and A. Allamand. 2002. *Democracies in Development: Politics and Reform in Latin America.* Washington, DC: Inter-American Development Bank.

Penfold, M. 1999. Institutional Electoral Incentives and Decentralization Outcomes: Comparing Colombia and Venezuela. Ph.D. dissertation, Political Science, Columbia University, New York.

Stein, E., E. Talvi, and Alejandro Grisanti. 1999. Institutional Arrangements and Fiscal Performance: The Latin American Experience. In James M. Poterba and Jürgen von Hagen, eds., *Fiscal Institutions and Fiscal Performance.* Chicago and London: University of Chicago Press.

5

Institutional Reforms, Budget Politics, and Fiscal Outcomes in Ecuador

Andrés Mejía Acosta, Vicente Albornoz, and M. Caridad Araujo

BUDGET POLITICS IN A VOLATILE ENVIRONMENT

The Ecuadorian budget process offers an excellent policy arena for examining the extent to which multiple political actors, acting in a changing policy environment, have shaped the nature of fiscal outcomes over time. This chapter analyzes the impact of economic and political shocks on Ecuador's budget process between 1979 and 2006; the ways through which political agents have reacted to such shocks; their formal and informal influences during the formulation, approval, execution, and monitoring of budgets; and the subsequent fiscal outcomes.

The budget process in Ecuador takes place in an environment characterized by the presence of multiple political actors, institutional instability, and few incentives to cooperate over the long run. Oil rents, when available, have triggered politicians' rent-seeking behavior in the form of increasing discretionary spending or earmarking allocations to different stakeholders. While the mechanism for hardwiring budget allocations (*partidas de gasto*) has facilitated some political compromises with the opposition in the short run, it has preempted the government's ability to adjust and respond to oil price volatility in the long run. A brief historical analysis of the budget process since the country's return to democracy in 1979 reveals that politicians' rent-seeking behavior has prevailed, despite major constitutional and economic reforms aimed at rationalizing the budget process. For example, important constitutional reforms and other legislation approved between 1994 and 1998 sought to increase the president's agenda-setting powers over the budget process while eliminating legislators' ability to bargain for provincial allocations. These reforms removed politicians' incentives and currencies to form budget coalitions at the national level; at the same time, subnational (municipal and provincial) governments became important political players with formal rights and prerogatives to influence budget allocations and shape the budget process.

This chapter documents a significant "shift" of budget politics that took place from the national to the subnational arena in the late 1990s. The adoption of dollarization in 2000 and the subsequent adoption of the fiscal responsibility law (FRL) in 2002 are other examples of reforms that imposed restrictions on political agents as they sought to enforce fiscal discipline. Although these legal changes helped improve the fiscal outlook after 2001, this chapter suggests that subsequent fiscal surpluses are better explained by the dramatic increase in the international price of oil, rather than by austere political actors. In fact, in the context of rising oil prices, Congress and the president abolished key aspects of an FRL in 2005 to allow for greater government spending during an electoral campaign year.

An evaluation of budget outcomes suggests that the combination of stronger executives and the influence of high oil prices contributed to generating more efficient and sustainable budget outcomes. The political shift from the national to the subnational arena contributed to a more representative—though not unbiased—allocation of government spending. Despite the apparent successful adoption of ideal public finance reforms, the chapter argues that the budget process would not be sustainable in the long run for two reasons. In the first place, politicians in the national and subnational arenas still lacked incentives to form credible, effective, and durable coalitions around the redistribution of ever-growing government revenues. The other source of instability is the significant dependency on oil revenues caused by the resource bonanza. As a result, even oil stabilization funds, originally created to help sustain a dollarized economy, have been further earmarked with projects of short-term interest.

Since the completion of this chapter in 2006, the course of events in Ecuador has reshaped the budget process in two significant ways.

In the first place, the election of Rafael Correa as president at the end of 2006—and his subsequent political success in proposing, elaborating, and adopting a new constitution in 2008—strengthened the influence of the executive over a highly fragmented and demobilized opposition. This political influence affected the budget process, for example, through the adoption of a special law to "recover the use of oil revenues," which eliminated existing earmarks on oil revenues, thus centralizing oil wealth in the General Government Budget (GGB).[1] Other important reforms—induced by the effects of the oil bonanza—included increased government spending on education, health, social security, and new or greater subsidies for domestic fuels, housewives, and the unemployed. The second development, namely, the collapse of world financial markets and the corresponding fall in commodity prices, has affected Ecuador's reliance on abundant oil revenues. The dramatic drop in oil prices combined with OPEC-induced production cuts is likely to leave a sizeable fiscal gap in the Ecuadorian budget.

Without making predictions about future fiscal performance, it is clear that the sustainability of the Ecuadorian fiscal situation will be affected by the decline of oil prices and the lack of fiscal reserves. On the other hand, it is unclear that the uncontested power of the executive over the budget process would improve the representativity and efficiency of budgets; instead, it could promote greater discretionality and rent-seeking behavior from those in the government coalition. These concerns, however, remain empirical questions for future research.

FRAMEWORK: THE POLITICS OF THE BUDGET PROCESS IN ECUADOR

The Ecuadorian policymaking process is characterized by a permanent tension between a player with very strong agenda-setting interests (the

[1] This special law is called the Ley para la Recuperación del Uso de los Recursos Petroleros y Racionalización Administrativa de los Procesos de Endeudamiento. The law calls for the transfer of all current and future resources from oil funds (Fondo de Estabilización Social y Productiva y Reducción del Endeudamiento Público, FEIREP; Cuenta Especial de Reactivación Productiva, CEREPS; and Fondo de Estabilización Petrolera, FEP) to the GGB.

president) and multiple players with veto capabilities who are active in the national legislature, the subnational governments, and organized interest groups, and on the streets. Through this perverse configuration of diverging interests and actors with few formal incentives to support government coalitions over the long run, Ecuador has gained a widespread reputation for being "a very difficult country to govern." In the last decade alone, high levels of ethnic and regional conflict, military (in)action, economic decline, and congressional deadlock have at different times played contributing roles in the demise of three presidents before the end of their terms. Box 5.1 describes the main features of the policymaking process in Ecuador.

The dollarization of the economy in January 2000 had an additional effect on the Ecuadorian policymaking process. The adoption of the U.S. dollar as the national currency rendered the role of the Central Bank of Ecuador in setting monetary policy ineffective and de facto eliminated one of the two paths for policymaking by executive delegation. Thus, fiscal policy became a highly contested policy arena in Ecuador.

CRITICAL SHOCKS THAT HAVE AFFECTED THE ECUADORIAN BUDGET PROCESS

The Oil Factor

Oil is Ecuador's main export and its primary source of fiscal revenues. Between 2000 and 2005, oil revenues made up, on average, 26.4 percent of nonfinancial public sector revenues and 35.1 percent of central government revenues. Given the high dependence of public revenues on oil exports, the Ecuadorian economy is particularly vulnerable to fluctuations in the global price of oil (Fernandez and Lara, 1998) or natural disasters that may affect the steady supply of oil (such as the 1987 earthquake that broke the oil pipeline). An interruption in oil revenues could rapidly trigger a fiscal crisis. This vulnerability explains, in part, the country's unstable economic performance during the last democratic period.

Between 1998 and 2006, Ecuadorian oil prices fluctuated greatly. Observation of prices during that time enables the price change behav-

BOX 5.1 | The Ecuadorian Policymaking Process

Presidents, acting in a highly fragmented scenario, have pursued two paths to produce policy change. The first one has been to submit legislation to the national legislature where, on average, only 30 percent of the presidents' agenda gets approved as a result of the high number of opposition parties and the lack of political incentives to form government coalitions. To overcome institutional constraints on cooperation, governments and legislators have often assembled ad hoc, clandestine (ghost) alliances to trade pork barrel projects, provincial investment projects, patronage, particularistic policy concessions, etc., in exchange for legislative support. The overall effect has been a highly ineffective and costly bargaining process that has produced very little policy change.

The second avenue for policy change has been to delegate decision-making power to a technical bureaucracy, which has adopted reforms through bypassing political parties in the legislature. Although decisive policies have emerged from the Monetary Board, the Central Bank of Ecuador, and the National Council for Modernization, such reforms have responded to very specific interest groups, and policies have been reversed with every change of government or even with every new cabinet minister. At the end of the day, political parties have reasserted themselves in the policymaking game by accelerating the removal of unpopular cabinet ministers: between 1979 and 1998, the average mandate of a finance minister was approximately 12 months.

At the end of both paths, a set of formal and informal "last ditch veto players" has been ready to oppose, stall, or reverse unwanted policy decisions. Some formal channels of opposition have included appeals to the Constitutional Tribunal. Nonconventional policy channels have included protests by the indigenous, the military, and popular groups. Some of these "last ditch" players became protagonists in the ousting of three Ecuadorian presidents between 1997 and 2005.

Source: Mejía Acosta et al. (2008).

ior to be classified according to three periods. During the first period, between January 1998 and October 1999, prices remained at an average low price of US$12.6 per barrel. During the second period, between November 1999 and April 2004, prices increased to an average of US$23 per barrel. During the third period, between May 2004 and April 2006, the price of a barrel rose to an average level of US$39.1, with an upward price trend. The periods that characterize the evolution of oil prices are consistent with the general pattern of variation in fiscal outcomes between 1998 and 2005, as illustrated in Table 5.1. During 1998 and 1999, the budget reflects large deficits; the trend is reversed and the budget even produces positive net balances between 2000 and 2005.

This chapter argues that fluctuations in oil prices have affected the institutional aspect of the budget-making process in Ecuador, as well as the incentives for fiscal discipline available to budget players. In the

TABLE 5.1 Evolution of Fiscal Results in Ecuador, 1998–2005
(relative to the nonfinancial public sector and in percentage of GDP)

	1998	1999	2000	2001	2002	2003	2004	2005
Budget global deficit	–5.2	–4.9	1.5	0	0.8	1.1	2.1	0.7

Source: Central Bank of Ecuador.

aftermath of a significant fiscal crisis—falling oil prices and the subsequent dollarization of the Ecuadorian economy—political parties in Congress adopted the FRL to limit the expansion of public expenditure and produce an overall sobering effect on fiscal policy. Three years later, when oil prices had reached their highest levels, the same congressional parties voted to amend the FRL. This amendment de facto eliminated constraints on public expenditure as well as other fiscal controls. This fluctuation was not an isolated event; instead, this chapter argues that movements in oil prices have been closely related to changes in preferences and behaviors of the actors of the budget policymaking process.

Given the contentious nature of the policymaking process and the high dependency on oil revenues, Ecuador has not demonstrated a capacity to adapt to shocks (policy rigidity), nor have governments improved their ability to sustain agreements over time (policy volatility). Fiscal policy is set within a complex frame in which the budget plays an important role, not only because of the magnitude of the resources it allocates, but because of its rigid structure due to earmarking. A rigid budget imposes one additional constraint on the capacity of fiscal policy to adapt to external shocks. This constraint has been enhanced with the adoption of dollarization, which de facto has limited the range of adjustment instruments available to the executive. The windfall effect of rising oil revenues can temporarily alleviate the fiscal rigidity imposed by dollarization, but this factor does not eliminate the need for deeper structural reforms. During the last 35 years, the inability to make necessary fiscal reforms has been one of the elements hindering the success of adjustment programs (Hurtado, 2006).

The 1998 Constitution

The national assembly that produced a new constitution between 1997 and 1998 was inspired by the need to strengthen political institutions that promoted increased governability and improved political representation. In practice, the approved reforms of the 1998 Ecudorian constitution strengthened presidential powers over Congress (governability), while at the same time the reforms aimed to strengthen the connection between citizens and politicians (representativity). Together with other closely related reforms, these reforms introduced a mixed set of incentives for political cooperation.

In the first place, the reforms increased the president's level of influence in the budget process, at the expense of legislators. Presidents were granted exclusive rights to initiate the budget process, and their decree and veto powers were increased. Congress was banned from increasing expenditures or creating new revenues, and legislators were no longer allowed to bargain provincial allocations or discretionary—off budget—funding for their districts, but rather had to approve budgets based on sectoral spending (*partidas de gasto*). Secondly, the reforms sought to reduce the number of actors participating in the budget process. Accordingly, the number of legislators was reduced from 123 to 100. After 1998, Congress became more provincially oriented, as provincial legislators were elected through a personalized vote and the existence of national legislators (elected on a national slate) was eliminated. Internally, the seven-member budget committee gained greater agenda-setting power to revise the executive's proposed budget, but the decision-making power for budget approval was devolved to the entire congressional floor. Lastly, the reforms extended the temporal horizons of budget players. Legislators had been allowed to seek reelection since 1996 and, through the new constitution, their mandate was extended from two to four years (thus eliminating midterm elections). Legislative appointments and committee service were also extended from one to two years. In theory, this should have contributed to expanding the legislators' incentives for making intertemporal agreements, since legislators were appointed for longer periods in Congress while they accumulated more experience over time.

In practice, the reforms of the 1998 constitution produced a perverse combination of results. On the one hand, as a result of increased budget powers, the president became less dependent on gathering legislative support for budget approval and gained greater ability to execute budget allocations. On the other hand, legislators gained greater political representation vis-à-vis their constituents (they enjoyed longer terms in office with no term limits and were elected through personalized voting), but lost the ability to access investment projects for the benefit of their constituencies. This combination severely hindered politicians' prospects for developing an "electoral connection" with their voters. Concurrently with the drying out of coalition incentives at the national level, a series of institutional reforms strengthened the abilities of local governments to become successful lobbyists in the budget process and to develop successful electoral connections with voters. Suffice it to say here that traditional political parties, which lost their influence over the national budget process, reappeared as crucial actors in a new policy arena: the subnational governments.

Dollarization in Ecuador

The decision to dollarize the economy in January 2000 came as a drastic response to contain—or at least mitigate—the effects of a financial crisis that threatened Ecuador with hyperinflation, a stagnating economy (with GDP decreasing by 6.4 percent in 1999), falling oil prices, and a generalized lack of belief in the government's ability to produce economic recovery. Positive effects of dollarization are that it brought inflation down to levels that the country had not experienced in over two decades and provided economic agents with signals of stability that had been very much sought after. Dollarization formally reduced the possibility that the devaluation-inflation cycle could erode the real value of budget allocations. By bringing economic stability, dollarization decreased the discount rates of economic agents.

By renouncing monetary policy, the government gave a strong signal of its commitment to a structural reform in the hopes of stabilizing the economy and recovering some credibility at home and abroad. In terms of the budget process, Ecuador's drastic move to full dollarization eliminated one of the policy arenas where presidents did have some discretionary power to adopt policy decisions and the resoluteness to carry them out. By renouncing monetary policy, dollarization reduced the number of policy instruments available to the economic authorities, thus imposing an additional burden of responsibility over fiscal policy.

In the aftermath of dollarization, and while the country was still paying the economic price of the financial crisis, many government policymakers, as well as development banks, favored the adoption of reforms that would secure responsible fiscal management. Policies such as the adoption of an FRL and the creation of an oil fund—which reveal a change in the intertemporal preferences of agents—were put in place in the years following dollarization and were consistent with a change in agents' discount rates and with higher public regard for the benefits of sound fiscal policy.

THE RULES AND POLITICS OF THE BUDGET PROCESS

The budget process in Ecuador is the product of relentless institutional changes combined with rapidly adjusting responses from relevant budget actors. Since 1994, a series of changes to norms and budgetary procedures have been adopted to produce what could be considered a "wish list" of reforms to ensure fiscal sustainability and discipline. A review of the actual workings of such norms reveals that, for the most part, budgetary actors produce alternative patterns of cooperation around their most preferred outcomes. In this sense, Ecuador illustrates a case in which the adoption of constraints on political actors' spending abilities has improved fiscal discipline in the short run, but at the expense of diluting political incentives to sustain longer-term cooperation between the executive and the legislature.

To illustrate the discussion of the formal and actual workings of the budget process, Figure 5.1 maps the influence of the main political actors and lobby groups along different points of the fiscal year time line. The fiscal year in Ecuador follows the calendar year, from January 1 to December 31. Three types of budget actors are identified: (1) decisive players who have the formal or informal power to influence policy formulation (i.e., the executive, business lobbies, local governments), (2) veto players whose cooperation is needed to adopt policy changes (i.e., the legislature, political parties), and (3) last-ditch veto players who may exert effective pressure to demand budget execution or reverse unwanted policy decisions (i.e., courts, unorganized groups) (Mejía Acosta et al., 2008). Budget formulation takes place between May and September and it includes the executive, the Ministry of Economy and

FIGURE 5.1 | Political Timeline of the Budget Process

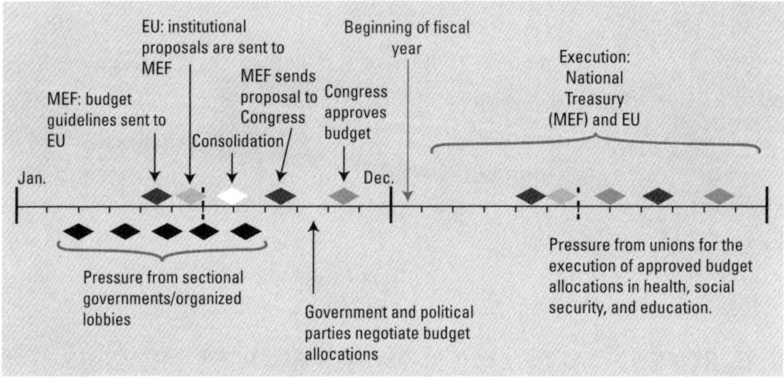

Source: MEF.

Finance (MEF), and the Executing Units (EUs) including subnational governments.[2] According to Article 258 of the 1998 constitution, the proposed budget is submitted to Congress in September and must be approved, amended, or rejected within 90 days (by November 30). Budget execution begins in January and during this time, different interest groups demand the effective execution of budget allocations. All unspent resources are returned to the MEF to be deposited in the Single Treasury Account at the beginnning of the following year.[3] Finally, the figure shows how the proximity of the subsequent budget cycle leaves very little room for legislators or other political actors to undertake budget monitoring.

Budget Formulation

Budget formulation is largely a prerogative of the executive branch. The president, through the MEF, elaborates a GGB proposal according to guidelines established by the National Planning Office (SENPLADES)

[2] MEF website, SIGEF terminology. An Executing Unit is the administrative unit (organization or group) that executes an assigned budget.

[3] The Single Treasury Account (Cuenta Única del Tesoro) is an instrument for fiscal management at the hands of the MEF.

and macroeconomic forecasts from the Central Bank of Ecuador (BCE). The MEF then requests that the EUs submit their budget estimates before April 30, taking into consideration the government's macroeconomic guidelines and fiscal responsibility principles. The fiscal budget is made up mainly of salary and wages, maintenance, and basic services expenditures, categories that are indexed to inflation and represent an inertial amount in the elaboration of the GGB (Almeida, Gallardo, and Tomaselli, 2005). Additional investments have to be approved by the SENPLADES and their financial viability certified by the subsecretary's Office of Public Investment. The MEF analyzes, verifies, consolidates, and can even amend information submited by EUs if the macrofiscal rules have not been followed. The budget proposal is submitted to Congress, which must analyze and approve it by September 1.

Like those in the rest of Latin America, Ecuadorian presidents remain the most influential budget players in the country. Traditionally, presidents in Ecuador gained a reputation for being "fiscally conservative" at the beginning of their four-year terms (1979–1996), but their discipline gradually relaxed as their mandate elapsed and the fragmented coalition partners began to engage more. Presidents also had an ample range of discretionary spending lines (*gastos reservados*) before 1997. While the availability of these funds allowed them to extract legislative support from the opposition, it also led to corruption scandals for misuse of public funds during the Durán Ballén, Bucaram, and Alarcón administrations (1992–1997). Reforms adopted after 1997 sought to reduce or control the budget powers of the president: new legislation introduced spending caps to ensure greater fiscal responsibility and long-term planning, and the General Comptroller's Office imposed a ceiling on the discretionary spending lines, which could only amount to 0.25 percent of the General Government Budget, and limited their use to the Ministries of Defense and Internal Affairs. Eventually, the 1998 constitution eliminated the executive's access to discretionary spending lines.

Despite formal limitations, presidents exert political and technical agenda-setting powers over the budget process through the MEF. Since 1979, the technical responsibility over fiscal policy had been shared between the MEF, the Monetary Board, and the BCE, but after the 1998 constitutional reforms and dollarization, the MEF became a powerful budget actor. Interest groups, such as teacher and doctor unions, pensioners, the military, and the police, consistently began to approach the MEF with requests to increase recurrent and capital spending during the budget formulation stage. Subnational governments (municipalities and provincial governments) also began to lobby the president or the finance minister to demand increases in capital spending, especially during the month of April. Despite the MEF's political role, nearly 80 percent of all finance ministers were chosen from a pool of technical government pundits without an explicit partisan affiliation. In the eyes of the opposition, the "technocratic" status of the finance ministers made them politically vulnerable to congressional impeachments or politically motivated resignations. Thus, the MEF was a political fuse whose official needed replacing every time the government achieved a new legislative agreement with the opposition, and a new minister—most likely another independent—was appointed. Between 1979 and 1998, the average tenure of finance ministers was 11.5 months in office (346 days). Ministers did not stay longer in office after 1998 despite the fact that Ecuador's 1998 constitutional reforms aimed at protecting cabinet members from legislative impeachment and censorship. If anything, the reforms produced the opposite effect: until December 2005, the average tenure of a finance minister was reduced to 7.3 months (220 days) (Mejía Acosta et al., 2008). Despite ministers' agenda-setting abilities, no minister stayed long enough to formulate and execute the same budget; thus ministerial volatility may have further contributed to strengthening the effective control of the president over budget formulation and execution.

A new set of influential actors in the budget formulation stage emerged in the mid-1990s: subnational governments. Subnational governments comprise elected local authorities (or the *regimen seccional autónomo*) and president-appointed provincial governors. Elected officials include provincial prefects who preside over the provincial legislature, which is made up of provincial counselors. The 326 mayors preside over the municipal councils and, since 2000, local authorities are elected in off-years without term limits. The strengthening of local governments in Ecuador is due to the gradual transfer of greater resources, better technical planning, and increased legal responsibilities and prerogatives. Since the early 1990s, the Association of Ecuadorian Municipalities (AME), a lobby group of mayors, has received and channeled international assistance to strengthen the capacity and technical planning of local governments. The AME has also lobbied for greater government resources for intermediate and small municipalities with less bargaining power than Quito or Guayaquil. The 1997 adoption of a special State Decentralization and Social Participation Act (Ley Especial de Descentralización y Participación Social) that earmarked 15 percent of the GGB for sectional governments further strengthened the AME's capacity to deliver public works in their districts. Together with other transfers, it is estimated that sectional governments benefit from at least 20 percent of the GGB and that they retain around 50 percent of the public sector's investment capacity. Finally, mayors have initiated important reforms to have greater prerogatives and responsibilities over resource allocation in their districts. Through reforms to the Organic Law of Municipal Regime (Ley Orgánica de Régimen Municipal), the State Decentralization and Social Participation Act, and the subsequent 2004 reform to the Organic Law of Municipal Regime, mayors have gained greater agenda-setting power during the budget formulation stage.[4]

Budget Approval

According to Article 130 of the 1998 constitution, Congress is in charge of approving the GGB and ensuring its proper execution. The president of Congress receives the executive's proposed budget and generally sends the bill to the Committee of Tributary, Fiscal, and Banking (CTFB). This committee is made up of seven members; each member serves a two-year term and can be reelected. In the absence of a congressional budget office, committee members rely on government entities such as the Internal Revenue Service (Servicio de Rentas Internas, SRI) or the EUs to elaborate their own revenue and expenditure estimates. The committee's detailed report is submitted to the Plenary of the Legislative Commissions (Plenario de las Comisiones Legislativas, PCL) of Congress, which is a council composed of 35 legislators who serve on five permanent committees. This report is discussed in only one debate by income and expenditure sectors. All legislators can ask for specific changes to the proposal based on the general guidelines established in the report from the CTFB. Congress has until November 30 each

[4] The Organic Law of Municipal Regime coordinates and regulates the roles of municipal governments in Ecuador.

year to approve or reform the proposal, but if the proposed budget is not approved, the original proposal submitted by the executive is the reversal point.

Although the budget approval stage is the policy stage at which congressional parties should maximize their influence over the budget process, the effective influence of these parties in practice has diminished over time. All things equal, the high party fragmentation and malapportionment of the Ecuadorian Congress has generally increased transaction costs of budget approval. First, legislators have had plenty of electoral incentives to cultivate a personal vote: in 1998, Congress was composed of 123 legislators from 22 provinces (100 legislators after 2002) who were elected through an open-list electoral formula.[5] Legislators were elected for four-year terms with no term limits. Secondly, the heterogeneous territorial distribution has created severe malapportionment in the transformation of votes into seats: for example, a legislator elected in 2002 from a large district, such as Guayas, represented approximately 22 times as many voters than a legislator who represented the constituency of a a scarcely populated province, such as Galápagos (Snyder and Samuels, 2001). Such disparities have skewed the proportional allocation of government spending in favor of overrepresented provinces.

There are two additional factors that have diminished the role of Congress as an effective arena for budget approval: the formal reduction of legislators' agenda-setting powers and the diminishing availability of resources used to facilitate political alliances. Together, these changes have eliminated political incentives for actors to cooperate in the national arena and have pushed budget coalitions to the subnational arena.

Changes in Legislators' Agenda-Setting Powers

The 1998 constitutional reforms formally reduced the overall influence of Congress on budget approval by withdrawing its ability to create spending lines in addition to those submitted by the executive and by allowing the president's proposed budget to become law if no budget

---

[5] This is a personalized form of voting, adopted in 1997, through which voters can elect as many representatives as seats are available in the district, regardless of party lists or party affiliation. Before 1997, the electoral system in Ecuador featured a "closed list" system that gave party leaders strong prerogatives over candidate nomination and selection.

agreement emerges from Congress by November 30. Through the reforms, the legislative procedure for budget approval also changed. Between 1979 and 1997, the budget committee reviewed the president's proposal, but budgetary amendments had to be approved by a simple majority of the PCL. The practice of approving budgets in the PCL generally benefited parties with larger contingents in Congress: party leaders bargained the direction and the amount of budget allocations directly with the executive. Although such agreements were not cheap for the executive, the mechanism ensured the credibility of budget coalitions: legislators' constituencies benefited from investment projects and some pork (or *troncha*), and the president obtained budget approval with a simple majority of PCL members.

The approval of the 1997 budget introduced important changes into the budget bargaining process. At the time, President Bucaram, who lacked the support of traditional political parties, managed to assemble a minimum coalition in the PCL with the support of his own party, the Roldosista Party (Partido Roldosista Ecuatoriano, PRE), and some independent legislators. The following year, opposition parties that were excluded from the Bucaram coalition—including the Social Christian Party (PSC), Democratic Left (ID), Christian Democratic Party (DP), Popular Democracy (MPD), and Pluri-National Pachakutik United Movement (Pachakutik)—promoted a reform to centralize agenda setting in the budget committee, but opened budget approval to the entire floor. Although the reform was approved amid the rhetoric of increased budget accountability, party leaders sought insurance mechanisms to prevent the executive from assembling budget coalitions with individual legislators. Predictably, traditional parties invested more resources in influencing the budget process through the budget committee. Whereas partisan affiliation on the CTFB had been evenly distributed across five or six political parties, 93 percent of the total number of committee assignments after 1998 were in the hands of four major political parties: DP, PRE, PSC and ID. The partisan takeover of the budget committee also reproduced regional patterns of party competition (PRE against PSC on the coast, DP against ID in the highlands). Evidence suggests that the budget committee reinforced the representation of larger provinces. The proportion of committee members who came from the three largest provinces (Pichincha, Guayas, and Manabí) nearly doubled, increasing from 31 percent to 57 percent. While there was an effective takeover of budget approval by political parties, they saw an effective decrease in their influence on the budget-making process.

Changes in Coalition Currencies

A second factor that reduced legislators' influence over budget approval was the 1994 reform that eliminated legislators' abilities to negotiate budget allocations for their provinces. Instead, legislators were required to approve the budget allocations by sector. The proposed reforms were initiated by President Durán Ballén (1992–1996) and approved by popular referenda with the purpose of eliminating legislators' rent-seeking incentives during the budget approval process (Mejía Acosta, 2006). Why would the executive voluntarily relinquish its ability and discretion to distribute funds and bargain budget coalitions with legislators? The Durán Ballén administration perceived that budget bargaining with political parties had become too expensive to sustain. According to Vice President Dahik:

> (A group of PSC legislators) would ask for provincial funds in return for supporting some of our laws. . . . And their family members would be the contractors. It was an absurd situation because their leaders were in opposition, but meanwhile some of the deputies were constantly sitting down with us, demanding money. It was collective bargaining, and the whole process was very expensive (Landau, 2001: 47).

By limiting the ability of Congress to reallocate provincial funds, the government had hoped to decrease the particularistic demands for government spending and allow a smoother, more technical process of budget approval. But the government's strategy of "drying out" the availability of budgetary allocations backfired, as party leaders refused to approve the 1995 budget by sectors unless their districts would benefit from government allocations. Eventually, disgruntled PSC leaders clashed with government officials over a scandal involving alleged vote buying, which forced the resignation of Vice President Dahik in 1995 and destroyed the PSC's presidential hopes in the 1996 general election. In the aftermath of additional corruption scandals during the Bucaram and Alarcón administrations, in 1998 the newly elected

Congress passed a code of ethics, which threatened legislators with dismissal if they were found negotiating with the executive for material or political resources for their districts or themselves. Although the code was never used in practice, it effectively eradicated existing coalition incentives between the executive and legislators. According to a party leader:

> In the past, corruption was very functional for governance. The Presidency, the administration's Secretary General, the Minster of Defense and the Minister of the Interior all had discretionary expenditures. Even if many don't like to accept it, these served in the past to buy legislators, to buy loyalties in detriment of (the discipline of) the political parties. A Budget Committee existed where, if conflicts arose, they were taken to the Plenary. It was a functional system: 18 years of democracy and there were no problems associated with the approval of the fiscal budget. The amount of the budget was negotiated by sectors, and legislators negotiated the amounts by entries, by allocations. It was an open secret. Legislators in the Budget Committee . . . negotiated giant allocations for themselves: they (arbitrarily) selected contractors, and it did not encounter problems with the Comptroller's Office because they (political parties) controlled the provincial comptrollers, the judicial branch, etc. These mechanisms no longer exist. While there is more transparency (in the budget process), sectors feel powerless to obtain gains and vent their frustration by radically opposing government initiatives.

In the end, the (failed) institutional attempts to depoliticize the budget process by eliminating legislators' incentives and means to cultivate a personal vote not only contradicted existing electoral incentives, but also increased the costs of budget bargaining in the legislature. Some informal and clandestine mechanisms for increasing capital spending and facilitate budget bargaining between the executive and the legislature prevailed, but overall, the lack of available and legal currencies affected the stability and reliability of budget coalitions.

The combined effect of institutional reforms on the process of budget approval has produced an interesting contradiction. On the one hand, the most prominent political parties sought to strengthen their presence and influence on the budget committee after 1998, even when the executive has retained significant powers of budget formulation and execution. On the other hand, legislators after 1998 lost access to key budgetary resources that would have facilitated more durable and reliable budget coalitions with the executive. Thus, the pending question is: why would legislators remain interested in budget politics at the committee level if the legislature has lost access to effective resource allocation? One proposed explanation is that parties and legislators in Congress have become indirect agents of provincial interests through the influence of their regional, provincial, and municipal governments.

Subnational Governments As *New Budget Actors*

As discussed earlier, the political context after the 1998 reforms offers an interesting combination of stronger subnational governments (especially mayors) that have gained influence over the budget process with weaker parties and legislators at the national level who have lost access to resource allocation. Not surprisingly, political parties quickly identified this asymmetry and quickly shifted their political activism from the national legislature to the subnational arena. In this arena, the parties enjoyed better access to budgetary allocations, which allowed them to deliver better constituency services and maintain an important electoral connection. The fact that mayors could also pursue immediate reelection (previously banned in the 1990s) gave politicians clearer opportunities to develop long-term relations of accountability with their constituents. Following this logic, prominent legislators and influential party leaders have abandoned the much discredited legislative arena to run successfully for local office: Paco Moncayo (ID) became mayor of Quito (in 2000 and 2004), Jaime Nebot (PSC) became mayor of Guayaquil (in 2000 and 2004), and Jorge Marun (PRE) became prefect of the Los Rios Province (in 2000 and 2004), to name a few. This "downward" move appeared to be a good political strategy, as city mayors had enough leverage to bargain budget allocations directly with the office of the president, to run some public services of their own, and even to influence some aspects of national policymaking. From a public standpoint, mayors also escaped the discredit of congressional parties while appearing as guardians of democracy and governability in their cities during times of national political crises. When the partisan affiliation of mayors elected before and after 1998 is examined, evidence suggests that that the four most influential Ecuadorian parties captured 332 city governments, nearly two-thirds of the total number of mayoral posts available in the 2000 and 2004 elections (75 percent if Pachakutik is included). Mayors' partisan affiliations reproduced regional trends of party competition.

While evidence suggests that political parties have reallocated to the subnational arena, more empirical research is needed to understand the mechanisms by which parties have influenced the subnational budget-making process. The case of Simon Bustamante, a PSC legislator from the province of Manabí, is a good example to illustrate this possible link. Bustamante has presided over the CTFB three of the four times in which he has been a member, and it is believed that he has played a critical role in helping channel budget allocations and regional development programs to his native province. Furthermore, his political party has gained an important presence in the provincial and municipal government since the mid-1990s.

Budget Execution

According to the 1998 constitution, the executive is responsible for the elaboration and execution of fiscal policies. Once the GGB has been approved by Congress, the MEF ensures that it complies with fiscal responsibility principles, and the MEF's Office of Budgets and the National Treasury establishes a priority order to assign resources according to its governance needs (Ecuadorian Political Constitution, Article 260) and then transfer the approved resources to the EUs, which are ultimately responsible for budgetary execution. Sometimes, the government faces cash flow problems because tax collection revenues tend to increase in April, whereas budget expenditures tend to be constant throughout the year. Thus, the MEF has the ability to reassign and adjust approved budget allocations by up to 5 percent in government expenditures during the fiscal year, without congressional approval.

The priority order for assigning resources is directly related to the budget structure by expenditure accounts, and this order is applied when the effective current nonoil revenues in the GGB are less than what has been budgeted for the quarter. The MEF can amend allocations in the expenditure budget as long as the amendments do not affect those allocations determined by the constitution. In the event that amendments are made to investments, they are subject to prioritization according to the multiannual plan of government and to the hierarchy of the executive's projects. The MEF can also reallocate funds within the approved budget based on the spending capability of the EUs or through the interpretation of *budgetary classifiers* (although this is not officially established). In general, the minister of finance has significant leverage in establishing the rules of transfers, spending increases or reductions, and other budgetary modifications.

The actual allocation of resources across spending items at each stage of the budget process between 1990 and 2006 reveals that nearly half of the spending included in the executive's budget proposal is absorbed by four sectors: education, defense, health, and social welfare and labor. In general, these sectors have the largest share of civil servants and thus contribute with a higher wage bill. Throughout the budget process, allocation across sectors remains relatively stable with few exceptions. Perhaps the sector with the most dramatic decrease in its total spending allocation is social welfare and labor, which at the proposal stage is set to receive 6.7 percent of total spending, but at execution stage receives only an average of 3 percent of total spending. At the other extreme (and consistent with the high degree of discretion of the MEF throughout the budget process), the MEF has the most dramatic average budget increase, from a projected 2 percent of spending at the proposal stage to an actual 6 percent of spending when the budget is executed.

Further research is needed to understand the political mechanisms by which some sectors are better able to protect their original budget allocations and effectively execute allocated spending. At this point, the executive—through the MEF—appears to be the most influential player in determining the degree and direction of budget execution.

Budget Monitoring

The follow-up on and control of budgetary execution are responsibilities of Congress and the General Comptroller's Office, through its system of Control, Censuring, and Auditing of the State. This system, in turn, has mechanisms for internal and external control. The EUs have to ensure the creation and maintenance of the EUs' internal control system, through which public servants and functionaries report on and make themselves responsible for the execution of their attributions, the use of public resources, and the results obtained. The internal control exercise has to be applied before, during, and after through specialized units in each of the EUs, which have to comply with legal regulations. Even the MEF has some role in enforcing internal control of EUs, in that it can adjust the corresponding cash programming based on the unit's budgetary execution record. External control is exercised by the General Comptroller's Office, which is an independent institution, and Congress, as it is the active participant in this office. Even though there is a constitutional mandate for Congress to follow up on budgetary execution, in practice it has no technical capacity to do so. The participation of the General Comptroller's Office is ex post the budgetary execution; therefore, timely alerts on the quality of expenditure execution of the EUs have to come from internal control. It is worth mentioning that because of the large number of EUs, it is impossible for the General Comptroller's Office to exercise external control on all of them systematically.

The approval of the Access to Public Information and Transparency Law (LOTAIP) in 2004 established a legal framework for facilitating the participation of citizens in the supervision of governmental actions and decision making. The LOTAIP mandates that government agencies disclose information regarding their legal status, directory board, budget, auditing results, plans and executed programs, and forms of accountability to citizens. Furthermore, the law also establishes specific sanctions for illegitimate acts of omission or denial of access to public information by state functionaries. A number of citizen observatories have also been organized to supervise the allocation and execution of fiscal expenditures. Some of the most relevant organizations that have an influence on the fiscal exercise are the Observatory of Fiscal Policy, the Observatory of Human Resources of the Health Sector, the Social Contract for Education, the Observatory of Children and Youth, the Observatory of Public Services, and the Observatory of Public Policies in the South, among others. In the long run, these watchdogs can play a complementary role to that of governmental institutions to improve the quality of budgetary execution and distribution.

INSTITUTIONAL CHANGES AND THE QUALITY OF BUDGET OUTCOMES

This section presents empirical evidence to assess the impact of institutional reforms on the sustainability, efficiency, and flexibility of budget outcomes. The level of detail and type of analysis chosen are contingent on data availability.

Improved Sustainability with Fiscal Vulnerability

Between 2000 and 2005, Ecuador experienced an improvement along several dimensions of its fiscal standing, reflected in healthier debt and current account indicators. This is not too surprising for various reasons. First, the period coincides with Ecuador's recovery from the severe crisis of 1999. Second, Ecuador's budget relies heavily on oil revenues—which were stable for a period (2002–2003) and then grew, as the result of a dramatic increase in the international prices of oil (2003 onwards).

This analysis of Ecuador's recent fiscal improvements leads to two questions of relevance. First: to what extent have the constitutional reforms and dollarization also had an effect on the improved sustainability of budget outcomes? Second: is this trend sustainable over time?

Unfortunately, there are no studies that attempt to disentangle empirically the effects of the different factors that influence the sustainability of budget outcomes. An exception is the paper by Barnhill and Kopits (2003) that explores the impact of dollarization. Their main finding is that dollarization substantially reduced fiscal vulnerability (the order of magnitude is between 14 and 16 percent of the net worth of Ecuador's public sector). They also identify the components of the government's balance sheet whose volatility makes the largest contributions to fiscal vulnerability: oil income, profits from state-owned enterprises, outstanding external liabilities, and liabilities of the pension system.

This chapter argues that the Ecuadorian economy remains vulnerable to external shocks and therefore, its capacity to maintain fiscal sustainability in the future is, to a large extent, tied to the evolution of oil prices. This claim is based on three facts and is supported by related research (Barnhill and Kopits, 2003; Díaz Alvarado, Izquierdo, and Panizza, 2004). First, as long as oil remains the principal source of government revenues (taxes account for less than half of current revenues), variations in oil prices constitute a meaningful source of volatility. Second, expenditures are quite rigid, which is in part because public wages represent a high share of primary spending in Ecuador and have been experiencing an increasing trend between 2000 and 2006. Other aspects of budget rigidity are discussed herein in the section on earmarks. Third, rigidity in expenditures becomes even more critical in a dollarized regime in which government's main policy tool is on the fiscal front.

FEWER BUDGET REALLOCATIONS AND MORE EFFICIENT OUTCOMES

The role of institutional changes in efficiency of budget outcomes in Ecuador is explored by assessing the trends in the magnitude and direction of budget reallocations at different stages of the budget process between 1990 and 2006. The focus is on changes in budget reallocations before and after the reforms of the 1998 constitution and dollarization.

Following the model proposed in this volume, this section presents a measure of the total change in the composition of spending for each pair of stages in the budget process. Specifically, the changes in the composition of spending are defined by the following variables:

- *CBL*: Total change in the composition of spending based on the executive's proposal and the budget law *formally* approved by Congress.
- *CBR*: Total change in the composition of spending based on the executive's proposal and the budget law *really* approved by Congress. This indicator accounts for the hidden costs of the budget that are present in the detail of the real budget, but not in the summary text that is formally approved by Congress.
- *CRD*: Total change in the composition of spending based on the budget law *really* approved by Congress and the executed budget.
- *CBD*: Total change in the composition of spending based on the executive's proposal and executed budget.

Both *CBL* and *CBR* are approval intervals, in which the main actor responsible for budget reallocations is Congress. Congress decides on these reallocations based on the laws (and the "acceptable" loopholes around them). Political pressure for reallocations—through different interest groups—can and does affect the behavior of Congress. Alternatively, *CRD* and *CBD* are execution intervals, in which the executive has the largest discretion. At these stages, organized groups—especially those with capacity to mobilize—are the most likely to succeed in obtaining budget reallocations in their favor.[6]

Figure 5.2 depicts the evolution of the annual total spending reallocations at each stage of the budget process. It illustrates that for every year, the total magnitude of the changes during the execution stage is much larger than that of those which occur during the approval stage. In other words, the executive plays a more important role than Congress in budget outcomes. Second, it is clear that after the 1998 constitutional reforms, the real reallocations in the budget approved by Congress are smaller than the ones that appear masked in the budget law. Third, the shape of the lines reveals that the overall magnitude of the reallocations in spending at all stages of the process (and in particular execution) decreased after dollarization to levels comparable to those in the early 1990s. Although the interval is short, the magnitude of reallocations also seems to decrease for approval, especially in the interval when the FRL was in place. However, further research and longer time series would be needed to conclude that the FRL was effective in restraining budget reallocations during the approval stage. While all of the actors of the budget process seem to have experienced a reduction in their capacity to reallocate resources across items, the postreform series are not long enough for this evidence to be found conclusive.

An alternative way of looking at the data is to focus not on *total* reallocations by year (i.e., the sum of the absolute value of reallocations across items), but on the yearly *mean* budget reallocation across items.[7] These measures quantify whether the dispersion in reallocations across items has experienced any systematic differences over

[6] The data allow CXY_{it} to be computed for years $t = 1990 \ldots 2005$ (and thus time subscripts to be added) across 19 budget items. 2005 data were available only for proposal and approval stages.

[7] Data on these means are not reported but can be obtained from the authors upon request.

FIGURE 5.2 **Budget Reallocations at Different Stages of the Process**

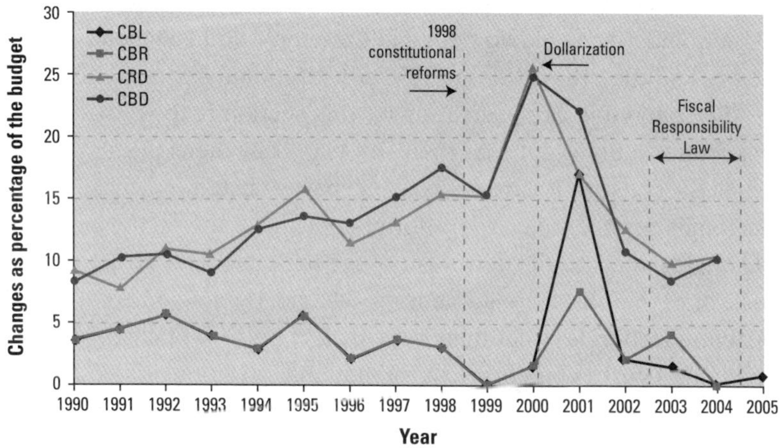

Source: Data collected by the authors for this chapter from Congress and the MEF.
Note: B = composition of spending in executive budget proposal. L = composition of spending in budget law approved by Congress. R = real composition of spending in budget law approved by Congress. D = composition of spending in the total executed expenditure. Within each year, $n = 19$ expenditure items. For comparability, debt payments have been excluded from the budget.

time. Although sample sizes are small ($n = 19$), t-tests of the equality of means comparing t to $t + 1$ reveal two trends. First, most differences that are statistically significant concentrate in the post-1998 period and at the approval stage. Second, the magnitude of the dispersion in reallocations across items at the approval stage seems to be decreasing, in particular after 2001. These data seem to support the hypothesis that the period after the institutional reforms analyzed herein was indeed characterized by smaller reallocations and more efficient budget outcomes.

SMALL, POORER PROVINCES ARE BETTER REPRESENTED IN THE BUDGET

The 1998 constitution and related reforms adopted significant electoral changes that affected the level and quality of representation. This section discusses how these changes affected the representativity of budget outcomes. Representativity is measured as the provincial per capita spending: the higher the per capita spending of a province, the better represented its residents have been in the budget process (Albornoz, 2000; Hidalgo, Albornoz, and Hurtado, 2007). Available data allow comparisons of two points in time, 1997 and 2004, one of them before and the other after the 1998 constitutional reforms.

Since the unit of observation for this section is the province, it is important to point out that there are two likely mechanisms through which the constitutional reforms could have affected provincial budget outcomes. First, the electoral reforms could have altered the incentives of congressmen, to the detriment of the national party structures and in favor of their local constituencies. Second, the implementation of a decentralization law that mandated that 15 percent of all government spending be distributed across subnational governments could have altered the provincial budget dynamics.

An inspection of the provincial-level spending data reveals a few facts. First, there is a large dispersion in per capita spending across provinces. Second, spending in per capita terms is inversely correlated with population size. Third, spending in per capita terms is positively associated with poverty, suggesting a relatively progressive pattern of spending. These are not surprising findings. Differences in spending could be explained by (a) differences in provinces' needs (or poverty), (b) differences in their characteristics (geographic, ethnic, historic, and other), or (c) the presence of economies of scale in the provision of services in areas with higher population densities.

Figure 5.3 illustrates the changes in per capita expenditure between 1997 and 2004 in Ecuador. Each diamond or square represents one province. The vertical axis depicts the ratio of the 2004 per capita expenditure to that in 1997. The horizontal axis illustrates per capita expenditure in 1997, the base year. This figure also distinguishes across provinces above and below median provincial poverty. Most provinces experienced increases in their per capita spending, with two exceptions (one of them an outlier) that were taken out of the figure for clarity. The growth in per capita spending was larger in provinces where per capita spending was also greater in 1997, as the scatter plot would seem to follow a positively sloped trajectory. Poorer provinces were also more likely to see bigger increases in their per capita expenditure. It seems then that provinces that are found to be more marginal (and possibly smaller in population and more remote) would experience higher increases in the per capita spending

FIGURE 5.3 Changes in Per Capita Expenditure, 1997–2004

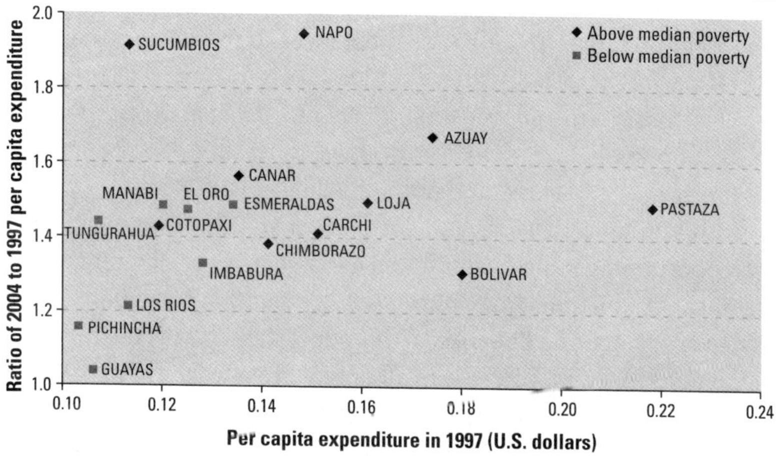

Sources: Provincial expenditure data from Albornoz (2000) and from data collected by the authors for this study. Population data from Instituto Nacional de Estadística y Censos (INEC). Poverty data from 1990 poverty map constructed by the World Bank.

Note: Galápagos and Morona Santiago are not included in figure.

determined by the budget. This is interpreted as evidence of improved representativity of the budget.

The institutional reforms introduced after 1998 significantly altered the electoral dynamics in Ecuador. Electoral reforms were adopted to elect legislators through a personalized vote, first by simple plurality (1998) and then through some form of proportional representation rule (2000, 2002). The reforms also allowed an increase in the total number of legislators, which rose from 82 in 1996 to 100 in 2002, *and* eliminated the election of national legislators. In theory, these changes should have encouraged legislators to cultivate personal and local followings as opposed to prompting them to be responsive to their party leaderships, and should have contributed to the proliferation of political parties and the fragmentation of the legislative landscape. From the president's perspective, these reforms would, in turn, increase transaction costs for forming budget coalitions, since more fragmented and provincial players were involved in the budget process.

One useful measure of equity in electoral representation is captured by the concept of malapportionment, defined as the discrepancy between the share of legislative seats and the share of population held by geographical units (Snyder and Samuels, 2001). The measure of malapportionment illustrates deviations from the democratic "one man, one vote" principle, and it shows differences in the relative weights of citizens' votes across districts.

It is possible to track the evolution of provincial malapportionment in the periods before and after the 1998 constitution. The malapportionment measure computed at the provincial level suggests that the constitution led to a very small decrease in malapportionment (mean malapportionment diminished from 41 to 37, and the difference is not significantly different from zero). This means that the reform had a minuscule effect. The direction of this effect was towards the reduction of the relative weight of a vote in all but four relatively small provinces. This change could be consistent with the change in representativeness of budget outcomes in favor of smaller provinces that was observed after the reform.

BUDGET OUTCOMES ARE RIGID ON THE EXPENDITURES AND REVENUES SIDES

Budgetary rigidity comes from factors that limit the government's capacity to modify its budget in the short run. When analyzed from this perspective, the rigidity in Ecuador's fiscal budget presents itself in various ways. To the extent possible, Ecuador's budget rigidity is quantified in this section. The main finding is that Ecuador's high budget rigidity has only worsened since the adoption of the 1998 constitution.[8]

Estimates suggest that 92 percent of the central government's budget is inflexible (Almeida, Gallardo, and Tomaselli, 2005). The discussion that follows focuses on earmarks as a factor behind such inflexibility. However, other causes of budget rigidity are the various subsidies—many of them of a regressive nature—that are perceived as entitlements and thus difficult to remove (for example, electricity or fuel subsidies).

[8] The significant changes to earmarks that were introduced since 2006 are beyond the scope of this chapter.

Two types of factors prevent the budget from showing all real revenues and expenditures and make quantifying budget rigidity complex. First, some earmarked revenues are handed directly to the beneficiaries before they enter the National Treasury (i.e., earmarks on revenues). Second, certain expenditures, such as fuel subsidies, are accounted for as costs for the state oil company and thus subtracted from total oil revenues even before these are registered in the budget (i.e., earmarks on expenditures).

Earmarks are revenues and expenditures that are assigned by law to specific purposes. They were created as a means for Congress to ensure the allocation of resources to determined constituencies and to offset legislators' lack of formal access to provincial budgetary allocations (Gallardo, 2001; Almeida, Gallardo, and Tomaselli, 2005). The laws establish contradictory rules regarding the existence of earmarks. In general, the 1998 constitution bans the creation of any new earmarks, yet it earmarks 30 percent of government spending for education.

A disaggregation of the central government's 2006 budget proposal illustrates the large magnitude of earmarks. For example, in the 2006 proposed budget, 20.9 percent of total tax collections were earmarked to be distributed among a number of institutions. The main beneficiaries of tax revenue earmarks are universities and sectional governments, which receive 32 percent and 11 percent of such earmarks, respectively. In this proposed budget, 14.52 percent of total oil revenues are earmarked for the following: education, health, roads, and autonomous and decentralized entities. In addition if oil revenues are larger than what has been budgeted, they are transferred to an oil stabilization fund managed by the BCE. All of the surplus of this fund is also earmarked: 45 percent towards the management of liabilities, 35 percent for roads in the Oriente region where oil is produced, 10 percent for development projects in five provinces, and 10 percent for the police.

In terms of earmarks on expenditures, the main earmarked resources are those that benefit sectional governments. By law, 15 percent of all current income ought to be transfered to municipalities and provincial governments. On the expenditure side, there are also other sources of budget rigidity, specifically inflexible expenditures such as wages, subsidies, projects with domestic and foreign debt, and foreign debt interest payments (Almeida, Gallardo, and Tomaselli, 2005). The rela-

FIGURE 5.4 | **Fiscal Budget by Expenditure, 2006**

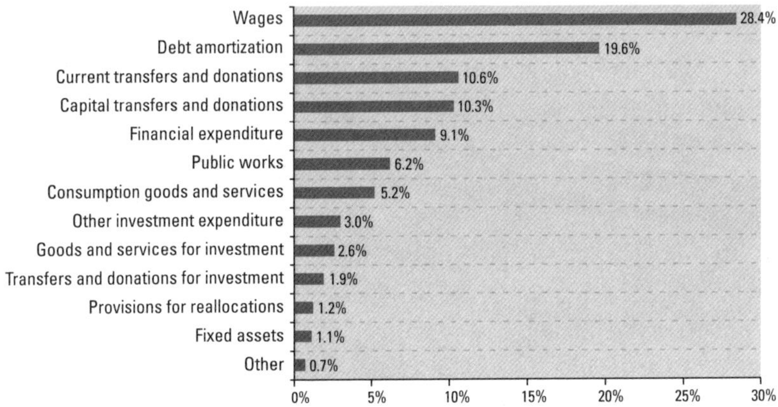

Source: MEF, 2006 budget.

tive weight of these and other expenses in the 2006 budget proposal is depicted in Figure 5.4.

SUMMARY AND CONCLUSIONS

Ecuador offers an interesting case study for analyzing—from a political economy perspective—the impact of major political and economic reforms on the budget process and, consequently, on budget outcomes. The focus on budget outcomes reflects this chapter's concern with finding a comprehensive account of the changing incentives for cooperation that budget players have under different political and budgetary arrangements.

The chapter finds that the set of constitutional reforms adopted in 1998 and other political reforms adopted in previous years (1996–1998) offered relevant budget players in Ecuador a contradictory set of incentives for cooperation. On the one hand, these reforms gave legislators incentives to be more responsive and accountable to their constituents by allowing them to seek reelection and stay longer in office. On the other hand, the reforms constricted the role of Congress in the general budget process by giving the executive greater agenda-setting power over formulation and execution, and by banning legislators from accessing or negotiating budget allocations for provinces. In the end, the greater agenda-setting powers of the executive contributed to a more sustainable budget process. From a political standpoint, the budget became more efficient, as fewer budget reallocations took place. The electoral reforms aimed at adjusting the proportionality of the electoral system were also reflected in more representative budget outcomes. Finally, legislation approved since 1998 contributed to greater instances of earmarking and therefore more rigid budget outcomes, despite constitutional provisions to the contrary.

Dollarization reforms and the subsequent FRL significantly constrained the choice of fiscal policy instruments available to governments. Dollarization imposed a de facto need for fiscal discipline, as the government could no longer print money. By eliminating the role of the monetary authority, dollarization also contributed to shifting policy choices to the legislative arena, where policy change has traditionally been rigid. At the same time, a rise in international oil prices and consequently an increase in oil revenues further encouraged earmarking of oil reserve funds and therefore greater budget rigidity. The lower discount rates that came with dollarization are likely to have contributed to greater budget sustainability and efficiency. Although it is not possible to calculate the net effect of different reforms on budget outcomes, institutional changes have improved budget governance (in the sense of producing more sustainable, representative, and efficient budget outcomes), at the expense of the budget's being less adaptable to unexpected shifts in market conditions, such as downward changes in commodity (oil) prices.

Although current budget outcomes appear desirable, this chapter claims that they are outside an equilibrium path, largely because budget players do not have incentives to sustain political agreements over the long run. This instability is due to the prevailing asymmetry of powers between a strong executive, weak legislatures, and newly empowered subnational governments, and the disrupting effects of rising oil revenues on actors' incentives for budget discipline. While the 1998 constitution improved the representativity of legislators, it also reinforced the powers of the executive over the budget process at the expense of the legislature. Under the 1998 rules, legislators had very little space to influence budget allocations in favor of their constituencies. As a result, rational politicians migrated from a resource-dry policy arena to local governments, where they could access government resources and develop clearer electoral loyalties. The mechanisms through which municipal governments accessed government resources (through legislative parties or directly with the president) remain unclear and deserve further research. Oil dependency also had negative effects on sustained budget cooperation. While politicians were willing to adopt legislation to ensure fiscal responsibility in the aftermath of an economic crisis at the end of the 1990s, the rapid growth of oil revenues in the following years reversed incentives for fiscal austerity. In the context of high oil prices and in anticipation of an electoral year, Congress effectively eliminated spending constraints imposed by the FRL in 2005.

The migration of politicians to subnational governments and the eroding incentives for fiscal discipline during an oil bonanza are examples that illustrate the fickle nature of budget coalitions in Ecuador. Most importantly, perhaps, they illustrate politicians' success at influencing the budget process despite institutional reforms aimed at depoliticizing the process. This permanent tension between changing budgetary rules and politicians' cooperation incentives has challenged the long-term sustainability of quality budget outcomes in Ecuador.

REFERENCES

Albornoz, V. 2000. *Gobierno central, autonomías y finanzas provinciales.* Quito: Corporación de Estudios para el Desarrollo (CORDES).

Almeida, M. D., V. Gallardo, and A. Tomaselli. 2005. Gobernabilidad fiscal en Ecuador. German Development Cooperation (GTZ), Quito. Unpublished.

Barnhill, T. M. Jr., and G. Kopits. 2003. Assessing Fiscal Sustainability under Uncertainty. IMF Working Paper No. WP03/79. International Monetary Fund (IMF), Washington, DC.

Díaz Alvarado, C., A. Izquierdo, and U. Panizza. 2004. Fiscal Sustainability in Emerging Market Countries with an Application to Ecuador. Working Paper No. 511. Research Department, Inter-American Development Bank, Washington, DC.

Fernandez, G., and C. Lara 1998. Los shocks exógenos y el crecimiento económico del Ecuador. Nota Técnica No. 48. Banco Central del Ecuador.

Gallardo, J. 2001. Reforma fiscal. Ministerio de Economía y Finanza, Quito. Unpublished.

Hidalgo, J., V. Albornoz, and F. Hurtado. 2007. *Las finanzas provinciales del gobierno central.* Cuadernos de Descentralización. Quito: Corporación de Estudios para el Desarrollo (CORDES).

Hurtado, O. 2006. *Los costos del populismo.* Quito: Corporación de Estudios para el Desarrollo (CORDES).

Landau, D. 2001. Policy or Pork? Presidential Strategy Choice and the Legislature in Ecuador. B. A. thesis, Department of Government, Harvard University, Cambridge, MA.

Mejía Acosta, A. 2006. Crafting Legislative Ghost Coalitions in Ecuador: Informal Institutions and Economic Reform in an Unlikely Case. In G. Helmke and S. Levitsky, eds., *Informal Institutions and Democracy: Lessons from Latin America.* Baltimore Johns Hopkins University Press.

Mejía Acosta, A., M. C. Araujo, A. Pérez-Liñán, and S. Saiegh. 2008. Veto Players, Fickle Institutions, and Low-Quality Policies: The Policymaking Process in Ecuador. In E. Stein, M. Tommasi, C. Scartascini, and P. T. Spiller, eds., *Policymaking in Latin America: How Politics Shapes Policies.* Washington, DC: Inter-American Development Bank, and Cambridge, MA: DRCLAS.

Snyder, R., and D. Samuels. 2001. Devaluing the Vote in Latin America. *Journal of Democracy* 12(1): 146–59.

DATA SETS

Estudio de finanzas provinciales a nivel provincial (Corporación de Estudios para el Desarrollo (CORDES)

Indicators from OECD-IDB-WB Budget Survey Project

Monthly Statistical Information from the Central Bank of Ecuador

Development Data Platform time series data from the World Bank

Ecuador 1990 and 2001 poverty maps prepared by the World Bank

Ecuador 1990 and 2001 population censuses from Instituto Nacional de Estadística y Censos (INEC)

Sistema Integrado de Indicadores Sociales del Ecuador (SIISE), 2006

6

Weakened Policymaking Process, Deteriorating Fiscal Outcomes: The Case of Paraguay

José R. Molinas, Aníbal Pérez-Liñán, and Mark Hallerberg,
with the collaboration of Audrey Morgan

DISENTANGLING THE BUDGET PROCESS IN PARAGUAY

By the end of 2000, as Paraguay recovered from a failed military uprising and the approval rate of the president dwindled, alarming press reports indicated that the Central Bank of Paraguay had recommended the firing of ten thousand public employees, which constituted about 5 percent of the total public workforce. The political context was too sensitive for seasoned politicians to follow such technical advice. Instead, a few weeks later the administration floated bonds for US$85 million in order to cover the mandatory end-of-the-year bonuses (*aguinaldos*) for public employees and retired citizens.

This story from Christmas of 2000 illustrates a type of situation that existed from after the introduction of a new constitution in 1992 through 2002. Over this period, each successive Paraguayan administration faced greater political challenges and financial pressures than its predecessor. The result was chronic fiscal deficit from 1995 through 2002. The budget then approached a balanced status in 2004 and was in surplus for the next three years (Figure 6.1).

How does one account for these fluctuations in the budget balance? A recent study of the Paraguayan policymaking process suggests that the relatively new Paraguayan democracy has rapidly expanded the number of formal and informal veto players. A growing number of parties and

FIGURE 6.1 | Budget Balance in Paraguay, 1989–2007

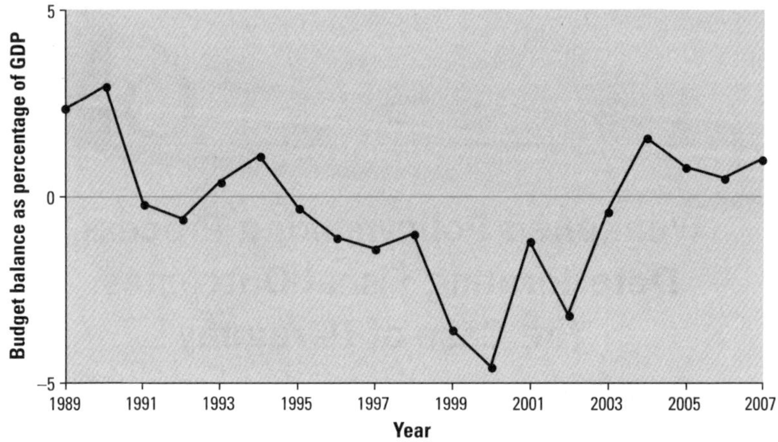

Source: http://www.hacienda.gov.py (retrieved on June 3, 2008).

factions in the legislature have constrained the ability of the executive to control the budget process, and emerging social movements (in particular, the peasant movement) have operated as noninstitutional veto players (popular protests, for instance, forced the cancellation of the privatization program in 2002). The Paraguayan system thus seems to provide relative flexibility for the provision of particularistic benefits, but relative rigidity for the control of overall national expenditures (Molinas, Pérez-Liñán, and Saiegh, 2004).

This chapter proposes to disentangle the budget process by studying the key players that influence the budget cycle in Paraguay, as well as the players' powers and incentives. It briefly reviews the most significant points of the general theoretical framework—introduced in the opening chapter of this volume—that are relevant to the budget process in Paraguay. The chapter emphasizes the interactions between historical legacies, the overall institutional design, and the budgetary procedures as factors that shape politicians' incentives to display cooperative behavior in the elaboration of the budget. Then, the chapter addresses the formal and informal rules that guide the budget policymaking process. The analysis herein is based not only on formal instruments, such as the constitution and related laws, but also on in-depth interviews with several policymakers in the executive branch and in Congress. The chapter also explores how such procedures interact with the overall political context to create specific incentives for critical actors in the process. The concluding section discusses how the generally low incentives for cooperation have created negative conditions for the sustainability of public expenditures, the efficient allocation of resources, and the representative quality of the spending.

THE BUDGETARY FRAMEWORK IN PARAGUAY

This chapter addresses the Paraguayan budget process from the perspectives of both a transaction cost theory of the policymaking process (Spiller and Tommasi, 2003) and the public expenditure management literature (Schick, 1998). The chapter analyzes the "outer features" of the budget process and builds on the prior findings of research on the political institutions, policymaking processes, and policy outcomes in Paraguay (Molinas, Pérez-Liñán, and Saiegh, 2004).

The ability of political leaders and bureaucrats to coordinate their long-term goals and actions lies at the core of the budget process. In the absence of cooperation, public officials are trapped in a common pool problem: multiple agents intend to extract resources from the same treasury without much concern for the sustainability of the aggregate outcome in the long run. The likely result is thus a tragedy of the commons.

The relative performance of the budget process ultimately translates into the "outer features" of fiscal policies. Three features of public finances deserve careful consideration. First, the **sustainability** of public expenditures indicates to what extent the level of expenditures is consistent with the government's intertemporal budget constraints (the ability of the government to comply with its obligations in the long run). Second, the **efficiency** of public expenditures reflects the degree to which the allocation of public resources is devoted to the most valuable activities. Third, the **representativeness** of expenditures maps the extent to which the allocation of resources reflects the preferences of the population at large or, alternatively, the preferences of concentrated interest groups (IDB, 2004).

Following this scheme, the interpretation herein of how the framework for the current Paraguayan budget process developed over time can be summarized as follows. Between 1954 and 1989, Paraguay was ruled by General Alfredo Stroessner, who imposed a centralized pattern of policymaking characterized by the support of the armed forces, the government bureaucracy, and the "granitic" Colorado Party. In February of 1989, a coup led by General Andrés Rodríguez ousted Stroessner and ignited the transition to democracy. One of the main legacies of "Stronismo" was an intense internal struggle for the control of the ruling Colorado Party after Stroessner was removed from office in 1989. Factionalism was in part compounded by the very nature of the democratic transition—which made it more difficult for the president or military officers to assert unilateral control over the party—and in part by a series of institutional choices adopted with the 1992 constitutional reforms, including the mandate for competitive primary elections for all parties. Mandatory primaries washed away the effects of the closed-list proportional representation system: rather than concentrate power in a few national party leaders, the electoral system encouraged the formation of political machines under the control of multiple party factions. The performance of these political machines depends on their leaders' access to, and ability to distribute, patronage and pork to their voters. The result has been a policymaking process that emphasizes particularistic policies rather than regulatory statutes or redistributive programs.

The incentives generated by this political context have encouraged the emergence of informal procedures that operate in parallel to the formal rules of the budget process. For instance, although the minister of finance is formally in charge of negotiating the approval of the central government's budget with Congress, individual agencies often bypass the minister and lobby members of Congress directly. The Paraguayan Ministry of Finance can later use its de facto control over the disbursement of funds to reassert its priorities, but bureaucrats and party politicians have responded to this problem by expanding public employment, given that the ministry is highly constrained in its ability to tamper with public salaries.

This dynamic has created a serious problem of coordination, which has led to a common pool dilemma. Multiple veto players want to maximize their share of the public budget without endogenizing the costs of growing public expenditures. To the extent that the ability of the president and the finance minister to enforce cooperation among the players has declined over time, the consequences have been lower levels of budget sustainability (illustrated by the deficit levels displayed in Figure 6.1) and declining allocative efficiency and representativeness.[1]

SPECIFIC FORMAL AND INFORMAL RULES FOR THE BUDGET PROCESS

The specific rules for the budget process have been established in the 1992 Paraguayan Constitution, in Law 1535 sanctioned in 1999, and in entrenched uses, customs, and informal rules. This section provides a description of a few general rules and then discusses the particular rules for the different budget stages.

The elaboration of the Nation's General Budget (NGB) rests formally on the following principles: *universality* (it should include all public revenues and expenditures), *legality* (estimated revenues can be exceeded in practice, but authorized expenditures represent a maximum ceiling), *unity* (all decisions should be included in a single document), *yearly periodicity* (a new budget must be approved every year), and *balance* (expenditures cannot exceed estimated revenues and financing). The NGB includes the structure of revenue and expenditure (current and capital); the financing arrangements; a personnel annex that includes the number, type, name, and salary; and the budget of public enterprises, which includes data on cost and performance of goods and services. Expenditure and personnel are presented separately for each public institution.

Although the annual law of the NGB may not contain any statement that modifies other laws, this law may, in practice, contradict the permanent law. The Paraguayan legal system does not rank laws, and therefore any law can suspend the effect of a previous statute.

---

[1] It does not follow from this statement that concentration of power in the executive branch would be sufficient to solve problems of sustainability, efficiency, and representativeness. An unconstrained president could, for instance, compromise the budget balance in order to reassert his short-term priorities and then happily transfer this legacy to the next administration. As will be discussed in the "Conclusions" section of this chapter, problems in the budget process are not solved by eliminating veto players, but rather by "calibrating" their incentives.

Budget Preparation Stage

Budget Guidelines

The coordinator of the budget preparation stage is the Ministry of Finance (MF). The executive issues an annual decree within the first four months of the calendar year to establish the guidelines of NGB preparation, according to the executive's policy objectives. The MF prepares a draft for the general budget guidelines, which are established by a presidential decree.

Institutional Budget Projects

The institutional budget projects must be consistent with each institution's operating plan. There are differences in the projects for institutions within and outside of the central government. The institutional projects must be presented to the MF within the first semester of each year. In case of delay of any institution, the MF will prepare the institutional project.

In the budget consolidation process, there are some informal negotiations among the minister of finance and the other ministers. Indeed, any item that exceeds the general guidelines has to be negotiated between the minister of finance and his peers. If the MF deems it necessary to cut a ministry's budget proposal substantially, it provides the agency with new specific guidelines for revising its original proposal. In other cases, when the revisions are not considered substantial, the MF simply proceeds with the changes on its own. The MF may also increase the budget proposals of the institutions. The consolidated budget can be discussed in the Council of Ministers, or cabinet, but more often it is presented by the MF directly to Congress as the executive proposal. The executive-consolidated NGB project must be presented by September 1.

Budget Approval Stage

The budget must be initiated by the executive on September 1 every year and must be passed (or rejected) by Congress by December 20. If Congress rejects the executive proposal, the reversionary point (what will become the status quo) is the previous year's budget. Starting on September 1, a joint bicameral commission, composed of 15 deputies and 15 senators, studies the budget for 60 days before issuing a nonbinding recommendation. On October 30, the revised proposal moves to the Chamber of Deputies, the lower house of Paraguay's bicameral legislature, where it is studied by the Chamber Budget Committee—the largest of the chamber's committees, with 26 members including the ones participating in the joint commission—and must move to a floor vote within two weeks.

On November 15, the budget bill moves to the Senate Budget Committee, where it is further revised and must move to a floor vote within two weeks. The Senate can alter any item of the lower chamber's version by simple majority, virtually drafting the "final" version of the budget.

On November 30, the bill moves back to the Chamber of Deputies, which has until December 10 to submit a second-round vote. During this stage, the lower house can treat only the budget items that have been previously rejected or altered by the Senate (all other items are already fixed), and the deputies confront a closed rule: they can only reject the Senate's proposal, without modifications, by an absolute majority of the chamber's members. The items modified by the Senate are treated item by item by the deputies, and if the proposal is rejected, the fallback point is the deputies' original proposal. Between December 10 and December 20, the Senate must vote the whole budget bill up or down. This treatment provides an incentive to reject the changes introduced by the deputies. It takes a two-thirds majority to reject the bill, and if it is rejected, the fallback point is the revised Senate proposal. Congress cannot reallocate investment resources to finance current expenditures, nor can it reallocate resources affected by special laws.

The executive-legislative relations in budget matters will be exclusively maintained through the MF. This office can propose changes to the executive NGB project after it is presented; however, this formal rule does not apply in practice. All of those interviewed for this project in ministries and in the legislature state that ministers and top public managers contact legislators directly to defend their budget proposals.[2]

---

[2] The only exception in recent years seems to be the approval process of the 2003 budget, because there was a new administration and Congress in place, as well as an explicit order from the executive to ministers and top managers not to approach legislators.

The executive has, in principle, constitutional authority to sanction this type of behavior; however, in practice, it seems too costly to the executive to charge these players with lobbying Congress for their budget.

Budget Execution Stage

The MF has an active role in the budget execution stage. The minister keeps the budget equilibrium and oversees compliance with the budget execution plan. In accordance with this role, all public institutions will present to the MF an annual plan of revenue and expenditure installments based on their activity time frame.

The MF, in coordination with public institutions, will propose to the executive a monthly financial plan of revenue and expenditure for budget execution. Given monthly cash limits, each ministry decides how to allocate its funds internally. The MF manages the funds allocated to rigid expenditures (public salaries, external debt service, and pension funds). Because the MF has some discretion in the execution of the budget, there is also room for the introduction of political criteria in the release of funds.

Evaluation and Control of Budget Execution Results

According to the text of the law, the executive establishes the guidelines for the evaluation and control of results from the budget execution. Formally, the internal and external control of public institutions is handled by the Internal Institutional Audits (IIAs), the Executive's General Auditor Office (EGA), and the Republic General Comptroller Office (RGC). The internal control comprises the ex ante control by public managers and the ex-post control by the IIAs and the EGA (L1535). The IIAs comprise 21 specialized units of controls for each public institution that proceed according to generally accepted audit norms. Internal auditors depend on the highest manager of each institution. The EGA depends upon the president and is a unit of internal control for the executive. The EGA supervises the functioning of the IIAs and must proceed according to generally accepted audit norms. External control is a responsibility of the RGC. Also, with executive authorization, public institutions can hire independent external auditors, according to their special laws and/or international treaties. The evaluation measures the results for each program according to the objectives and goals initially established in the budget proposal, and it is expected to incorporate an assessment of the results and recommendations for corrective actions.

However, the formal rules regarding evaluation are not enforced in Paraguay. All interviewees concur regarding this statement and point out that no government institution takes seriously a performance evaluation of the allocation of public funds. On a scale of 1 (not adequate) to 20 (very adequate), the interviewees' average ranking of the quality of evaluation of results is only 4.5.

Despite the lacunae of the established norms and procedures, the internal and external control places excessive importance on the policymakers' following the rules at the expense of evaluating results. All the interviewees coincide on this point. Moreover, despite the high attention given to them, the actual control of the norms and procedures is only marginally adequate. On a scale of 1 (not adequate) to 20 (very adequate), the interviewees' average ranking of the quality of control of norms and procedures is only 8.5.

THE FORMAL AND INFORMAL INCENTIVES OF THE PLAYERS AND THE DEGREE OF POLITICAL COOPERATION THROUGHOUT THE BUDGET PROCESS

In terms of the budget process, political cooperation refers to the solving of coordination problems throughout the different stages to generate a management system of public funds that is efficient, representative, and sustainable. This management system has public good features; that is, it is nonsubtractable by its use and it is nonexcludable from its use. The achievement of political cooperation implies the solution of prisoner's dilemma–type problems among public agencies and political actors.

The level of political cooperation depends, as stated above, upon the specific rules that govern the players' interaction within the budget process, the overall policymaking process, basic institutions, and history. The degree of political intertemporal cooperation is low in Paraguay. In the current political context, there has been a multiplication of veto players, as mentioned earlier. This situation has imposed low decisiveness on the policymaking process.

The current Paraguayan policymaking process has limited capacity to modify major policies. As a proxy for this process, Molinas, Pérez-Liñán, and Saiegh (2004) observe that regulatory bills initiated by the executive have faced declining rates of success: 87 percent were approved by Congress during the last year of the Rodríguez administration, 69 percent during the Wasmosy term, 60 percent during the short Cubas period, and 48 percent during the González Macchi administration. Low decisiveness is the product of a weakened executive coupled with legislators with little interest in policymaking.

Corruption exposés have delegitimized the policymaking process, thus preventing the emergence of cooperation and blocking substantial policy change. Also, in a context of declining formal and partisan powers, particularistic policy may be one of the few resources left to the executive for negotiating with Congress. An expansion of pork barrel politics may be consistent with a strategic attempt by the executive to overcome its increasing weaknesses. In the current context, the president may have limited capacity to adopt new regulatory or redistributive schemes, but he or she could be even weaker in the absence of distributive policy.

To understand how the low level of political cooperation around the system for management of public funds takes place, this section will describe the players—both formal and informal—that participate in the budget process and their incentives, as well as how these players interact in the different budget stages.

Political Leaders

Political leaders do not have a formal role in the budget process; however, they informally intervene in all of its major stages. It is through the political parties that the overall policymaking process mainly affects the level of political cooperation around the budget.

In the preparation stage of the budget process, party leaders—local and national—lobby with public managers over public employment for their supporters. Public employment is the main currency of exchange in the transaction between the government and political parties. This practice is not restricted to the different factions of the National Republican Association (ANR), usually known as the Colorado Party (a conservative political party in Paraguay founded in the late 1800s).

It is, rather, a widespread behavior among both ANR and opposition parties.[3]

In the preparation stage, it is common for party leaders to approach multiple agents, including top public managers, ministries, the executive, and the MF. In the approval, execution, and control stages, the interaction between party leaders—locally and nationally—and legislators is continuous. Moreover, several party leaders are legislators.

The increased political competition has increased the incentives for clientelistic public hiring, since party leaders need to strengthen their leadership. This has negatively impacted fiscal sustainability in Paraguay. On a scale of 1 (no effect) to 20 (very important effect), the interviewees' average ranking of the impact of clientelistic public hiring on fiscal sustainability is 15.3.

Public Institutions

The Top Management

Within the budget process, it is important to distinguish two types of public institutions: the central government institutions and the decentralized public institutions. The main difference between the two types is that negotiations with the MF over transfers of funds are more involved for central government institutions.

All types of public institutions must comply with the formal rules of budget preparation. However, public institutions do not comply with the formal rule that states that the executive-legislative relations in budget matters must be exclusively maintained through the MF. Ministers and top public managers contact legislators directly to defend their budget proposals. This situation increases the number of players in the game, which jeopardizes the prospects of reaching a cooperative outcome between Congress and the MF. The lower perspective of cooperation between Congress and the MF may decrease both efficiency and sustainability in the budget process.

The relationship of the MF with institutions outside the central government in the approval process can be more complex. These institu-

[3] There are, however, honorable exceptions.

tions are less dependent on the MF than their centralized counterparts. In several cases, decentralized institutions have their own institutional revenues and do not depend on MF transfers. For these institutions, the incentive to negotiate directly with Congress is stronger.

Central government institutions must follow a more difficult path to achieve their desired budget. A successful direct negotiation with Congress during the approval process is a necessary step. Then, these institutions have to negotiate successfully with the MF during the execution stage to get the funds released.

Ministers and top public managers must reconcile in their budget proposal both the anticipated expenditure due to clientelistic reasons (i.e., often the public employment due to political patronage may not coincide with the position requirements) and the necessary expenditure for fulfilling their institutional tasks. Incorporating the clientelistic expenditure may also increase the probability of success of their budget proposal, since this creates compatibility of incentives of the political leaders who may lobby for the institution's budget.

During the execution phase, negotiations between the MF and line ministries can be very long and frustrating, as pointed out by several interviewees. The objectives of line ministries and the MF differ greatly. While line ministries seek resources in order to carry out needed activities to achieve their institutional objectives, the MF is primarily concerned that the public expenditure does not exceed the Treasury's ability to pay the institutions. There is a high transaction cost in the relationship between line ministries and the MF. Line ministries have to obtain MF support to adjust their budget among different items in the same program or executive support to adjust their budget among different programs within the same institution. If resources fall short, line ministries have the option to adjust their objectives or to lobby for more resources with the MF. This lobbying process has at least three stages of negotiation, according to one interviewee. First, there is a negotiation at the minister's level. If this negotiation is successful, there is another level of negotiation between the budget director of the MF and administrative director of the line ministry. The budget director has to be independently persuaded of the merits of the planned expenditure by the line ministry. If this director is not persuaded, budget execution is not possible. If he or she is convinced, there is a third level of negotiation. Once the budget modification is approved and there is authorization to spend, a negotiation over the effective transfer of resources is initiated between the line ministry treasurer and the MF treasurer.

As demonstrated above, there are many different levels of approval in the MF for releasing funds. This difficult process generates incentives for "informal" negotiations with MF officials. The currency of exchange at this level could be several exchanges, to include "favor" exchanges. The transaction costs associated with this informal procedure are huge. First, there is a financial opportunity cost of the delay that is not being considered by the public management. In several cases, private contractors incorporate this shadow price into their pricing for the provision of goods and services to the government, while in others the currency is a transfer from contractors to the government. Frequently, *gestores* (specialists in dealing with specific transactions) have to be hired to do the follow-up with the MF.

Public managers have incentives to spend, independently of the budget execution results. An interviewee pointed out that "if an administrator does not execute 90 percent of his budget, he will be told next year that he does not need that money. This situation inhibits the efficient use of resources." The interviewee gave this example: if an institution has US$10,000 to spend on computer equipment before the end of the year, but the most current software will not be ready until the following year, it would be better to wait to buy the most modern hardware and software. However, the risk in this case is that those funds may no longer be available for next year. It should be noted that many public managers have incentives to spend to earn commission on the purchase of goods and services.

It is clear that there are many incentives to pursue particularistic behavior and not as many to search for efficiency and representativeness in public management. These incentives make cooperation during the budget process more difficult to achieve.

The Bureaucracy

In spite of democratic formal institutions, Paraguay has not been able to develop an effective, relatively independent bureaucracy that is accountable. In 2000, Law 1626/00 sought to modernize the public service career by establishing a clearer system of selection, training, promotion, and retirement for public employees. Among its key measures was the creation of the Secretaria de la Función Pública (Secretariat for Civil Service) with the rank of a ministry. This secretariat was created to take charge of increasing rationalization, transparency, and efficiency in human resource management. However, the law has been challenged as unconstitutional, substantially delaying its full application (Marió, Silva-Leander, and Carter, 2004). Thus, a clear description for public positions, procedure manuals, a consistent scale of public salaries, performance evaluations of public employees, and effective training systems do not currently exist in Paraguay (Marió, Silva-Leander, and Carter, 2004).

According to Ugo Panizza (1999), while the average Latin American public sector employee earns roughly 4 percent more than workers with similar characteristics employed by the private sector, the wage premium for a Paraguayan public employee is around 17 percent. This indicator can be used as a measure of the relative inefficiency of the public sector with respect to the private sector. The greatest challenge faced by the Paraguayan bureaucracy, though, has to do with corruption. As Kaufmann, Kraay, and Zoido-Lobatón (1999) show, multiple observers view corrupt and dishonest practices as a distinctive feature of the Paraguayan bureaucracy.

Several people interviewed in Paraguay for this project stated that the typical public employee in Paraguay does not see corruption, under its standard definition—the abuse of public position for private benefit—as wrong. For the typical public employee, it is normal to receive "an incentive" to accelerate the process in the public sector. From the standpoint of these employees, such payments are for personalized services that have to be charged separately and are part of their compensation packages. For the typical public employee, the concept of corruption is restricted to direct stealing of public money or government assets. Also, "traffic of influence" is an informal rule in Paraguayan bureaucracy. This is not perceived as wrong, but rather as a manifestation of power, something very close to a source of prestige.

The Ministry of Finance

The role of the MF is central in the budget process and comprises three fields of activity: economics, public management, and politics. That is, the ministry's formal duties include designing a macroeconomically sound fiscal policy; coordinating the government's economic team; representing the executive in negotiations with Congress over budget matters; coordinating the use, accounting, and reporting of public funds; and coordinating the tax collection process, among others.

It is possible to categorize finance ministers into two types.[4] The first type displays a stronger profile on management, followed by political and economic capabilities. The second type displays a stronger profile on economics, followed by management and political capabilities. Among the first type of ministers are H. Gerhard Doll, who served under Raúl Cubas, and Federico Zayas, Francisco Oviedo, and Alcides Jimenez, who served under Luis González Macchi. Among the second type are James Spalding, who served under Luis González Macchi, and Dionisio Borda, who served under Óscar Nicanor Duarte Frutos.

In the budget preparation stage, the economic and management dimension of the MF dominates. The MF is the coordinator of the budget preparation process: it drafts the general budget guidelines; receives, revises, and prepares (for delaying institutions) the institutional projects that are later consolidated as the executive proposal to Congress; and drafts the explanation on fiscal policy, the policy objectives, and the technical details of revenue estimation.

During the approval process, the political dimension dominates. The MF faces two strategic fronts of negotiation: one with managers of public institutions and one with Congress. To enhance chances of political cooperation between the executive and Congress, it would be better to present a consistent executive proposal represented by the MF. However, as mentioned before, with the exception of the approval process for the 2004 budget, this does not usually happen. Some of the interviewees pointed out that oftentimes, public institutions do not present a technically sound proposal to the MF, deciding beforehand that they will make their highest effort in lobbying Congress directly. This situation, explains another interviewee, depends upon the profile of public managers, the executive, and the MF. If the MF is relatively powerful or it is strongly backed up by the executive, the incentives to negotiate directly with Congress decrease for public managers. If pub-

[4] In this categorization, each minister is compared against himself, relatively, on the dimensions. There is no comparison across ministers.

lic managers are relatively powerful and the MF does not have a good working relationship with Congress, the incentives for public managers to negotiate directly with Congress increase.

In the execution stage, transfers of funds to central government agencies are managed by the MF, through a monthly cash flow plan that is prepared following quarterly indicative planning. In practice, however, the MF has some leeway to administer the transfers. Even when dealing with rigid expenditures (public salaries, external debt service, and pension funds), the MF has some discretionary power in choosing what expenditures will be prioritized in times of financial hardship. The most rigid expenditures account for approximately 80 percent of the total budget for the central government. The allocation of the remaining 20 percent is another source of relative discretionary power for the MF, because there is no law that establishes the procedure through which the "residual" budget should be allocated.

In summary, the MF has less discretion when allocating funds for the most rigid items and more discretion with the least rigid ones. The exercise of such discretionary power, of course, is subject to presidential approval. Regarding the control stage, the MF coordinates the reporting mechanisms of the government, which includes consolidating and checking the budget, financial, and patrimonial information of public institutions.

The Executive Branch

The 1992 constitution grants the executive power exclusive initiation over the budget. If Congress rejects the budget or if the president fails to present a proposal, the status quo (the current year's budget) becomes the reversionary point. The Paraguayan president has limited resources for imposing unilateral budget decisions. The president lacks proper decree powers (although he or she may submit "urgent" bills to Congress), and as with other policies, the president's line item veto of the budget can be overridden by an absolute majority of Congress.

In terms of budget coordination at the preparation stage, Paraguay has a relatively hierarchical budget procedure (Alesina et al., 1999: 260), and it has avoided the formation of coalition cabinets. In fact, only five coalition cabinets (in 1874, 1904, 1912, 1946, and 1999) have been formed throughout Paraguay's history (Pangrazio, 2000: 324–25). The last one, during the González Macchi administration, crumbled within a few months when the Liberal Party abandoned the government because the president refused to give the party control over 40 percent of all political appointments (Paredes, 2001).

In practice, the responsibilities that the executive and the MF have over the budget process are interconnected. The executive oversees the MF in the preparation, approval, execution, and control stages. The executive also has the responsibility for establishing the guidelines for evaluation of results. Neither the establishment of the guidelines nor the evaluations themselves are regularly undertaken.

Congress

Given the powers of the executive, Paraguay is one of the three South American countries where the constitution gives Congress unrestricted power over the budget process (the others are Argentina and Bolivia). In the remaining countries, legislators can alter budget items but cannot raise total expenditures, or they are only allowed to cut the budget (Payne et al., 2002: 202).

The unrestricted congressional power over the budget process threatens aggregate fiscal discipline. As Schick (1998) points out, aggregate discipline requires that budget totals be set independently of and before decisions are made on the various parts of the budget; otherwise, the spending totals will be raised to accommodate demand. Unrestricted power allows Congress to alter revenue estimates to accommodate demands.

The lack of adequate technical aides and procedures prevents Congress from effectively using program evaluations in making budget decisions. Congress makes its budget decisions also on a yearly basis, with no reference to a medium-term expenditure framework.

Regarding the control stage, Congress evaluates the executive report on the execution of the previous year's budget, based on the Republic General Comptroller's report. As mentioned before, the tendency is for Congress to accept the comptroller's assessment of the executive's report.

Some words are also in order about the electoral system. Members of **Congress** are elected in concurrent elections every five years and can be reelected indefinitely. The Paraguayan lower house is formed by 80 deputies who are elected from 18 districts (*departamentos*) for five-year terms. These deputies are elected from closed party lists using proportional representation in relatively small districts (the average district magnitude is 4.4). In theory, the closed-list system creates little incentive to cultivate the "personal vote" (Shugart and Carey, 1992; Hallerberg and Marier, 2004), but as claimed elsewhere herein, legally mandated party primaries and relatively small districts have encouraged particularistic politics in the Chamber. The Senate is composed of 45 members elected from closed party lists in a nationwide electoral district. The Paraguayan bicameral system is highly congruent—meaning that the partisan composition of the Chamber and the Senate is usually quite similar (Lijphart, 1999; Llanos, 2002). Although congressional reelection is not banned by the constitution, the electoral context, marked by competitive primaries, increasing party factionalism, and new political parties, has created greater uncertainty about the political survival of legislators. In 1998, 54 percent of the deputies were reelected; in 2003, only 21 percent of the deputies remained in their seats. The available evidence, which is limited, suggests that there is no high degree of specialization in the committee system.

Political Parties

Since the nineteenth century, two major **political parties** have dominated the local landscape: the Colorados (ANR) and the Liberals (Authentic Radical Liberal Party, PLRA). Although the ANR has remained the largest party (winning 67 percent of the seats in the lower chamber in 1989, 50 percent in 1993, 56 percent in 1998, and 46 percent in 2003), the Liberals were able to capture the vice presidency in the 2000 election (scheduled to fill in the vacant position after Vice President Argaña was killed in 1999). Following the democratization process, smaller middle-class parties (Encuentro Nacional, País Solidario, and Patria Querida) and General Oviedo's UNACE Party were able to capture several seats in Congress. As a result, the effective number of parties in the lower house grew from 1.0 in 1960 to 1.9 in 1989, 2.4 in 1993, 2.3 in 1998, and 3.2 in 2003.[5] During 2003 and 2004 the ANR was forced to

---

[5] The "effective number" is based on the size of the parties (here measured in legislative seats). The formula for the index is $ENP = 1 / \Sigma(p^2)$, where p represents the proportion of seats controlled by each party in the lower chamber (Laakso and Taagepera, 1979).

rely on informal coalitions with the Patria Querida (on tax reform) and the Liberals (to appoint the ombudsman), and even on a political pact with all legislative parties (to pursue the reform of the Supreme Court) in order to pass its major policy initiatives.

Increasing Factionalism

Political fragmentation led to an increase in the number of factional veto players in Congress during the 1990s. Herein, to assess the magnitude of this problem, the Rice index of party unity was estimated for the Colorado and the Liberal Parties in the Chamber of Deputies for all budget-related votes since 1996. The Rice index ranges from zero, when the party is evenly split in a budgetary vote, to 100, when all the members of the party vote together (Rice, 1925).[6] It is possible to identify two categories of budgetary bills: the articles of the annual budget, voted on at the end of the previous year, and the amendments to the budget, usually introduced by the executive branch to correct provisions of the original budget during the course of the year. On average, more than 40 bills that amend different parts of the budget are introduced in Congress every year—although roll call data do not exist for all of them. In more than 90 percent of the cases, these bills attempt to transfer or reallocate resources across public agencies.

These figures lead to two conclusions. First, party cohesion tends to be greater when the party is dealing with specific amendments than when dealing with the national budget bill. This finding reinforces the idea that the system is more capable of dealing with particularistic decisions than with nationwide policies, but it may also result from the fact that the president is legally mandated to submit the budget bill to Congress, although he or she can strategically withdraw specific amendments that are expected to fail. Second, and more important, it is clear that internal party crises can directly affect the budget process. At the peak of the confrontation between Colorado factions (1999, in the preparation of the 2000 budget), cohesion dropped drastically, and a surprisingly cohesive PLRA stepped in to approve the bill. Party disputes within the ruling ANR also hindered the party's ability to approve amendments to the current budget during that year.

---

[6] The formula for the index is $R = |Ayes - Nays| / (Ayes + Nays) * 100$.

The Judiciary Branch

The 1992 constitution included a broad definition of human rights and established a new framework for the **judiciary**. The Assembly sought to promote judicial independence by mandating an allocation of at least 3 percent of all public expenditures to the judiciary. In addition, reforms barred judges from holding any partisan posts, created a jury to prosecute judges (independent from the Supreme Court), and established a Consejo de la Magistratura to select judges. However, many of these reforms were never fully implemented (or not implemented at all). The result was a somewhat more autonomous, but hardly competent, judiciary. According to a survey conducted by the World Bank Institute in 1999, the judiciary's institutional performance in Paraguay is relatively poor and its officials are perceived as being particularly corrupt (CISNI, 2006). The judiciary's institutional performance is ranked below average in different dimensions, such as quality of service, quantity of service, cost of provision, and accessibility (CISNI, 2006). In April of 2004, President Nicanor Duarte Frutos convinced Congress to remove six of the nine justices on the Supreme Court, in an attempt to reshuffle the judiciary.

THE BUDGET'S LIFE CYCLE

This section traces the budget's life cycle from its inception to the execution phase using data for 2002 and 2003. The first part maps the evolution of the budget through the stages of executive preparation and legislative approval. The second part analyzes the volatility of the budget during the different phases of elaboration and focuses on the execution stage (obligations and disbursements).

Absolute Spending Levels: Initiation and Approval

In his analysis of the 2004 budget, Uña (2004: Table 2) identifies three items that represent a majority of national expenditures: wages (*servicios personales*, 24 percent of the 2004 budget), transfers (17 percent of the budget, mostly devoted to social security), and debt services (13 percent). Other high-spending categories are physical investment (13 percent, although with a high component of foreign credit) and inventories (*bienes de cambio*, 16 percent). In contrast, other categories comprise lower levels of spending, such as nonpersonnel services (5 percent) and consumption goods (3 percent).

The analyses herein of the 2002 and 2003 budgets indicate a similar distribution and lead to three conclusions. First, the specific role of the MF in relation to the institutions and the president does not emerge with clarity. In an analysis of the budgets from 2000 to 2003 there were no significant differences between the institutions', the MF's, and the executive's proposals. It seems that the MF budget guidelines worked well, although the measure of the consistency across the proposals was exaggerated by the lack of data for the 2001 executive proposal and the 2003 MF proposal. However, for the remaining two years (2000 and 2002), the MF *increased* the institutional requests. The expansion was slight in 2000, but substantial in 2002 (from 3.3 to 3.8 trillion guaranies). A possible explanation for this fact could be that the institutions did not present their proposals on time and the MF corrected the previous year's budget. In 2000 and 2001, the executive slightly increased the MF proposal. However, the general perception of the interviewees for this chapter is that the MF budget proposal is usually the executive's proposal, which is consistent with what is observed in the 2001–2003 period. For this reason, the MF and the executive proposal can be viewed as interchangeable in comparing the behavior of the two chambers of Congress.

Second, in three of the four years, the bicameral commission did not substantially modify the executive's proposal over the public wage bill. In 2002, however, in an effort to roll back personnel spending, the bicameral commission proposed a substantial reduction in the total wage bill (from 3.9 to 3.6 trillion guaranies). This episode contrasts with the image of patronage-seeking legislators. But more research is needed to establish whether this was an isolated episode or an indication of a more systematic pattern.

Third, it seems that the lower house is not a major player in the shaping of high-spending items. The Chamber of Deputies may alter the relative share of the budget for particular items (a topic discussed below), but for the most part, it does not challenge the aggregate spending levels set by the bicameral commission. In contrast, the Senate seems to be willing to modify aggregate spending in order to approach the requests of the MF. These institutions seemed to struggle with the Chamber of Deputies for greater authorizations, which contradicts theoretical expectations that the MF and the senators (elected in a nationwide district) would be inclined to cut spending. This pattern is confirmed by the Senate's request for physical investment in 2002. The extraordinary increase in personnel spending in the last phase of the legislative process in 2000 and 2001, however, was probably not a unilateral decision of the Senate—since senators are not allowed to tamper with specific items at this stage. This last-minute expansion of the wage bill deserves further research.

In summary, in the preparation and approval stages, while the MF and the executive do not cut the total wage bill from the institutional proposals, it seems that they do reduce spending on other items, such as physical investment. That is, the executive is not as strict with public employment, but it tries to compensate with other types of expenditures. It is also evident that the executive finds a friendlier partner in the Senate than in the Chamber of Deputies.

Relative Spending Levels: Volatility and Execution

How stable is the composition of the budget from one phase to the next? To what extent is the MF able to reassert its priorities during the execution phase? In order to address these questions, herein the degree of volatility of the budget proposal is estimated at different stages following Abuelafia, Braun, and Díaz Frers (2005: 38). Given a number of government agencies, *N*, the coefficient of volatility for the budget at the *t*th stage of elaboration equals

$$C_t = 0.5 * \sum_{i=1}^{N} \left| \frac{S_{i,t}}{\sum_{i=1}^{N} S_{i,t}} - \frac{S_{i,t-1}}{\sum_{i=1}^{N} S_{i,t-1}} \right|.$$

In this equation, C_t is the coefficient for budget phase (t) and S_i is the proposed spending for the *i*th agency. The estimation of *C* is akin to the estimation of electoral volatility coefficients in the analysis of party systems (e.g., Pedersen, 1983). The figure captures the total share of the budget that is transferred from "loser" agencies to "winner" agencies from one phase of the budget process to the next.[7] Because the share of the

[7] In this estimation, agencies are winners or losers in relative, not absolute, terms. All agencies may lose part of their budgets if, for instance, Congress consistently cuts their requests in the

budget lost by one agency is transferred to others in the next version of the budget, the absolute aggregate change is divided by two.

Herein, this equation is used to assess five phases in the budget process: (A) the agencies' initial requests; (B) the executive's proposal; (C) the budget approved by Congress (at the second vote in the Senate); (D) the operating budget (after amendments are introduced during the year); (E) the obligations contracted by the government; and (F) the executed budget. In the following analysis, those capital letters are used to identify the phases. As such, for instance, A-B denotes the coefficient for the volatility of the budget observed between the initial requests and the executive proposal submitted to Congress.

Table 6.1 presents the coefficient for the different phases of the budget process between 2002 and 2004 (data for the initial phases of the 2004 budget are not available). The values reflect the evolution of the following: the total budget (in the top panel), central government spending, the decentralized institutions, and social sector spending (a subset of central government spending comprising health and education). Figures in boldface indicate levels of budget volatility above the 10 percent mark.

The evidence suggests that some "wrestling" takes between the agencies, the MF, and the López Palace (which serves as the workplace for the president) during the preparation phase prior to September 1. This process seems to be more acute in decentralized institutions. At the same time, the MF seems to use obligations as instruments to reassert its priorities. In 2004, the volatility between the budget bill and the obligations amounted to more than 40 percent of the total budget. At the same time, volatility in the social sector budget seems to be consistently lower, which suggests two alternative—but not exclusive—interpretations: (a) that social policy is seen as a priority by all players and (b) that spending on health and education is politically sensitive (and thus respected by all players), not only because of its social impact, but also because of its capacity to generate sources of patronage.

Herein, the volatility rates are also examined for one particular type of spending: the wage bill. Information for personnel services is available between 2000 and 2004. The evidence gathered for wage bill spending suggests that (a) Congress is more likely to modify the presi-

budget bill. But if Congress preserves the relative size of their budgets (e.g., by cutting a uniform 10 percent for all agencies), the volatility coefficient is zero.

TABLE 6.1 Volatility Index for Total Spending, 2002–2004

Total budget	A–B	B–C	C–D	D–E	E–F
2002	0.069	0.045	0.020	0.063	0.049
2003	0.083	0.055	0.065	0.084	0.043
2004	NA	NA	0.061	**0.204**	0.026
Central government					
2002	0.056	0.038	0.021	0.035	0.029
2003	0.078	0.078	0.094	0.083	0.046
2004	NA	NA	0.065	0.063	0.023
Decentralized institutions					
2002	**0.106**	0.054	0.022	0.091	0.013
2003	0.034	0.034	0.028	0.074	0.010
2004	NA	NA	0.057	**0.417**	0.018
Social sector (education and health)					
2002	0.026	0.038	0.000	0.029	0.031
2003	0.006	0.006	0.009	0.054	0.043
2004	NA	NA	0.002	0.028	0.032

Key:

A-B Agency requests – executive's proposal
B-C Executive – senators II (budget approved by Congress)
C-D Senators II – operating budget
D-E Operating budget – obligated
E-F Obligated – executed

dent's requests in this field than in others; (b) the MF is willing to use obligations aggressively as an instrument for budget control (and this is also true for decentralized institutions); and (c) the public wage bill in the social sector remains relatively uncontroversial. It is tempting to interpret the data as proof that Congress intends to expand patronage politics beyond the social sector while the MF contains this expansion. However, the evidence is very inconclusive.

THE OUTER FEATURES OF THE BUDGET PROCESS

Sustainability

The increased rigidity of public policies is reflected in the budget, which also presents a high degree of rigid expenditures. The lack of capacity to take advantage that the context presents (low policy adaptability) jeopardizes policy innovation and growth. The effect of high rigid expenditures combined with the opportunity cost of lack of policy innovation and growth threatens the sustainability of public finance. In fact, there have been chronic fiscal deficits in Paraguay since 1995. Since the democratization process started in 1989, each administration has confronted greater financial difficulties. Whereas the Rodríguez administration achieved on average a fiscal surplus of 1 percent of GDP, the González Macchi administration faced an average fiscal deficit of 3 percent of GDP. This situation occurred despite both an increase in tax revenues as a proportion of GDP and an increase in nontax revenues (arising mainly from royalties of the binational electric dams).

The driving force behind the increasing fiscal deficit is the steady increase in public expenditures, especially current expenditures. In turn, the main factor behind the rise of current expenditures is the expansion of the public wage bill. The public wage bill almost doubled, as a proportion of GDP, during the González Macchi administration compared to the Rodríguez administration. At the same time, expenditures on goods and services have remained rather fixed as a share of GDP. This situation might create imbalances that will erode public employees' productivity, since they do not have access to nonlabor complementary inputs to perform their duties.

Efficiency

Efficiency considerations in public finance refer to the ability to reallocate resources from lesser to higher priorities and from less to more effective programs (*allocative efficiency*), as well as the ability to operate efficiently to be competitive with market prices (*operational efficiency*). Regarding allocative efficiency, after 1989 the policy preferences of the Stroessner and the Rodríguez administrations proved divergent. This can be seen from the significant change in budget allocation that has taken place since 1989. In fact, it can be argued that the significant increase in the public wage bill was propelled by the interaction of three factors: (a) the need to strengthen key institutions after the demise of the dictatorship in 1989, (b) the new social priorities of the democratic period, and (c) the increased number of political veto players demanding pork for their constituencies.

TABLE 6.2 Congress, Judiciary, and Executive Expenditures
(percentage of total central government expenditure)

	1988	1992	2002
Congress	0.3	0.6	1.2
Judiciary	1.1	1.6	5.4
Executive	56.8	73.1	58.3

Source: Financial reports of the MF (1980–2002).

Table 6.2 illustrates that new institutions put in place with the 1992 constitution, such as an enlarged Congress and a renewed judiciary, naturally demanded more resources. The percentage of the budget allocated to Congress doubled as a proportion of central government expenditure in the 1992–2002 period. The participation of the judiciary more than tripled during the same period.[8]

The new priorities in social spending following the demise of the Stroessner regime also help explain the growth in the public wage bill. Expenditures in education and health significantly increased in the 1992–2002 period. In fact, the combined budgets of the Education and Health Ministries rose from 30 percent to 46 percent of the executive's total budget between 1992 and 2002.[9]

The transition to democracy also prompted the multiplication of veto players. The effective number of parties in the lower house grew from 1.0 in 1960 to 1.9 in 1989, to 2.4 in 1993, to 2.3 in 1998, and to 3.2 in 2003.[10] In addition, the ruling Colorado Party has been increasingly divided; factional disputes led to the collapse of the Cubas Grau administration in 1999 and permanently threatened the survival of the González Macchi administration. In this context, the transaction costs of legislative policymaking have risen substantially. Because in Paraguay most pork barrel spending takes the form of patronage, these costs have been mostly funneled through the creation of positions in the public sector.

---

[8] Financial reports of the MF (1980–2002).

[9] Ibid.

[10] The effective number of parties is an index akin to the Hirschman-Herfindahl index of market concentration applied to the distribution of legislative seats among political parties. The formula for the index is $ENP = 1 / \Sigma (p^2)$, where p represents the proportion of seats controlled by each party in the lower chamber.

It is possible to hypothesize that the increased demand for pork, combined with a legitimized agenda for social expenditures, has produced an inefficient allocation of public jobs in the social sector. This will affect the operational efficiency of the social sector. In contrast to other bureaucratic domains, the education and health systems have a nationwide employee network, and positions in this network may be precious tokens of exchange with deputies and local party leaders.

Representativeness

In a context of low public regard, the budget representativeness is also expected to be low. As mentioned above, the current policymaking process displays a very low level of public regard. In Congress, for example, controversy over bills (and thus a greater role of veto players) is expected to concentrate on comprehensive (nationwide, region-wide, or sector-wide) policies of regulatory or redistributive intent. In contrast, particularistic policies (distributive bills with a local focus) of low visibility and low marginal cost will be less likely to generate frictions within the legislature or in executive-legislative relations. It is possible that the Paraguayan system may provide relative flexibility for the provision of particularistic (privately regarded) policies, but relative rigidity for the provision of comprehensive regulatory or redistributive policies.

It is more difficult for a set of particularistic policies to reflect the preferences of the population at large. As such, it might be the case that the low representativeness of the budget jeopardizes the equity of public expenditure.

CONCLUSIONS

The degree of political cooperation around the budget is a major determinant of budget features such as sustainability, efficiency, and representativeness. However, the degree of political cooperation depends upon the rules (formal and informal) of the budget process, the overall policymaking process, the incentives created by the broader institutional framework, and other historical legacies.

This chapter identifies several shortcomings in the current budget process. This concluding section suggests some clear reforms that could be enacted to address them. Although changing some rules would require constitutional reforms, many rules can be altered through administrative procedures. The discussion herein focuses on the latter cases. Given the low degree of political cooperation in Paraguay, political actors may require clear signals of commitment to reforms from the executive before cooperating in more ambitious reforms of the legal system. Thus, successful administrative reforms will make future legal and constitutional reforms easier. If designed correctly, changes in the rules for the budget policymaking process could trigger a virtuous circle of political cooperation and development. In order to identify potential areas for improvement in the rules of these budget processes, the formal and informal rules are summarized in Table 6.3.

Given that under the current policymaking process, implementing any major change represents a challenge, this section focuses on five administrative measures that are expected to effectively improve the rules of the budget process. Recommendations in this area involve two basic components: a set of changes in administrative procedures and a set of proposals to collect and disseminate budgetary information.

First, this chapter suggests that public employment and other particularistic policies are essential for the survival of competitive factions; these instruments have therefore become the main currency for building coalitions for the executive. One way for the executive to counteract this tendency is to signal a credible commitment with respect to certain policy priorities. The proposal herein has four components. First, early during the term the president should announce a medium-term (e.g., four-year) spending plan. The plan would indicate the main programs that constitute the president's agenda. Second, those priorities would be translated into a scoring system to assign "points" to requests for new funding from public agencies. Third, during the preparation phase, the executive would rank agency requests based on these criteria. Fourth, the ratings and the justification for the allocation would be released together with the presentation of the budget proposal to Congress by September 1 every year. The document explaining the decisions about allocations (including the scoring of requests) would be presented to the press, in order to reinforce the commitment of the administration to its agenda.

TABLE 6.3 Formal and Informal Rules in the Budget Process

Formal rules	Informal rules
Within the annual Law of the Nation's General Budget, there will be no statement that modifies other permanent laws.	The Paraguayan legal system does not rank laws. Any law could suspend the effect of a previous one.
Public employees who generate a misuse of public funds will personally be responsible for repairing damages with their assets.	The sanction mechanisms are extremely weak in Paraguay, due to (a) incomplete legislation, (b) weak evaluation and control systems, and (c) judicial mismanagement, among others.
Preparation phase	
Revenue estimation based on technical assessment.	Congress modifies revenues at will.
Expenditures should be a function of objectives and goals, and should be based on performance indicators.	Often expenditures replicate those of the previous year.
The executive-legislative relations in budget matters will be exclusively maintained through the MF.	Ministers and top public managers contact legislators directly to defend their budget proposals.
Execution phase	
The MF will keep the budget balanced.	The minister's scope in the execution of the budget is severely limited by the high proportion of rigid expenditures.
	High degree of discretion by public managers in budget execution due to the lack of proper definition of procedures.
	Public managers have incentives to spend resources independently of their results. Those resources that the managers do not spend are lost.
Evaluation and control phase	
The executive will establish the guidelines for evaluation and control of results.	No government institution takes seriously a performance evaluation of the allocation of public funds.
The Internal Institutional Audits are specialized units of controls for each public institution.	IIAs are technically weak. They do not have incentives to "disagree" with top managers.
	The internal and external control focuses excessively on norms and procedures and not on results.
	Even though the comptroller's revision should be ex post, public agencies are often asked to perform ex ante revisions. This creates potential conflicts of interest.

This proposal would serve as an informal equivalent of the multiyear budget plan. This approach would likely improve the representativeness of the budget by making the preparation phase more systematic and transparent and by increasing the levels of public debate and accountability even before the congressional phase. It would also promote sustainability by giving the executive an instrument to fend off the demands of powerful players within and outside the administration—unless they can frame those requests in terms of the president's public agenda.

Second, the policymakers interviewed emphasize the lack of a link between public expenditures and performance indicators. The adoption of performance indicators should be a key component of the preparation phase, and performance evaluations could be incorporated as part of the scoring system for the agency requests suggested in the previous section.

Third, a core problem identified herein is that public employment is a major resource to build political support—support that flows from voters to factional leaders and from those leaders to the executive. As explained previously herein, a law passed in 2000 attempted to modernize the public service by establishing a clear system of selection, training, promotion, and retirement for public employees. The law, however, was challenged on constitutional grounds, failing in the end to establish a consistent scale of public salaries, an effective training system, or a procedure for performance evaluation of public employees. Clearly, government needs to strengthen the public service career system. The adoption of a tenure system for the public administration, which was proposed by a policymaker, would be a step in the right direction. Under this system, public officials would not acquire job security during their first two years in the civil service. After this period, the officials' performances would be evaluated by the Secretariat for Civil Service and they would be either confirmed in their posts or dismissed.

Fourth, corruption also remains a problem. In place of the presentation of anticorruption as a moral crusade, a recalibration of the incentives for public managers throughout the system would likely be effective. First, all public institutions should undertake a reliable risk map by identifying procedures' lacunae—potential weaknesses of the control systems—and by adopting anticorruption preventive measures. Second, it would be useful to create a procedural manual to guide the preparation of the budget requests by the agencies and the ensuing decision-making process by the executive (the cabinet and the *equipo económico nacional)*. Third, civil society organizations should be encouraged (and allowed) to monitor efficiency and the proper use of public resources.

A final administrative measure should be considered with regards to executive-legislative relations. Although executive-legislative relations in budget matters should take place only through the MF, under the current budget process, powerful ministers and public managers contact legislators directly and lobby them to protect their budget proposals. In turn, the MF uses its control over transfers to reassert policy priorities, although this practice is often constrained by the rigidity of public wages and of social policy spending. To confront this problem, it is necessary to strengthen the negotiation position of the MF in dealing with Congress.

Along with the administrative changes, this chapter proposes two additional measures, which would require constitutional revision. A formal multiyear budget system would encourage basic agreements on major policy issues and would facilitate intertemporal coordination. Although those advantages would be achieved to a degree through the commitment device proposed in our first recommendation, a constitutionally sanctioned multiyear budget would project in the medium run the high level of political cooperation obtained by every new administration. It might, however, introduce rigidities into the budget process if the system is exposed to exogenous shocks.

Furthermore, the adoption of a legal hierarchy would address the possible contradictions between the annual budget and the rest of the legal architecture of the Paraguayan state. It is necessary to have a binding general law that provides a clear set of criteria for formulating periodic budget laws. This requires a ranking system of laws currently absent from the Paraguayan legal order.

There are also measures that may seem obvious to observers that are not recommendable. Although Paraguay is one of the few countries in the Latin American region where the constitution gives Congress unrestricted power over the budget process, it is not advisable to impose constitutional budget caps during the approval phase. It would be tempting to propose a constitutional reform that would allow the executive to set expenditure limits and prevent Congress from modifying revenue estimations at will. But the evidence presented above suggests that under some circumstances, Congress is willing to cut spending below the requirements of the executive. This final point suggests that further research is necessary to pinpoint the precise *incentives* that drive public spending before a clear reallocation of *powers* across institutions is advocated.

REFERENCES

Abuelafia, E., M. Braun, and L. Díaz Frers. 2005. Coparticipación Federal: una mirada más allá del debate de corto plazo. Documento de Políticas Públicas N°3, CIPPEC, Buenos Aires, Argentina.

Alesina, A., R. Hausmann, R. Hommes, and E. Stein. 1999. Budget Institutions and Fiscal Performance in Latin America. *Journal of Development Economics* 59(2): 253–73.

CISNI (Consejo Impulsor del Sistema Nacional de Integridad). 2006. *Patrones de comportamiento y desempeño institucional, gobernabilidad y corrupción en el sector público en Paraguay, 2005* Programa de Apoyo al CISNI—Convenio ATN/SF 8962. Asunción: CISNI.

Hallerberg, M., and P. Marier. 2004. Executive Authority, the Personal Vote, and Budget Discipline in Latin American and Caribbean Countries. *American Journal of Political Science* 48(3): 571–87.

IDB (Inter-American Development Bank). 2004. Who Decides on Public Expenditures? A Political Economy Analysis of the Budget Process. Call for Proposals. Inter-American Development Bank, Washington, DC.

Kaufmann, D., A. Kraay, and P. Zoido-Lobatón. 1999. Aggregating Governance Indicators. Policy Research Working Paper No. 2195. World Bank, Washington, DC.

Laakso, M., and R. Taagapera. 1979. Effective Number of Parties: A Measure with Application to West Europe. *Comparative Political Studies* 12(1): 3–27.

Lijphart, A. 1999. *Patterns of Democracy: Government Forms and Performance in Thirty-Six Countries.* New Haven: Yale University Press.

Llanos, M. 2002. El bicameralismo en América Latina. Paper presented at the Tercer Congreso Internacional de Latinoamericanistas en Europa (CEISAL), July 3–6, Amsterdam.

Marió, E. G., A. Silva-Leander, and M. Carter. 2004. Paraguay: Social Development Issues for Poverty Alleviation. World Bank Social Development Papers no. 63. World Bank, Washington, DC.

Molinas, J., A. Pérez-Liñán, and S. Saiegh. 2004. Political Institutions, Policymaking Processes, and Policy Outcomes in Paraguay. *Revista de Ciencia Política* 24(2).

Pangrazio, M. A. 2000. *Historia Política del Paraguay.* Vol. 2. Asunción: Intercontinental Editora.

Panizza, U. 1999. Why Do Lazy People Make More Money? The Strange Case of the Public Sector Wage Premium. IDB Working Paper No. 403. Inter-American Development Bank, Washington, DC.

Paredes, R. 2001. *Los opositores y la transición.* Asunción: Grafía Press.

Payne, J. M., D. Zovatto G., F. Carrillo Florez, and A. Allamand Zavala. 2002. *Democracies in Development: Politics and Reform in Latin America.* Washington, DC: Inter-American Development Bank and New York: International Institute for Democracy and Electoral Assistance.

Pedersen, M. 1983. Changing Patterns of Electoral Volatility in European Party Systems: Explorations in Explanation. In Hans Daadler and Peter Mair, eds., *Western European Party Systems: Continuity and Change.* London: Sage.

Rice, S. A. 1925. The Behavior of Legislative Groups: A Method of Measurement. *Political Science Quarterly* 40(1): 60–72.

Schick, A. 1998. *A Contemporary Approach to Public Expenditure Management.* Washington, DC: World Bank Institute.

Shugart, M. S., and J. M. Carey. 1992. *Presidents and Assemblies: Constitutional Design and Electoral Dynamics.* Cambridge: Cambridge University Press.

Spiller, P. T., and M. Tommasi. 2003. The Institutional Foundations of Public Policy: A Transactions Approach with Application to Argentina. *Journal of Law, Economics, and Organization* 19(2): 281–306.

Uña, G. 2004. Análisis del proceso presupuestario. Background paper for Institutional and Governance Review, World Bank, Asunción, Paraguay.

7 

Success in Sustainability? The Case of Peru

Luis Carranza, Jorge F. Chávez, and José Valderrama

TESTING THE STABILITY OF PERU'S FISCAL STANCE

From a macro perspective, Peruvian fiscal policy has shown a spectacular turnaround since the early 1990s: after averaging near 6 percent of the GDP in the 1970s and rising to near 9 percent of the GDP in the 1980s, the budget deficit decreased to 2.4 percent in the 1990s. As illustrated in Figure 7.1, the evident deficit bias in the fiscal balance decreased drastically between 1991 and 1992—a result that was determinant for the success of the stabilization process undertaken in that decade in reducing inflation and creating a more favorable climate for economic growth—and since then has remained under relative control. Even though the fiscal stance deteriorated in the late 1990s (in part because of the impact of the international financial crises of these years), the deficit resumed its decreasing trend, passing from –3.3 percent of GDP in 2000 to a positive balance of 2.1 percent in 2006.

However, this recent improvement in the fiscal results has been strongly influenced by substantial improvements in the international prices of the commodities exported by Peru (mainly metals), jointly with the recent upturn of the Peruvian economy after the recession of 1998–2001, factors that are cyclical by nature. Estimates indicate that since the significant adjustment that was registered in 2001, the structural deficit has stayed constant, around 1.5 percent of GDP. Moreover, given the strong increase in fiscal revenues, the government between 2001 and 2006 could have been more "fiscally responsible" in its last

FIGURE 7.1 Nonfinancial Public Sector: Overall and Primary Balance, 1970–2006
(percentage of GDP)

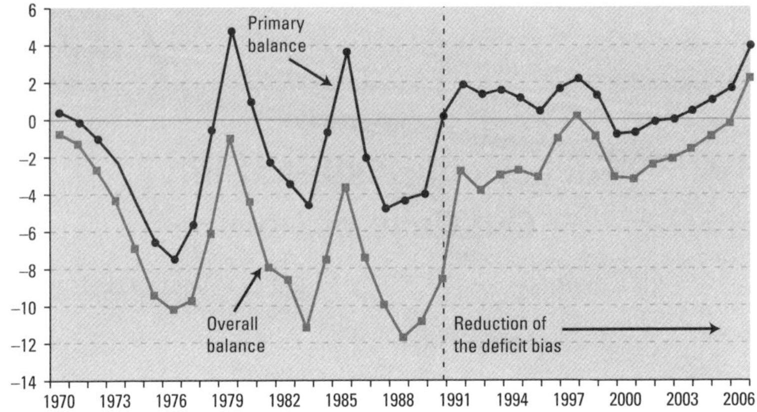

Source: BCRP.

two years, therefore further reducing the structural deficit to be in line with the principle of the current fiscal responsibility law adopted in 1999, which will be discussed later in this chapter.

Thus, despite the relative stability of the fiscal stance, there are some issues and concerns in terms of the outcomes that result from the features of the budget process. These are the dependent variables that can be explained by the institutional setup and by the policymaking process that shapes the features of the budget process that will be analyzed in the following sections of this chapter. Among the most outstanding are the following:

- **Strong political business cycles** (Nordhaus, 1975) **are common, as was the case of the 1995 and 2000 elections.** The political business cycle was particularly pronounced in 1995 and 2000, years in which President Alberto Fujimori sought reelection. The government strongly increased nonfinancial public expenditures in the months prior to the election, seeking to influence voters with public works and patronage distribution.
- **Public debt has decreased significantly as a percentage of GDP in recent years, from 46 percent of GDP in 2001 to less than 33 percent by the end of 2006.** However, this ratio is still similar

to that which prevailed at the end of 1997 after the implementation of the Brady Plan yielded a significant reduction in the debt-to-GDP ratio, and about 75 percent of the total public debt is still denominated in foreign currencies. It should also be recalled that the Peruvian economy has been affected by recurrent and strong external shocks, generating episodes of high volatility. For those reasons, despite this recent improvement in the debt-to-GDP ratio, Peruvian public finances should still be considered vulnerable to exogenous shocks and cannot be considered fully sustainable.

- **Besides the reforms in fiscal policy management, the reduction of the deficit bias observed in recent years has also been possible because of higher tax revenues that, in turn, came as a consequence of higher commodity prices (particularly metals), tax rate increases, and measures to improve tax administration.** These latter measures included an increase in the rates of the value-added tax (Impuesto General a las Ventas, IGV)—the main source of tax revenues for the Peruvian economy—and those of the income taxes, as well as the creation of new (*supposedly*) transitory taxes, such as a financial transaction tax and a transitory tax on net assets. On the other side, current expenditures have increased significantly in recent years, especially those for wages. That is, transitory revenues have been used in recent years to finance permanent expenditures, creating a dangerous situation for subsequent years.
- **In line with the increase in current expenditures, the budget composition has become more rigid in recent years.** Budget rigidities may become an important constraint on fiscal management and reduce the efficiency of fiscal policy. It is understandable that relatively flexible expenditures could rise during upturns, so that they can easily be reduced in downturns (when the speed of growth decreases). However, as previously mentioned, since 2002, the growth in public expenditures has been accentuated in wages and salaries and other recurrent expenses. Budget rigidity has increased in recent years of relative economic peacefulness.
- **Higher increases in current expenditures have not translated into an increased quality of key public services, such as public health and education, or into a higher efficiency in social policies.** Despite the strong increase in current expenditures in

recent years, the quality of public services has not improved, and subsequent governments have failed to apply adequate corrective measures for this situation. Two examples are the dramatic deterioration of the quality of public education—described in more detail in a later section herein—and the estimated inefficiencies in the administration of the resources allocated to the biggest social program in Peru: the "Glass of Milk."[1] In the latter case, a recent study estimates that around 30 percent of the approximately US$100 million devoted yearly to this program has been lost through inefficient practices, outrages, and corruption, which has also yielded serious targeting problems (see Alcázar, Wachtenheim, and López-Cálix, 2003).

- **Finally, the representativeness and the transparency of budgetary decisions have improved in recent years.** The perception of transparency in the Peruvian budget increased between 2003 and 2005, according to the last Index of Budgetary Transparency (IBT) constructed by the International Budget Project (2005). Two factors may be behind this improvement. First, the introduction of bottom-top mechanisms of participative budgets for certain components of the budget corresponding to subnational governments has allowed the participation of civil society in budgetary decisions pertaining to public investment projects that benefit districts and provinces. Second, from 1999 to 2006, there was a substantial decrease in modifications made to the approved budget through presidential decrees ("decrees of urgency"), which do not require previous authorization by Congress.

In this context, the main objective of this chapter is to present an analysis of the political economy of the budget process in Peru. For this purpose, the analysis herein focuses more on the policymaking

[1] The Glass of Milk feeding program (Vaso de Leche) is the largest social transfer in Peru and the second-largest component of the transfers from the central government to subnational governments (local and regional governments). Formally introduced in Lima in 1984, currently the program covers around four million beneficiaries nationwide. Despite its name, the program is not confined to the distribution of milk, but also involves cereals and other substitutes. The objective of the program is to improve the nutritional level of infants, small children, and pregnant or breast-feeding mothers and also to improve the quality of life of the poorest segments of the population.

process that lies behind the Peruvian budget process than on the outcomes it yields. The chapter identifies key actors that influence public expenditures, the incentives and restrictions the actors face, and the formal and informal rules that determine their behavior and influence the way they interact. Also, this type of analysis may contribute to explain three issues that may allow a better understanding of potential developments of the Peruvian economy. First, how easy would it be for future governments to dismantle the results of all the efforts made since the 1990s? Second, why has Peruvian fiscal policy remained procyclical despite the success of the reforms undertaken during the 1990s and the introduction of fiscal rules? And finally, why have successive governments since the 1990s allowed the current critical deterioration of the efficiency of public expenditures?

The rest of the chapter is structured as follows: the subsequent section presents a general description of key actors inside and outside of the government, while the third section analyzes the actors' interactions in the different stages of the budgetary process. The fourth section analyzes three concrete results: the dominance of the executive branch throughout the whole budget process, the procyclicality of the Peruvian fiscal policy, and the relationship between opportunism and efficiency. The last section concludes.

KEY ACTORS IN THE PERUVIAN BUDGET PROCESS

One characteristic common to every budget process is the inherent presence of conflict: resources are always scarce and insufficient to satisfy all requests or needs, which generates competition among actors inside the government (ministers, public bureaucrats, and legislators) and outside the government (interest groups in the society). With this particularity in mind, a detailed description of the main actors in the budgetary process is presented in this section as well as the incentives these individuals face. In total, 10 types of players are analyzed who interact in four spheres: the executive branch, Congress, the judicial branch, and civil society. This analysis will include a description of the main features of each one of these spheres as well as details about the other agents that are involved and the characteristics that they adopt in the policymaking process.

The Executive Branch

Traditionally, the political science literature emphasizes the conflicting situations that arise between the executive and the legislative branches of government, and in some countries between the central and subnational governments or other regional entities. Although the relationship between the executive and Congress is important, in the Peruvian case the understanding of the conflicts that arise inside the same executive is also a key element. This is because the behavior of actors inside the executive explains many of the problems with budgetary issues.

To simplify the analysis, the executive will be decomposed in a very general way: as the presidency, the Ministry of Economy and Finance (MEF), and the different spending units (or *pliegos*)—each with their respective representatives or heads. Although in principle, central objectives common to all institutions inside the executive are captured in general in the multiyear macro framework (Marco Macroeconomómico Multianual, MMM: a framework with a three-year forecast published yearly at the end of May), it may not be in line with the framework of the central government. Thus, when these objectives become contradictory, situations of open conflict may arise.

Historically, the Peruvian political regime has been characterized as highly presidentialist, meaning that the president is invested by the constitution with strong powers. In this line, the current constitution of 1993 grants the president wide legislative powers, such as veto power over bills approved by Congress; the ability to issue de facto laws through decrees of urgency; and nonlegislative powers, such as the appointment of cabinet ministers and the definition of government priorities. Also, the president can request from Congress a delegation of the authority to legislate, a practice that has been common in Peru, especially in the first year of a new government. The president uses this power to introduce complex technical changes, which include the creation of new taxes and the increase of existing tax rates—changes that entail a high political cost that members of Congress prefer to avoid.

The president can then be interpreted as an actor who has the objective of maximizing his or her popular acceptance and political sustainability. To achieve this objective, he or she has the incentive to increase public expenditure aimed at sectors with more power of political pressure or with more public opinion support (or to grant tributary benefits to these sectors, thus reducing total fiscal revenues). For this reason, presidents face both economic and institutional constraints. First, any presidential decision that entails an increase in public expenditure needs to be financed either by an increase in tax revenue, which is limited by the large size of the informal economy, or by the reallocation of existing expenditures, which is also limited given the rigidity of the budget structure. Also, if needed, the government can seek sizeable loans from the international markets, and those markets tend to be volatile. In fact, these restrictions became more binding in the first half of the 1990s for two reasons: first, during this period there was a wide consensus against appealing to the inflationary tax after the deep economic crisis of the last three years of the 1980s, and second, at this time international debt markets were practically closed for Peru after almost a decade in which successive governments unilaterally limited sovereign debt service.

From the institutional side, the president also faces important constraints. During the 1990s, the necessity of agreements with the International Monetary Fund (IMF) was an important element in this respect. However, in more recent years the fiscal responsibility law, which imposes limits on the fiscal deficit and on the annual increment of public expenditure, has replaced the role played by IMF programs as an instrument for limiting the president's degrees of freedom to increase the overall expenditure ceiling and expand the deficit. Moreover, the current constitution prohibits the central bank from financing the government's deficit. The institutional constraints increase the political cost of enlarging the public budget during the execution stage, at least through the loss of credibility that comes from an exaggerated nonfulfillment of the fiscal rules, especially in relation to the limit on the increase of the fiscal deficit for a given year.

However, the consequences of violating these constraints of the fiscal responsibility law and the constitution do not appear immediately, so that in electoral times, the executive still has the incentive to increase public expenditure further, which generates political business cycles. As described in the introduction, this opportunist-electoral behavior was clearly evident in the presidential elections of 1995 and 2000. It is important to remember that this behavior was more accentuated in the 1990s in relation to the 1980s, a result that can be attributed, on one hand, to the fact that financial restriction diminished during the

1990s, and on the other, to the introduction of immediate presidential reelection during the same decade. Also, an opportunist-recurrent behavior or a *voracity effect* (see Tornell and Lane, 1998; Akitoby et al., 2006)—which implies that in the event of higher fiscal revenues (during upturns) there is still a strong incentive to increase the expenditures at a higher percentage than usual—cannot be discarded.

The second key actor inside the executive is the MEF, which is the one actor that explicitly has the objective of maintaining the sustainability of public finances. Operationally, one can conceptualize the MEF as having the intention of fulfilling the fiscal rules, and especially the objectives and commitments that it assumes in the MMM, subject to pressures from other line ministers and other spending units inside the executive (including the president), as well as from other political actors, to increase the overall expenditure ceiling. As discussed in the introductory chapter of this volume, the MEF may be able to solve the "common pool resource" problem that arises among the other ministers and spending units' representatives in the formulation stage of the budget process, as well as in the execution stage. In the Peruvian case, the problem arises because each one of those spending units has the incentive to appropriate a bigger proportion of the available resources for its own sector during both the approval and execution stages, through either formal channels (introducing its demands as part of the supplementary credits[2]) or informal means, such as getting political support from the president in the expectation that the total budget ceiling approved for its sector is exactly disbursed at the year end. This is why it comes as no surprise that the MEF has tended to support the implementation of formal rules or lock-ins to help in their quest to maintain the sustainability of public finances, such as modifications that strengthen the hierarchical role of the MEF in setting budget ceilings; fiscal policies that create more transparency to help uncover the incompatibilities of political decisions; and, in some cases, explicit rules to justify the MEF's negation before certain demands that come from other actors (particularly the president).

The third group of actors inside the executive comprises the heads of the spending units (e.g., other line ministers and chiefs of departments).

---

[2] A supplementary credit increases the overall budget ceiling. It differs from a transfer or reassignment among departments in that the total does not change.

These actors have the objective of maximizing expenditure assigned to their sectors, subject to the budgetary ceiling imposed by the MEF, since in practice their performance is evaluated by the amount of public works they can perform or the quantity of services they can provide, and in certain cases the wage increases they are able to grant to public workers are dependent on their sector (particularly in the case of public school teachers, doctors, policemen, etc.). In general, the spending units know that they have more information than the MEF and thus can have more control over the execution of expenditures. It is worth noting that before the implementation of the reforms undertaken in the early 1990s, the MEF had certain decision-making power in regard to the overall budget ceiling and to the allocation of resources among spending units. However, these latter entities tended to behave strategically, financing lower-priority expenditures with the assigned resources to force the granting of later increments. The MEF then had to reconcile the spending units' monthly demands with the budget ceiling (which was highly flexible due to constant increments) and the pressure on the central bank to limit its credits to the public sector.

This last group of actors is particularly active during the bilateral discussions with the MEF that take place in the formulation stage (see the subsequent section), if possible with the president's support, in order to have their resource allocation increased. In general, these heads of spending units avoid competing explicitly among themselves for the allocation of resources. They also tend to use bilateral negotiation in the execution stage to make sure they are ultimately authorized to use the total amount of resources that was originally allocated to them in the approved budget, as well as with the hope of eventually enlarging their budget for future years. In recent years, other types of bilateral negotiations have begun to proliferate in which future budget commitments are defined with some sector. For example, the government has approved investment projects undertaken through private-public associations that often require some kind of governmental guarantee. These types of projects represent an intertemporal predation of the macro framework.

The Congress

Since its dissolution in April of 1992 and the constitutional change in 1993 (see Morón and Sanborn, 2006), the Peruvian Congress has had a single chamber with 120 members elected in an open-list proportional-representation electoral system with personal voting. One key feature of the Peruvian electoral system is the simultaneity of legislative and presidential elections, which historically has allowed the governing party to have a relative majority or to build a majority coalition in Congress with relative ease. This has been the case since 1980, with the exception of the government of the period 1990–1992, which abruptly turned into a de facto majoritarian regime after the 1992 dissolution. However, despite this relative dominance of Congress by the governing party, the inherent characteristics of the political system (such as the weakness of political parties) means that the executive does not receive unconditional support from members of Congress who belong to the governing party. In other words, the Peruvian executive has to pay a price in terms of pork barrel projects or patronage distribution in exchange for legislative support.

This situation is a direct result of the electoral rules that are in place in Peru. Members of Congress are elected through an open-list proportional-representation system, which introduces an important trade-off: while the system favors the representation of multiple political groups in Congress, it also contributes to the weakening of political parties by favoring the personalization of the vote. Candidates are elected by citizens who base their selections on candidates' personal qualities instead of partisan characteristics—offering a strong incentive for legislators to develop direct links with their constituencies rather than to mediate their communication through political parties, especially when they are seeking direct reelection (Cain, Ferejohn, and Fiorina, 1987). The Peruvian parties or political groups (*movimientos politicos,* organized specifically for a given election) end up inviting public figures (artists, sportsmen, etc.) to participate in the elections with the deliberate purpose of attracting votes, and thus, the Peruvian Congress has been characterized as having "public figures doing political work" instead of "political figures doing public work." Also, initiatives prompted by members of Congress tend to be determined more by members' desire to be reelected or to be recognized by public opinion, which accentuates the issuance of populist norms—with geographically aimed or sector-specific benefits—that have a direct impact on the public budget and that impede the formulation of constructive policies for the long term.

This situation has also determined a high rotation of political parties between governing periods, as well as frequent party switching within a single period. Hence, as a result of the reduced expected duration of their legislative careers (which was an average of 5.5 years in the five-year legislative periods between 1980 and 2001), members of Congress are more prone to be influenced by interest groups and by legislative lobbying. Moreover, the high rotation of legislators reduces the benefits of beginning any relationship of intertemporal cooperation. In this context, members of Congress may prefer to follow strategies that would grant them short-term benefits, instead of trying to coordinate with other legislators and the executive, which could yield them certain benefits, but only in the medium or long term.

The Peruvian constitution allows members of Congress to introduce amendments to the composition of the budget proposal presented for consideration by the executive, but explicitly prohibits their legislative initiatives to have implications in terms of new expenditures. Notwithstanding this prohibition, some of their decisions regarding budgetary issues have had important macroeconomic fiscal effects. Frequently, initiatives prompted by members of Congress are aimed at indirectly enlarging tributary exceptions and approving legislation that implies future expenditure commitments that indirectly impact the budget—especially legislation aimed at increasing the public sector payroll by changing the status of some workers from temporary to permanent, recruiting new workers, or approving wage increases for certain professions. This has led the executive to veto a historically high number of legislative proposals that originated within Congress.[3]

The Budget Committee

The draft budget bill presented by the executive at the end of August each year is analyzed in Congress by the legislative standing Budget and Public Accounts Committee (henceforth, the Budget Committee), which should elaborate a verdict with amendment proposals and present it to the plenary by mid-November of the same year. During this two-and-a-

---

[3] According to Morón and Sanborn (2006), the president vetoed around 30 percent of the laws approved by Congress between 2001 and 2004, while between 1995 and 2001 this proportion was only 12 percent.

half-month period, the Budget Committee meets with the heads of the spending units, MEF officials, and officials of other public institutions that can contribute to the discussion. Nevertheless, as pointed out by Francke et al. (2003), Santiso and García Belgrano (2004), and Shack (2005), this committee faces an important constraint: it lacks sufficient technical capacity to make a deep analysis of the composition of the budget, because—besides the inexperience of most members of Congress on fiscal or budgetary issues—the committee also lacks the support of a permanent staff of advisors that are sufficiently specialized in these issues. Hence, in order to amend the structure of the budget proposed by the executive, the committee has to rely on the assistance of officials from the MEF's National Agency of Public Budget (DNPP).[4]

Membership in the Budget Committee is particularly attractive to members of Congress, because only committee members are allowed to headline legislators' amendments during the voting process on the plenary, giving these members important bargaining power within their parties or coalitions. Moreover, members of Congress particularly desire the position of president of the committee, because the process of approving amendments—including negotiation with MEF officials—is centralized with this actor, granting him or her high decision-making power. Therefore, nominations to the committee are the result of intense political bargaining between political parties in the Permanent Commission (or Mesa Directiva), which takes place every year. As in the rest of the legislative standing committees, the composition of the Budget Committee changes annually. The resulting internal composition of legislative committees tends to reflect the composition of Congress. As a result the legislative majority (the governing party or coalition) tends to chair the committee and consequently has a decisive influence on its agendas and work plans. However, this result depends on the ability of the governing party (i.e., its political *strength*) to dominate negotiations aimed at determining the composition of standing committees (for example, in 2004, a member of a nongoverning party was appointed as chair

[4] The National Agency of Public Budget is the senior body of the Ministry of Economy and Finance that is responsible for the formulation, approval, execution, and evaluation of the budgetary process of all entities and bodies of the public sector, except the autonomous public entities (Central Reserve Bank of Peru, Superintendency of Banking and Insurance, and Private Pension Fund Administration Companies).

of the committee). Finally, the yearly rotation of the Budget Committee negatively affects the continuity and quality of the work of members and prevents specialization and the consolidation of their institutional technical expertise (see Santiso and García Belgrano, 2004).

The Judiciary Branch

According to IDB (2005), the role of the judiciary in the formation of policies varies among Latin American countries, ranging from that of a veto player in the sense developed by Tsebelis (2001), to an impartial regulator of political transactions (impartial referee), to a political player, to a societal representative. In the Peruvian case, even though the Constitutional Court (CC) would fit into Tsebelis's definition of a veto player, ever since this entity has had the capacity to veto policy decisions for reasons of constitutional interpretation, the Peruvian judicial system as a whole has been designed to act as an impartial regulator.

However, there are some external and internal factors that have prevented the Peruvian judiciary from playing this role. On the contrary, these factors have granted the judiciary a more political role, and some of its decisions have had adverse effects on the budget. Among the internal factors, the most important are corruption issues and the limited specialization of judges in economic and budgetary topics, which determines the effect of decisions on these topics on the public budget—for example, decisions that allow the restoration of money cut for the employment of public workers, which are made following appropriate procedures, and those that obligate the homogenization of salary levels for certain public workers.

Among the external factors, one that should be highlighted is the intention of political parties to dominate the judiciary by influencing the appointment of judges and fiscal attorneys and also through the appointment of members of the CC by Congress. Besides this *politicization* of the "political regulator," the heads of the judicial power are tempted to participate in politics—a situation that may bias their decisions—to be consistent with the majority of the public opinion. Evidently, all these factors limit the impartiality of the judicial power and therefore have prevented it from having an effective role in the promotion of intertemporal cooperation among the key actors and from serving as a counterbalance to the power exercised by the executive.

Political Parties

Since the beginning of the Republican period in 1821, there has never been a strong party system in Peru, where parties with deep roots in society negotiate, cooperate, engage in sustained alliances, and make and ensure compliance with intertemporal agreements (Morón and Sanborn, 2006). Political parties are rather unpopular, and it is common for political movements or associations supporting *independent* candidates to appear for a specific election. The fact that the presidents elected in 1990, 1995, and 2001 came from political movements rather than institutionalized political parties corroborates this point.

In general, the main objective of political parties and movements is to exercise political power as a way to directly influence the policymaking process. However, once these parties get elected and have to exercise the power, they realize that there is a difference between what they proposed before being elected and what is possible once they face the institutional and economic constraints of the government. The historical institutional weakness of Peruvian political parties has often resulted in situations in which actors in the policymaking process do not cooperate; such situations favor big changes in the orientation of policies and prevent the population from reaching a national consensus on long-term public policies. Then, in this context the approval of structural reforms with high future benefits—but with certain immediate costs—is quite difficult, because while these latter short-term costs are easily estimated, the long-term benefits of this kind of policy action are not fully perceived.

Other Actors: Interest Groups and Public Opinion

Diverse interest groups attempt to influence decisions on public policies, but do so without direct participation in the government. These groups defend union, industrial, and regional interests—among others—and they do this either directly, through lobbying, or indirectly, by methods such as organizing social protests or strikes or influencing the media to gain the support of public opinion and forcing a solution to the demands of the parties they represent. When the interaction of these groups is observed, the common pool resource problem is quite evident, because these groups try to persuade politicians to undertake policy decisions whose outcome will benefit highly the groups themselves, but whose costs will have to be paid for by the universe of citizens or taxpayers. In practice, these interest groups have the support of key political allies inside Congress or even inside the executive (ministers or other politically appointed officials) and exert pressure on the MEF to appropriate the resources required to implement these policies with particularistic benefits.

However, as in many other countries of the Latin American region, the relative strength of the different unions or industrial associations in Peru has been changing over the years, especially since the reform process of the early 1990s. Thus, for example, the liberalization of the labor market undertaken during the 1990s drastically reduced the strength of labor unions (of both private and public enterprises), and the result was that the number of strikes and labor conflicts diminished notably during this decade relative to the previous one. Indeed, on one hand, even though labor unions have partially recovered their strength since 2001, they have not been able to be as influential as they were before the 1990s. On the other hand, private business associations have increased their influential power, as they have centralized their actions in the National Confederation of Private Companies (CONFIEP), Peru's main business association.

Finally, public opinion plays an important role in the Peruvian political process because the public's reaction is a key factor for the survival of policy decisions, especially if these decisions entail budgetary implications. However, certain characteristics of Peruvian public opinion are adverse for the achievement of optimal public policies. In particular, public opinion

- Is strongly influenced by the media, which may bias such opinion in favor of an interest group or political party, if they are able to influence the media.
- Has not fully internalized the country's intertemporal budget constraint. After the dramatic consequences of the economic crises experienced in the 1980s, public opinion *does* reflect the perception that bad policies will undoubtedly yield high inflation rates. However, there is not a unanimous rejection of the implementation of policies that imply future costs.

- Still has a highly rooted concept of a *paternalistic* state, and therefore the notion of "socially fair policies" is quite distorted. In particular, practically *any* proposed policy decision that entails wage increases, change of status of public workers from temporary to permanent, and the creation or expansion of subsidies and of tax exemptions is considered "socially fair" by several sectors inside public opinion. This situation facilitates the strategic behavior of some political players.

THE INTERACTION OF KEY ACTORS IN THE STAGES OF THE BUDGET PROCESS

This section describes the formal and informal rules that determine the interaction of actors in the four stages of the budget process in Peru: formulation, approval, execution, and oversight.

Budget Formulation

According to the fiscal responsibility law of 1999, the formulation stage of the Peruvian budget process begins with the publication of the MMM in the second quarter of the year previous to the one for which a budget is being formulated. The MMM includes the official forecasts necessary for budget formulation and also the targets that the MEF is committed to achieving in the short term, and it should be approved by the cabinet of ministers and the president. The reason for publishing this document relatively early in the budgetary cycle is that the government attempts to set the overall ceiling for public expenditure administered through the fiscal budget in order to determine the allocation of this amount among the executing units at a later time.

This stage is highly hierarchical, with the MEF's DNPP as central player. The entire discussion around the MMM and the setting of budget ceilings is led by the DNPP, and no major conflicting situations arise, either with the president or with the rest of the line ministries. Immediately after the publication of the MMM, the DNPP sets the ceilings for the next year's budget for each sector and the formal rules that each spending unit has to follow in presenting its draft budget. The spending units present their requirements following those rules, and then a series of bilateral discussions are held between the DNPP and representatives of each spending unit. In this bargaining process, the DNPP holds the key decision power within the executive branch, and even though most of the negotiations are based on the ceilings imposed by the DNPP, the heads of certain spending units attempt to introduce new expenditures or projects into their individual budgets—sometimes with the support of legislators or other line ministers—in order to increase their ceilings for future years. A more collegial discussion on the relative assignment of resources across sectors is not usual practice, although legally both the budgetary macro framework and the executive's budget proposal are approved by the Council of Ministers with all representatives of the executive spending units present. Although here it could be assumed that spending units are homogenous, in practice there are important differences, especially among those that are legally more independent of the executive—particularly the judiciary and subnational governments—versus the ones that are inherently more dependent on this branch of government. In general, the latter institutions have a minister or a public official in charge who has directly or indirectly participated in the approval of the executive's budget proposal before it is sent to the Congress for approval. Thus, it is likely that their budget demands are less public, as in fact happened in the 1990s. However, more recently, even the ministers tend to disagree openly with the resources allocated to their sectors and demand higher resources in their presentations to the Budget Committee and even use the media to exert pressure on the MEF.

Also, the heads of the spending units take advantage of their enhanced access to information on the operative details of their sectors and are tempted to incorporate less crucial expenditures in the approved budget. This practice artificially reduces key expenditures, because these actors know that, during the execution stage, the government will be forced to appropriate their requests for budget increases. Otherwise the outputs of these units, in terms of goods or services they provide, will be adversely affected. Evidently the DNPP becomes aware of this situation, and even though it tries to detect these inconsistencies during the formulation stage, in certain situations the spending units get away with this practice. An emblematic example is the minister of the interior's underestimation of the Peruvian police budget for fuel for 2005. Because of this underestimation, at the beginning of the second quarter of that year, the minister "had" to request an urgent budget increase—which evidently had to be granted—under the excuse that "their patrols were not going to be able to run, and therefore this situation could bring security problems for the society." According to former directors of the DNPP, these types of strategic practices were common in the 1980s, then decreased substantially under the politically strong government that stayed in office during the 1990s, and apparently they were being used again in the government that reigned between 2001 and 2006, denoting the government's weakness in political terms.

At the end of the process, the DNPP reconciles the modification demands of the spending units with the estimated revenues for the year for which the budget is being formulated and presents a first draft for the budget to the MEF. After final adjustments, the MEF presents the draft budget bill to the president at the end of August.

According to the Peruvian constitution, the Council of Ministers has to approve the draft budget bill and send it to Congress for consideration before August 30 of each year. Before this deadline, the president and public officers from the DNPP, including the deputy minister of finance and the minister of economics and finance, have an informal negotiation around the draft budget bill. This final within-the-executive negotiation, although informal, is a crucial step in the overall budgetary process. During this step, requests are often made for an increase in funds for specific budget lines with high political value. Most of the time these requests come directly from the president, but sometimes, line ministers with high political status manage to power-channel their own requests through the president in this crucial stage. As the one actor who internalizes the economy's intertemporal budget constraint, the minister of economy and finance negotiates the presidential requests to minimize the impact on the expected budget deficit. After the inclusion of the agreed-upon presidential requests, the MEF publishes by mid-August a revised version of the MMM to avoid potential inconsistencies between the macro framework and the second draft budget, which includes the amendments introduced by the president. Finally, once the Council of Ministers approves this second draft, the president formally submits the budget bill to Congress. Two other bills, one stipulating and authorizing the contracting of debt and a second one showing the fiscal balance, must accompany the budget bill. According to the constitution, the budget must effectively be balanced, stating both expenditures and sources of finance, including any kind of debt.

Legislative Budget Approval

Congress has 90 days (between September and November of each calendar year) to review, evaluate, and propose amendments to the composition of the executive's budget proposal. After a formal presentation by the president of the Council of Ministers along with the minister of economy and finance, each ministry and spending agency must defend its individual budgetary needs to the Budget Committee. Then, an intense bargaining process takes place within this committee, as members and nonmembers strive to include budgetary amendments to support requests by spending agencies and—fundamentally—amendments aimed to benefit their constituencies in the form of pork barrel projects and patronage distribution.

Two closely related characteristics determine the dominance of the executive at this stage of the budget process in Peru. First, as previously mentioned, the Peruvian budget is highly incremental, as budgets are formulated using the previous year's budget as base, focusing only on the marginal variations that the variations in tax revenues allow. Then, even though global expenditure ceilings are determined within a framework of institutional objectives, in practice these procedures consist of the setting of expenditures for the next year on the basis of the expenditures of the current year. That is, institutional objectives are virtually obviated, and there is no connection between the determination of expenses for the next year's budget and the goods and services that would be additionally supplied, nor is there an exhaustive evaluation of the impact of the expenditures realized the previous year. Thus, introducing large amendments would distort the equilibrium of the budget structure, and members of Congress are aware of this.

Second, Congress lacks technical capacity to perform a true analysis of the executive's budget proposal, and thus members of the Budget Committee need to rely heavily on DNPP officials to review and negotiate their proposed amendments. Therefore, in practice the executive can influence which amendments will be appropriated. Considering the huge discretionary power in executing the annual budget, it is reasonable to expect that the executive will take advantage of this power to try to affect legislators' behavior and ensure that they will approve most of the executive's budget proposal. In general, the MEF is aware that it cannot avoid paying a price, in pork and patronage, for legislative support for the draft budget (see Pereira and Mueller, 2004). Hence, the MEF follows a *rabbit garden strategy* as proposed by Rubin (1999): it sets aside a small portion of the budget to satisfy amendments proposed by members of Congress (the *rabbit garden*, less than 0.5 percent of the overall budget, according to interviews with former DNPP officers) so that the main structure of the budget is left untouched (the *main garden*). The MEF is aware of this bargaining process and takes advantage of its technical capacity; thus the MEF is able to manipulate the draft budget formally presented to the legislature to include line items intended to be sacrificed to account for amendments introduced by legislators.

In terms of the theory of *political transaction costs* proposed by Dixit (1996) and North (1990), the combination of a fragmented Congress together with legislators with low expectations of being reelected makes political transactions between the executive and the legislative branches more expensive. Given the constitutional prohibition on Congress to increase public expenditures and the problems of time inconsistency, the resulting distrust favors the adoption of measures that tend to increase budget rigidity—as seemingly was the case in Peru between 1997 and 2006 (see Figure 7.2)—such as the expansion of earmarked revenues or the granting of higher autonomy to spending units or sectors over directly collected resources. Although this situation actually helps to address the conflicts that arise between the executive and the legislative branches of government, it harms the principles of "unique accounting" or "centralized tax collection" (*caja unica*) and often has generated an excessive expenditure or the existence of unused balances in certain sectors or line items. For example, the income source corresponding to "ordinary resources" (revenues that come principally from taxation and that are fully available to the Treasury) diminished among all income sources from near 80 percent of the approved budget in the early years of the 1990s to around 50 percent in the approved budget of 2006, as a result of the increase of special financing sources with more specific destinations.

The Budget Committee must issue its formal opinion on the three bills submitted by the executive by November 15, including both the majority and dissenting opinions on the budget bill, as well as the amendments the committee proposes. Then, the budget bill must be approved by the plenary and sent to the president, who decides either

FIGURE 7.2 **Estimated Budget Rigidity**[a]
(percentage of total expenditures net of debt payments included in the fiscal budget)

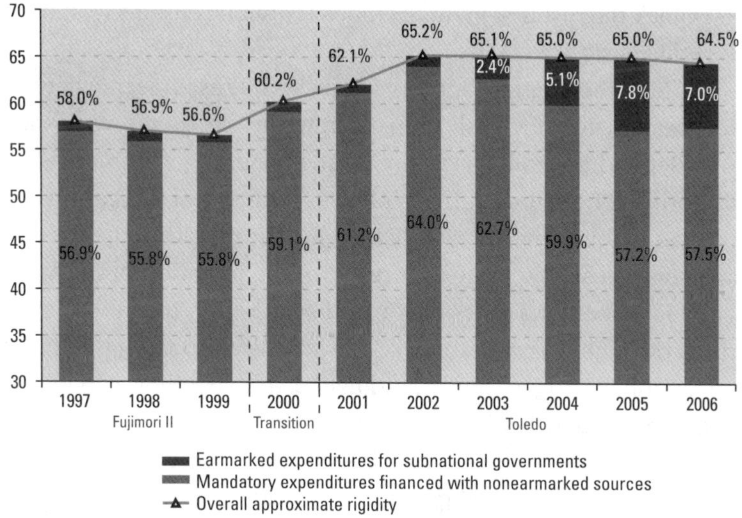

Sources: DNPP, authors' calculations.

[a] Includes (a) revenues earmarked for subnational governments and (b) rigid expenses (wages, social benefits, and debt interests) financed with nonearmarked revenues. The sum of (a) and (b) is presented as a percentage of the total expenditure, net of debt payments.

to pass the bill or to exercise his or her veto power. If by December 15 discussions in Congress do not yield a budget proposal because of legislative inaction or obstruction, or if the president decides to veto the draft budget bill, the Peruvian constitution stipulates that the executive's proposal automatically becomes law via a presidential decree. This clause is intended to avoid deadlocks in the budgetary process and is similar to clauses found in other Latin American countries' constitutions or legal frameworks for their respective budget processes.

Budget Execution and Oversight

The period of execution of the approved budget coincides with the calendar year following the formulation and approval stages. Budgets are modified through additional budget appropriation called *creditos suplementarios* and through transfers within and between spending units. Even though the spending units are partially able to modify the allocation of their own budget resources, this stage, like others, is highly dominated by the MEF. The execution of the approved budget is set by the cash management committee (Comité de Caja), which determines the disbursements of funds for public entities to spend on a monthly basis.

The MEF receives and approves requests for resource transfers from those responsible for cash programming in the spending agencies, which depend partially or totally on the general government, based on information regarding their inflows, payment of obligations, and financing disbursements. Conflicting situations within the executive can also arise at this stage as a result of the intention of the MEF to manipulate spending authorizations discretionally to smooth expenditures through the year, to avoid deviations of spending units from their opening budgets, and to adjust to the spending capability of the spending agencies.

Finally, legislative oversight of budget execution is quite limited for a variety of reasons, linked mainly to capacity constraints and skewed political incentives (see Santiso and García Belgrano, 2004; Shack, 2005), but also owing to the tendency of the majority party to chair key committees. However, the annual certification of public accounts (Article 81 of the Peruvian constitution) is a potentially powerful instrument available to the legislature for exerting control over budget execution and enforcing ex post government accountability.

THE INTERVENTION OF ACTORS IN BUDGET MODIFICATIONS, THE PROCYCLICALITY OF FISCAL POLICY, AND THE QUALITY OF PUBLIC EXPENDITURE

Who Sets the Agenda and Influences Most Decisions throughout the Budget Process?

In general, the Peruvian executive plays a preponderant role in determining the agenda and the decision process for national policies, and this preponderance is particularly high throughout the budgetary process; as such, a very secondary role is delegated to the legislature. To illustrate this point, this section analyzes the changes in the overall ceilings, as well as in the composition of the budget, in the different stages and examines those that are derived from decisions of the executive and those that could emanate of the legislative.

Based on an analysis of the budget proposals made by the executive to Congress for the years between 1996 and 2006, it was found that the overall ceiling of the budget law bill was modified in only five cases—it was reduced in four of the cases and increased in only one—and the modifications did not exceed 0.5 percent of the original approved budgets. It should be considered that these modifications did not come exclusively from Congress, but originated from pressures within the executive itself (often by request of the president).

Despite the lack of official records on budget modifications that result from the within-the-executive negotiation—prior to the presentation of the budget bill to Congress—former DNPP and MEF officers and other participants in these negotiations recognize that the amendments introduced during these substages of the formal formulation stage were greater in magnitude than the amendments introduced by the Budget Committee at the approval stage. For the years between 2004 and 2006, some indicators obtained from interviews with officials, along with information derived from changes to the MMM between its original publication (in May) and its revised version (published in August with modifications that result from the within-the-executive negotiation), point out that the portion of the budget amended inside the executive represented approximately 1.5 percent of the original expenditure ceiling determined by the MEF, while the amendments introduced by Congress at the approval stage represented only 0.3 percent of the approved budget. Hence, these indicators support the view that the budget process is highly dominated by the executive.

In contrast, the modifications that arise during the execution stage are much more significant. Between 1993 and 2006, the total effective credit was 12.5 percent higher on average than the approved budget.[5] Conversely, budget execution only accounted for 89.87 percent of the Presupuesto Institucional Modificado (PIM) on average, in the same period. Thus, this could be thought of as a compensation effect, because

---

[5] This is the so-called modified budget or PIM: the budget that includes all new appropriations resulting from supplementary credits granted by Congress at the executive's initiative and transfers between spending units introduced during the execution stage along a given fiscal year.

FIGURE 7.3 Changes to the Budget and Degree of Execution, 1991–2006
(total effective credit as a percentage of the approved budget, and execution as a percentage of the total effective credit)

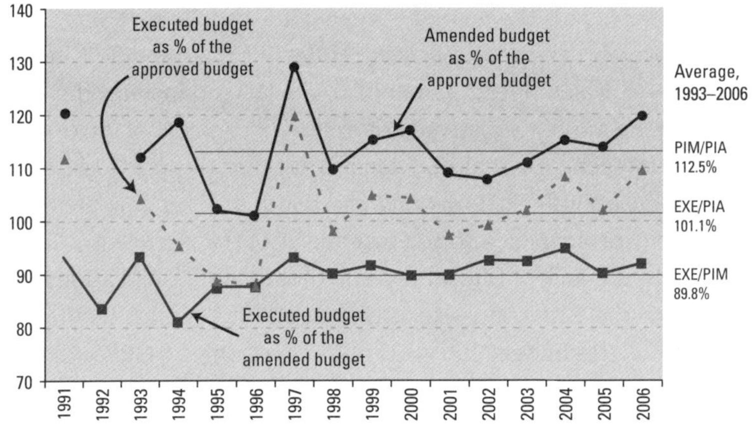

Source: MEF, Instituto Peruano de Economía.
Note: There are no official records for the year 1992. PIA: Presupuesto Institucional de Apertura (budget approved by Congress). PIM: Presupuesto Institucional Modificado (total effective credit). EXE: Presupuesto Ejecutado (executed budget)

the originally approved budget is modified either by increasing the total budget through on-the-go new appropriations or by the reallocation of resources for certain sectors or spending units; however, most of these modifications are not executed, and thus the executed budget ends up being closer to the amount originally approved than to the total modified budget (see Figure 7.3).[6]

Finally, it should be recognized that the difference between the total modified budget and the executed budget is caused not only by a lack of *calendarización* (that is, the authorization to commit expenditures granted by the MEF), but also by the managerial capacity limitations of many spending units to execute the resources that have been allocated for their utilization. Although there are no official records that strictly

[6] It is worth noting that the pronounced modification observed in the total budget approved for 1997 was due only to the decision to register the effects of the sovereign debt restructure that came from the culmination of the Brady Plan for Peru, in which the overdue debt with commercial creditors was formally recognized. This implied higher-than-expected principal and overdue interest payments that were financed with resources saved for this purpose. All these procedures were registered through new budget appropriations (supplementary credits).

differentiate between these two factors, informal data provided by DNPP officials suggest that, at least in recent years, the lack of *calendarización* has not been the preponderant factor, and the limited execution of expenditures is due, rather, to problems inside the spending units.

Can Institutions Explain the Reduction in the Procyclicality of the Peruvian Fiscal Policy?

Given the lack of a favorable environment to encourage intertemporal cooperation in Peru, actors have incentives to behave opportunistically to get the most short-term benefits from policy decisions, which in turn is highly detrimental for long-term commitments. Thus, the policies implemented tend to be easily reversed. Consistent with this situation, one could expect to observe a tendency toward procyclical policies owing to political reasons in good years: that is, when revenues are increasing, the government decides either to increase expenditures or to cut taxes, even though the higher revenues may be of a transitory nature, yielding a highly risky situation for the sustainability of the economy.

During the 1970s and 1980s, a procyclical fiscal policy clearly reigned in Peru. Although public revenues were stronger in good years, especially if accompanied by high international prices of the commodities that Peru exports (particularly metals), the fiscal deficits were higher than in bad years: the average deficit was 8.2 percent of GDP when the output gap was positive, while it averaged 6.3 percent when the output gap was negative. The coefficient of correlation between the output gap and the overall fiscal balance was –0.2 for the 20-year period. The pattern of nonfinancial expenditures also reveals the high procyclicality of fiscal policy: it increased on average 3.2 percent per year (in real terms) in the good years, while it decreased by an average of 6.7 percent when the output gap was negative (strongly affected by the crisis of the last years of the 1980s). As expected, the swings in capital expenditures were even more pronounced (with an average increase of 5 percent in the good years versus a fall of 8.1 percent in the bad years).

In periods of economic recuperation (the first part of and end of the 1970s, and the beginning and middle years of the 1980s) there was a clear relaxation of the fiscal stance, in part motivated by an explicit desire to stimulate the economy. However, this relaxation also reflected the opportunistic and voracious motives to spend the extra funds (especially in periods previously mentioned, through the abundance of petrodollars, very favorable international prices of commodities, and unilateral cessation of debt payments, respectively). It should then be no surprise that when a negative shock occurred or the initial stimulus could not continue, credibility deteriorated, the lack of available funds (except for the recourse to the inflation tax) began to dominate, and the necessity of a strong adjustment program developed as the only solution.

In this context, it is relevant to ask to what extent the introduction of fiscal institutions during the 1990s limited fiscal indiscipline and to what extent it helped to reduce the discretionality of policymakers, and hence, to what extent the procyclicality of fiscal policy was reduced. In particular, the commitment of the Peruvian government in the early 1990s to achieving progressive objectives in terms of fiscal outcomes as part of the agreements with the IMF was an important element that contributed to fiscal sustainability.

The role played by these agreements was later taken on by the fiscal rules introduced in the fiscal responsibility law of 1999. Two main reasons explain the enactment of this law. First, the implementation of an exaggerated countercyclical fiscal policy in 1998, which was a policy response to the international financial crises and the El Niño climate phenomena in 1998 and 1999, respectively, put the fiscal stance on a perceived unsustainable path. Second, there was a realization that the government had incentives to behave opportunistically, particularly in the context of electoral years. In general, the fiscal responsibility law's main objective was to obtain a positive fiscal balance over the cycle, allowing moderate deficits in bad years. Congress could grant waivers, but only in the event of economic crises or other emergency situations.

The fiscal responsibility law included the imposition of ceilings on the overall deficit and on the real growth of nonfinancial expenditures; measures to increase the transparency and accountability of public expenditure; and finally, the MMM to guide the approval stage of the budget process. Finally, the law was supplemented by a *sunshine law* in 2001, which was approved to increase transparency further and was modified in 2003 to incorporate the subnational governments created by the decentralization process.

Nevertheless, as was expected, the goals set by the fiscal responsibility law were not completely accomplished, since they were initiated because the governments continuously managed to get waivers on the rule on the deficit—in the 2000–2003 period characterized as recession years—and on the rules limiting expenditures in more recent years characterized as "good years." Notwithstanding this situation, these rules served as a useful *benchmark* by making explicit any strong deviations from the ceilings imposed, and progressively an ample consensus grew among independent analysts, certain political actors, and public opinion in general on the importance of reinforcing the accomplishment of the goals, rather than allowing a more discretionary behavior by the government.

Empirical exercises like the one presented in Carranza, Chavez, and Valderrama (2007) for the Peruvian case and in Mendoza and Ostry (2008), using a sample of both industrialized and emerging economies, confirm the view that although for the entire sample the fiscal balance has been procyclical, this behavior has been reduced significantly after 1990. Relative to other emerging countries, Peru since 1990 seems to have followed a less procyclical fiscal policy. Mendoza and Ostry estimate unconditional correlations between the fiscal primary balances (as a percentage of GDP) and output gaps for almost 50 countries for the period from the early 1990s to 2005. Their results suggest a lower procyclicality of Peruvian fiscal policy than that of the majority of other emerging countries and even lower procyclicality than the average of the industrialized economies.

The Misallocation of Public Expenditure as a Result of the Strategic Behavior of Key Actors

The executive has wide powers to alter the allocation of resources in the execution stage and to vary the total when the realized fiscal revenues diverge from those initially forecasted. These powers—although bounded by the degree of budgetary rigidity and by the reluctance of the president to be identified as an actor that tends to increase the deficit excessively—grant the government the capacity to adapt promptly to changing situations, a feature that in general is desirable in modern budgetary management. Nevertheless, this positive feature comes at the cost of facilitating the use of this discretionary power to seek short-term political benefits, and these pressures for "the execution of public works" or to attend to other demands can also yield a highly inefficient utilization of public resources.

An emblematic example of this situation is the case of the deterioration of the quality of the public education system in recent years, a direct consequence of the inadequate allocation of resources to this sector. In particular, there is evidence that supports this view in a context in which public expenditure on education—particularly on wages—has increased significantly in recent years. This increase was stimulated by the electoral promise of the winning presidential candidate of the 2001–2006 term to double the wages of public school teachers by the end of the government's mandate. Based on this promise, the government began to increase teachers' wages, but did not require a commitment to enhance the quality of public services, in a context in which the public administration lacked a system of performance indicators that could have been used for ex post evaluation of public expenditure.

Hence, even though over the period 2000–2006 the expenditure allocated to this sector increased by 31 percent in real terms, the indicators of the quality of the service did not improve and indeed seem to have worsened. For example, students in the last year of the primary level and those in the last year of the secondary level scored lower in the evaluation of logic and mathematics competences (basically the ability to solve elemental math problems) in 2004 compared to the evaluation in 1998, and the differences between the results in these two years are statistically significant. In the case of verbal and communication competences (the ability to understand basic texts), the average national score obtained by both groups evaluated was not statistically different in 2004 from that obtained in 1998. That is, student results were either worse or showed no improvement in six years, in a context of increasing wages for teachers. The results for the last year of secondary education are presented in Figure 7.4.

Thus, the strong increments in public expenditure devoted to the public education system in Peru have not translated into an improvement in the quality of the service. Because of the president's strong desire to fulfill his electoral promise, these increments took place unconditionally, that is, without a requirement for public school teachers to make any type of commitment to improve the quality of public education. In fact, the teachers' union (SUTEP) has been strongly opposed to any attempt

FIGURE 7.4 Performance of Public School Students and Public Expenditure in Secondary Education (5th Grade), 1998–2004[a]
(scores and millions of nuevos soles *of 2001, respectively)*

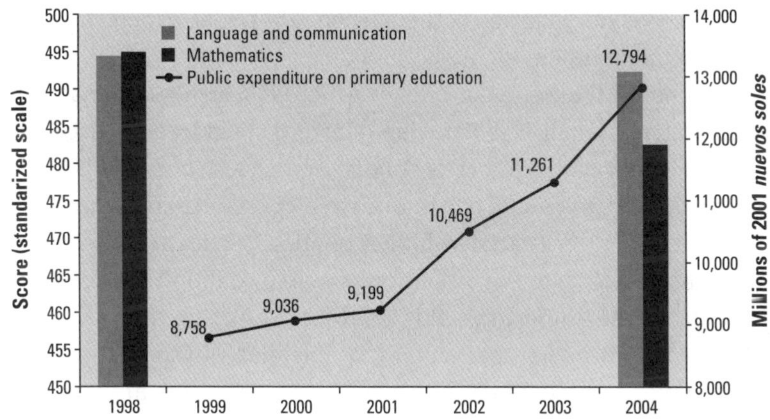

Source: Ministry of Education of Peru.
[a] The results for 1998 correspond to the CRECER evaluation, whereas the results for 2004 were collected in the National Evaluation of 2004, in which similar questions were applied for comparative purposes.

by the government to evaluate the performance of these teachers as a way of establishing a meritocracy-based system for wage increases.

CONCLUSIONS

The fiscal budget in Peru is the financial result of actions and policies that arise from the interaction between key actors. Moreover, it is a reflection of the political transactions among the different actors that intervene, formally or informally, in the formulation, approval, and execution of the public budget. History and the institutions that shape the policy decision-making process influence the resulting decisions. From this point of view, the political process is conditioned by the incentives and restrictions that the different actors face and by the institutional rules that affect the actors' interactions.

Herein, it has been made evident that even though stronger discipline and the reduction of the deficit bias have led to a reduction in the procyclicality of fiscal policy, this tendency has not yet been eliminated, and certain opportunistic behaviors still persist with respect to the political cycle (and not so much with respect to the business cycle). Finally, even though the transparency and representativeness of budget decisions have improved in recent years, there are still important issues to consider in terms of the efficiency of public expenditure and the consequent quality of public services.

In general, the Peruvian budget process is highly dominated by the executive branch. The Peruvian constitution grants the executive strong discretionary powers on budgetary issues, possibly because of the necessity to ensure governance in a country characterized by a fragmented political system with weak political parties and by electoral rules that do not favor the formation of stable coalitions in Congress. However, at the same time, this high level of discretion facilitates opportunistic behavior, particularly on the side of the executive, an effect that is accentuated by the high rotation of political actors and the resulting necessity for them to demonstrate active results in the short term.

The president wants to be perceived as "competent" through the execution of public works and the expansion of coverage of public services, while trying to fulfill electoral promises to keep the population's support. Given the weakness of political institutions, population acceptance is a key factor, not only to ensure that the governing party maintains certain representation in future elections, but also to rule out any possibility of the president's not being able to finish the period for which he or she was elected. The president also faces pressure from the heads of the spending units, certain members of Congress, and interest groups to increase public expenditure.

Evidently the president, although subject to financial and institutional constraints, attempts to maximize progress on these objectives. However, because of the severe economic crisis experienced in Peru during the 1980s, there is widespread awareness of the importance of maintaining fiscal discipline; thus the president has internalized the necessity of avoiding high deficits, which can increase the likelihood of facing a crisis in the short term. Nevertheless, policymakers still tend to engage in opportunistic behavior, that is, they try to take advantage of policy decisions that may have high costs in the long run, but that could bring them personal benefits in the short run. Some resulting outcomes of this situation are the observed tendency not to accumulate assets during upturns—that is, to spend all additional revenues in good times (a *voracity effect*) and to utilize public resources to influence electoral results.

Thus, given this strong discretionary power that has been granted to the president in particular, and to the executive in general, a set of institutional counterweights has been introduced to limit the high degree of flexibility granted to the executive in budgetary matters. In particular, these counterweights include measures aimed at enhancing the transparency of budgetary decisions, a greater hierarchical role for the MEF as the one actor in charge of maintaining fiscal discipline, and "external" limitations, such as the constitutional prohibition on the central bank in regard to financing the public deficit, the constant monitoring of economic policies by the IMF, and the introduction of fiscal rules.

Although some of these measures have already been implemented in Peru and certain types of fiscal discipline have been increasing in recent years, some of the issues that should be addressed by future governments are the following:

a. Even though the fiscal deficit and public debt have decreased in recent years, these outcomes are in part attributable to cyclical factors. Peru is still highly indebted and subject to strong economic swings, and thus it is highly recommended that fiscal discipline be further enhance to overrule problems of fiscal solvency completely—in line with the principle of a zero deficit for the long run included in the current fiscal responsibility law. Without this resulting room for maneuver, it will be hard to eliminate procyclicality from Peru's fiscal future.
b. The quality of public services (such as public education and health) and, in general, the efficiency of social policy are currently being questioned by the population, and this skepticism was reflected in the 2006 presidential elections. Actions aimed at solving these problems may imply future pressures for additional expenditures, especially on public infrastructure and social programs, and these expenditures should be undertaken with extra care to avoid affecting the sustainability of fiscal policy and to ensure that the resources are being utilized efficiently.
c. Based on the last presidential and legislative elections, and in general because of the fragmentation of the Peruvian political sys-

tem, it is not hard to believe that future administrations will lack strong parliamentary majorities, so politicians will have to learn how to make alliances and form coalitions to ensure a minimum level of governance. Thus, it is highly probable that future governments will face a higher *cost of governing* in terms of pork barrel projects and patronage that they will be forced to grant to ensure legislative support.

d. A more active role by Congress in budgetary decisions will be necessary and convenient, especially in terms of the oversight of the budget process.

e. Finally, the decentralization process will introduce new actors with increasing spending demands. This is particularly true for the case of regional governments that are not allowed to collect local revenues. Also, as international commodity prices continue to be high, regions that are not currently benefiting from the taxes collected from the exploitation of natural resources will exert pressure on the government to provide them with equal compensation.

REFERENCES

Akitoby, B, B. Clements, S. Gupta, and G. Inchauste. 2006. Public Spending, Voracity and Wagner's Law in Developing Countries. *European Journal of Political Economy 22*(4): 908–24.

Alcázar, L., J. R. López-Cálix, and E. Wachtenheim. 2003. Las pérdidas en el camino. Fugas en el gasto público: transferencias municipales, vaso de leche y educación. Instituto APOYO, Lima.

Alier, M. 2005. Budget Rigidities in Latin America. Paper presented at ECLAC's 18th Fiscal Policy Regional Seminar, Santiago, Chile.

Cain, B. E., J. A. Ferejohn, and M. P. Fiorina. 1987. *The Personal Vote* Cambridge, Massachusetts: Harvard University Press.

Carranza, L., J. Chavez, and J. Valderrama. 2007. La economía política del proceso presupuestario: el caso peruano. Working Paper No. Cs-102. Regional Department of Operations, Inter-American Development Bank, Washington, DC.

Dixit, A. 1996. *The Making of Economic Policy. A Transaction-Cost Politics Perspective*. Cambridge, MA: MIT Press.

Francke, P., J. Castro, R. Ugaz, and J. Salazar. 2003. Evaluación del proceso presupuestal peruano, con énfasis en su transparencia. Proyecto Análisis Independiente del Presupuesto Público, Lima, Peru.

IDB (Inter-American Development Bank). 2005. *The Politics of Policies*. Economic and Social Progress in Latin America: 2006 Report. Washington, DC: IDB.

International Budget Partnership. 2005. *Latin American Index of Budget Transparency, a Comparison of 8 Countries*. Washington, DC: Center on Budget and Policy Priorities.

Mendoza, E. G., and J. D. Ostry. 2008. International Evidence on Fiscal Solvency: Is Fiscal Policy "Responsible"? *Journal of Monetary Economics* 55: 1081–93.

Morón, E., and C. Sanborn. 2006. The Pitfalls of Policymaking in Peru: Actors, Institutions and Rules of the Game. Research Network Working Paper No. R-511. Inter-American Development Bank, Washington, DC.

Nordhaus, W. 1975. The Political Business Cycle. *Review of Economic Studies* 42: 169–90.

North, D. 1990. A Transaction Cost Theory of Politics. *Journal of Theoretical Politics* 2(4): 355–67.

Pereira, C., and B. Mueller. 2004. The Cost of Governing: Strategic Behavior of the President and Legislators in Brazil's Budgetary Process. *Comparative Political Studies* 37(7): 781–815.

Rubin, I. 1999. Understanding the Role of Conflict in Budgeting. In R. Meyers, ed., *Handbook of Government Budgeting*. San Francisco: Jossey Bass.

Santiso, C., and A. García Belgrano. 2004. Politics of Budgeting in Peru: Legislative Budget Oversight and Public Finance Accountability in Presidential Systems. SAIS Working Paper No. WP01–04. Paul H. Nitze School of Advance International Studies, Washington, DC.

Shack, N. 2005. Presupuestar en el Perú. Preliminary Working Paper. Economic Commission for Latin American and the Caribbean, Santiago, Chile.

Tornell, A., and P. Lane. 1998. Voracity and Growth. NBER Working Paper No. W6498. National Bureau of Economic Research, Cambridge, MA.

Tsebelis, G. 2001. *Veto Players: How Political Institutions Work*. Princeton, NJ: Princeton University Press.

8

Fiscal Rules That Fit Political Cycles: The Case of Uruguay

Juan Andrés Moraes, Daniel Chasquetti, and Mario Bergara

DEMOCRACY FIRST

Uruguay has been traditionally characterized as one of the most stable and representative democracies in Latin America. Part of this evaluation rests on the strength of Uruguay's political institutions and the clear preferences of citizens and elites to conceive of democracy as the best regime to solve political conflicts (Latinobarómetro, 2007). To a large extent, this view of democracy is based on the main features of Uruguay's policymaking process and particularly the form in which institutions and actors interact in generating most policy outputs. This interaction between a complex institutional design and a large number of veto players made Uruguay an outlier in regard to economic and state reforms in the Latin American region during the 1990s (Lora, 2001). It is in this context that budgetary policy in Uruguay represents one of the best examples for illustrating the extent to which politics and institutions affect policy outputs and particularly fiscal policy.

This chapter explores the extent to which Uruguayan institutions (interbranch relations, electoral rules, budgetary laws, etc.) and political actors (parties, factions, interest groups, and bureaucrats) involved in the budgetary process affect fiscal performance in terms of *sustainability, efficiency,* and *representativeness.* Since the early 1990s, throughout the structural adjustment and the economic reforms in the region, Uruguay has been temporally consistent with restrictive fiscal policies. However, unlike most Latin American countries, Uruguay has been able to sustain a large public sector and, particularly, one of the largest welfare states in the region. To a large extent, this combination has been the result of a singular small democracy where domestic political actors and institutions drive most policy outputs.

The chapter is structured in five sections. The subsequent section describes the broad policymaking process and the set of actors and institutions characterizing the Uruguayan political system. The third section combines the features of the policymaking process and the budgetary process, concluding with a set of hypotheses that deal with the level of *sustainability, efficiency,* and *representativeness* of the fiscal policy. The fourth section tests these hypotheses with evidence on public expenditures, indicators of efficiency of the public sector, and the process in which the budget bill is negotiated. The final section discuses the main findings and concludes.

THE URUGUAYAN POLICYMAKING PROCESS

Political Institutions

Political structures are composed by two sets of stable rules (see Bergara et al., 2006; Moraes, Chasquetti, and Bergara, 2005). On the one hand, rules concerning the balance of power or interbranch relations shape governmental institutions. On the other hand, electoral systems are orthogonal to executive-legislative relations, because electoral rules affect the number of agents or veto players in the policymaking process (Shugart and Carey, 1992; Cox and McCubbins, 2001; Spiller and Tommasi, 2003; Tsebelis, 2002). Additionally, direct democracy can complement executive-legislative relations and the electoral rules to complete the set of political structures that affect policy outputs. In this context, Uruguay is characterized by having solid democratic institutions with a large number of veto players that affect the policymaking process, as it occurs in most presidential governments with two separate branches of government, plus bicameralism and a number of parties and factions

First, Uruguay is a presidential regime in which—unlike the U.S. case—the president has an important set of legal tools to control the legislative agenda. For example, presidents have institutional devices such as total and item vetoes, the ability to initiate bills in strategic areas (such as tax policy or social security), the authority to introduce emergency bills, and, more importantly, the possibility of initiating the budget bill and the yearly revisions (Rendiciones de Cuenta). Besides, Uruguayan presidents hold important nonlegislative powers over cabinet appointments and other key bureaucratic spots within the public administration (Buquet, Chasquetti, and Moraes, 1998; Chasquetti and Moraes, 2000).

Second, presidents are elected for a five-year term without the possibility of reelection. Until 1996, presidents were elected through the plurality rule and double simultaneous vote (DSV). The plurality rule enabled parties to provide multiple candidates for the presidential race, allowing voters to cast their ballots primarily for a party and then for a presidential candidate, with an individual list of legislators for the senate and the lower chamber (González, 1991). Given that presidential candidates were able to sum up their votes (for the party), elected presidents were the most-voted-for candidates within the winning party, but not necessarily the most-voted-for candidate considering all competing parties. This singular set of rules was partially abandoned in a constitutional reform adopted in 1996, establishing presidential election by majority runoff as well as party primaries for all parties before the general election (Buquet, Chasquetti, and Moraes, 1998).

Third, Uruguay has a bicameral Congress. Senators and representatives are elected through a proportional-representation closed-list (PR–closed list) system for a five-year term without reelection limits. Until 1996, elections were held simultaneously at all levels of government (national and subnational) under DSV. Currently, legislative elections take place with the first round of presidential elections. Citizens cast their votes for a presidential candidate and a list of candidates for the legislature (Senate and Chamber of Deputies). The Senate has 30 members elected in a single national district, plus the vice president. The Chamber of Deputies has 99 members elected in 19 multimember electoral districts. In a first step, seats are allocated among parties applying the D'Hondt formula on a national basis.[1] Second, distribution takes place within parties (among factions), under proportional representation, and within districts, with a minimum of two representatives for each district.

[1] The D'Hondt formula, named after Belgian mathematician Victor D'Hondt, is a highest-averages method for allocating seats in party list proportional representation.

Last but not least, the institutional basis of the Uruguayan policy-making process provides important mechanisms of direct democracy (Altman, 2002). Among them, there are two remarkable devices that have been systematically used during the last 20 years. On the one hand, the constitution allows citizens to collect individual signatures of 25 percent of registered voters to call for a referendum that will endorse or revoke by majority vote a current law approved by Parliament. On the other hand, the constitution also allows the use of direct democracy to make constitutional reforms. In this case, reformers have to collect the signatures of 10 percent of registered voters in order to call for a plebiscite. Although the technical natures of these rules are essentially different, both legal devices have been widely used by the opposition against several policy reforms since 1985. In particular, it was intensely used by the Frente Amplio (FA), a left-wing Uruguayan political party founded in 1971, when it was in the opposition, and indeed it was successful in vetoing several reforms led by presidents of the Blanco and Colorado Parties. However, since the FA Party took office in 2005, traditional parties have failed to mobilize votes against the left-wing government using direct democracy.

Parties and Party System

Uruguay has one of the few institutionalized party systems in Latin America (Mainwaring, 1999). To a large extent, this characterization deals with the fact that two of the parties in the system, Nacional and Colorado, are two of the oldest in world history. These parties had a solid bipartisan dominance until FA emerged in 1971. Later, after the democratic restoration in 1985, the FA transformed the party system format into a multiparty system with three parties and "a half," if one considers the systematic presence of a small fourth party.[2] In any case, the party system reveals stability, unlike noninstitutionalized systems.

On the other hand, Uruguayan parties are factionalized. This type of internal organization is the direct consequence of electoral rules that facilitate the existence within parties of institutionalized and stable groups—or factions—generally led by presidential candidates or national senators. In this case, notice that the effective number of factions

[2] The Union Civica until 1989, and the Nuevo Espacio between 1989 and 1999.

has remained very stable over time, with an overall average of 2.8 for the period 1962–1999. The presence of factions within parties does not imply that parties are weak: parties are organized around factions, but they are still relevant agents in government, because there are rules and procedures for making joint decisions beyond factional divisions or policy preferences. In sum, it is important to note that although Uruguayan parties cannot be considered unified agents, factions are relevant and stable in the political system.

Given electoral rules characterized by PR–closed list, faction leaders have strong power to control the nomination process and, by implication, the party discipline in Parliament (Moraes, 2008). Because of this control, in general, legislators are extremely disciplined in Parliament (Morgenstern, 2001), and they have strong incentives to follow their faction leader and his or her policy preferences. Undisciplined legislators are unlikely to be endorsed for reelection, and their chances for gaining endorsement for other career paths are fairly low.

Characterizing the Uruguayan Policymaking Process

The Uruguayan policymaking process is determined by three broad institutional features: (a) a presidential regime that sets terms for both the executive and the legislature; (b) a president with strong agenda-setting powers in the legislature; and (c) a multiparty system with factionalized parties. The combination of these three features creates a policymaking process with a cyclical pattern composed of two periods within each presidential term, featuring cooperation and conflict.

The combination of a presidential regime and a multiparty system with factionalized parties explains the fact that most Uruguayan presidents since 1985 have been forced to build coalitions or specific agreements to pass their policies. But coalitions under presidential regimes tend to be weak because of the simple but crucial rule of the term mandate. Therefore, cooperation among parties is subject to the electoral calendar, and the evidence for legislative behavior in Uruguay confirms this pattern (see Chasquetti and Moraes, 2000). Once the presidential mandate lapses, presidents lose their political support. This implies that most important policies are passed during the fist two to three years of a government, when the president has a legislative majority. These conditions have changed since the Frente Amplio Party took office in 2005: for the first time since the democratic restoration, a majority party in Parliament does not need to make agreements, and thus the systematic cycle of cooperation and conflict is temporarily over.

From this brief description, it must be noted that the number of veto gates and veto players over policy decisions is large as a result of the set of institutions (presidential regime with bicameral legislature) and political agents operating within the system (fragmentation and party factionalization). Despite these different types of vetoes, the policymaking process has featured a systematic cycle of cooperation and conflict imposed by the presidential regime and the distribution of power among parties, in which no president had a majority status until 2005.

THE INTERACTIONS BETWEEN THE POLICYMAKING AND BUDGETARY PROCESSES

One of the main arguments in this chapter is that the Uruguayan policymaking process overdetermines the entire budgetary process. This means that despite the set of rules governing the budgetary process (which are certainly influential), systemic factors dealing with interbranch relations (executive-legislative) and the party system (number and organizational structure of parties) are more important for understanding the dynamics behind the budgetary process and outcomes.

The reason for this overdetermination of the policymaking process in budgetary politics is twofold. On the one hand, the institutional dynamics that affect the presidential regime constrain the ability of presidents to implement long-term strategies and regulations for the public administration as a whole beyond their terms. Presidents are elected for a five-year term, and the Uruguayan budget law is conceived as a medium-term development plan for each president. In turn, presidents attempt to pass their most important policy reforms within this law, which can be easily overturned by future budgets and ordinary laws. That is, the budget is conceived as the most important bill for all presidents, and yet budgets generally become typical omnibus bills, easily reversed by future budgets.

On the other hand, and more importantly, since the early 1990s Uruguayan presidents have been forced to build postelectoral coalitions because of their political weakness within and outside their parties.

The resulting political constraints have been far more powerful at the time budgets are prepared and endorsed than the set of rules of the budgetary process, by which presidents have a clear asymmetrical power vis-à-vis the legislature. Thus, institutional and political determinants that deal with the political system are largely more important than the specific set of regulations governing the budgetary process.

The rest of this section presents a set of interactions between the broad policymaking process described earlier herein (with its actors and institutions) and the specific actors and rules involved in the budgetary process. These interactions take place within each stage of the budgetary process, which is regulated by the constitution. The section concludes with a set of hypotheses emerging from this set of interactions.

Stages of the Budgetary Process

Preparation Stage

The preparation stage starts at the beginning of each new administration. According to the Uruguayan constitution (Article 214), the executive branch will prepare, along with the assessment of the Budget Office (OPP), the five-year term national budget for the newly elected government. This bill will be submitted to the legislature within the first six months after the new administration takes office (Umansky, 2006; Berreta, 2006; Moraes, Chasquetti, and Bergara, 2005).

In order to elaborate a first draft of the budget bill, the OPP and the Ministry of Finance (MF) deliver to the line ministries a set of directions or guides with the fiscal goals of the new government. These fiscal targets are the basis for each ministry to elaborate its own budget. After this process, each ministry delivers its budget to the OPP-MF so that the latter can adjust the differences between the fiscal goals and each project sent by the 12 ministries. During this time, there is a dense process of political negotiation within the party in office or among coalition members.

In this context, at least two factors introduce an important level of rigidity during the preparation stage: pensions and public wages. As happens in most OECD countries, the Uruguayan public sector has these rigid operative costs that force planners and politicians to focus on public investment as an adjustment variable. However, beyond these constraints that all governments have had to face since 1985—and particularly since 1990—budgets have served as a strategic tool for policy reform (Filgueira and Moraes, 1999). In other words, although governments have been constrained in their ability to implement major changes to their spending allocations as a result of severe rigidities in the composition of expenditures, they have used the budget bill as the most important legal instrument for reforming several policy areas.

Since the Uruguayan budget is a five-year term law with yearly revisions that can actually become new budgets, governments propose not only their fiscal program and allocations, but also several policy reforms. The inclusion of these reforms has been part of the preparation stage, since governments will not include policy changes in the budget bill unless they count on majorities in Parliament beforehand. Because of the "law of anticipated reactions" (Cox and Morgenstern, 2001), elected presidents negotiate within their parties and coalitions every single piece of legislation before it gets into the two branches of Parliament.[3] Essentially, during the preparation stage the budget bill becomes a set of windows (Kingdon, 1984) of policy negotiations between and within parties and factions. More specifically, the budget bill is mostly negotiated at the elite level between party or faction leaders outside the legislature.

Several important policy reforms have been passed within budget laws during the last two decades. To a large extent, the chance of passing a policy reform within the budget depends on its level of negotiation within the government party or coalition. The inverse is also true, which was demonstrated when part of President Luis Alberto Lacalle's fiscal adjustment and state- and market-oriented reforms were disarticulated before reaching Parliament in 1990. Originally, Lacalle was planning an omnibus bill with several reforms that were vetoed by some factions within his own party and coalition partners (the Colorado Party). More recently, President Julio María Sanguinetti's government (1995–2000) was able to pass important policy reforms in public administration and education (among other policy areas), but he failed to pass an important health care reform. This happened because at the time of reaching

[3] In the words of Cox and Morgenstern (2001: 172), "Carl Friedrich's 'law of anticipated reactions' expresses the single idea that if X's actions will be subject to review by Y, with Y capable of rewarding good actions and/or punishing bad ones, then X will likely anticipate and consider what it is that Y wants (Friedrich, 1963)."

Parliament, the reform had not been negotiated with coalition partners and the small but powerful set of medical interest groups.

In general terms, the preparation process is highly politicized, to the extent that parties and factions compete for a better slice of the cake. Since the system has an important number of veto players, high transaction costs created by intense political negotiations usually lead to concrete benefits with very diffuse costs. However, the budgetary process is relatively transparent in that political competition between and within parties compels these agents to "go public" in order to gain support for their demands.

Approval Stage

The approval stage is regulated by a set of constitutional devices involving executive-legislative relations. This process is characterized by six basic rules. First: (a) the executive branch has exclusive authority to introduce all legislation concerning budgetary policy; and (b) after a bill has been introduced in Parliament, both chambers have up to four months to pass or reject the bill. If the bill is rejected, the previous five-year budget is automatically endorsed. Otherwise, if the bill is passed: (c) the executive is allowed to veto the new bill (with either total or item veto); (d) the budget has to be approved by an absolute majority in each chamber; (e) the legislature cannot increase the amounts allocated to public spending without specifying the sources of new expenditures; and (f) the executive branch is allowed to deliver two complementary bills with changes to the original budget delivered to Parliament.

Once the bill has been introduced in one of the chambers (generally the Chamber of Deputies), it is automatically redirected to the budget committee. Occasionally, this committee works in coordination with other committees (those on health, education, transportation, etc.) in public hearings with the presence of bureaucrats and ministers, who illustrate, clarify, or support the budget bill. Finally, the budget committee has to pass the bill by majority rule in order for it to be considered in a plenary session.

Within the legislature, each chamber has the same authority over the budget bill. Each has 45 days to make a decision, and in those cases where differences arise, the bill has to be submitted to the first chamber, which will have 15 days to achieve agreement. If there is no agreement between the two chambers, the bill must be submitted to the General Assembly—a third chamber representing the meeting of deputies and senators—which has 15 days to decide.

Once the bill has been passed in both chambers of Parliament, or by the General Assembly, the president can use his or her veto power or facilitate an automatic endorsement after 10 days of legislative approval. However, at this point in the term, presidents are strong enough to sustain most of their policy preferences because they are still within their "honeymoon" with the electorate and coalition partners. Overriding executive vetoes is less frequent during the first half of presidential mandates than during the second half, when presidents generally lose their political support, coalitions fall apart, and parties and factions are inclined towards the electoral competition. In case of a veto, a supermajority of three-fifths in each chamber is needed to override the presidential veto.

Overall, budgets are passed without major contingencies in Parliament within the first year of each government term. For example, achieving legislative majorities to pass budget bills has not been necessarily difficult during the last four governments (under Presidents Lacalle [1990], Sanguinetti [1995], Batlle [2000], and Tabaré Vázquez [2005]). The fact that all presidents have been able to build governmental coalitions since the democratic restoration in 1985 has guaranteed enough political support in Parliament to endorse the presidential or coalitional agenda. Indeed, this political support can be observed in the way budget laws have been passed in plenary sessions during the last 20 years, where the party discipline has been perfect for those within the coalition and the presidential party (Moraes and Morgenstern, 1998; Koolhas, 2002).

Since the Lacalle administration (1990–1994), presidents have been able to "impose" that beyond the five-year term budget law, most yearly revision will not modify the spending allocations and the provisions set in the original budget law. This strategy has been followed in order to avoid negotiations every year, with the potential cost of political defeats for presidents after the second or third year of their terms. With only a few exceptions, presidents endorsed yearly revisions with a "single article, no new expenditures" between 1993 and 2002.

A variant of this scenario has been the establishment of a reversion point at which no budget bill can be passed as a result of the lack of votes in Parliament. In this case, the president gets what he or she wants: the original budget allocations made in the original five-year term budget law. This is well exemplified by the last two yearly revisions made by the Batlle administration. The Senate was unable to achieve enough votes to pass the bill approved by the lower chamber, and the president won his battle to sustain the original bill with the "single article, no new expenditures" strategy. This strategy forced parties and factions to negotiate their differences during the approval stage instead of delaying part of the negotiation for the annual revisions.

In 2005, when the Frente Amplio took office, the new administration decided to abandon the rigidities of designing a single budget for the entire period in government, without annual revisions. In this case, the government designed a middle-term fiscal program that was submitted by the minister of finance to the cabinet, which endorsed its contents in a plenary session. This fiscal program set the space or limits within which the left-wing party in office had to elaborate the new budget bill for the entire term in government. Yet the most important change in terms of strategy deals with the fact that the Frente Amplio rejected the "single article, no new expenditures" informally followed by traditional parties. In the current administration, every yearly revision is based on macroeconomic assumptions that build the fiscal programming on which the budget is designed.

Execution and Monitoring Stage

The execution and monitoring of the budget bill depends to a large extent on the executive branch. First, the execution takes place according to the budget allocations. However, unlike other cases in Latin America (Baldez and Carey, 1999), the way in which the budget bill is legally structured does not allow for discretion in the hands of bureaucrats or public servants. Each program has specified allocations on which public expenditures are structured (wages, investments, administrative costs, etc.). Thus, the execution process depends to a large extent on the level of cash (or credit) availability in the hands of the executive branch.

Although bureaucrats or public servants do not have discretion over budget expenditures, the fact that the executive has the authority to declare a lack of funds to finance specified allocations in the budget bill creates a de facto mechanism for shirking the budget law, which took place during the 2002 economic crisis faced by the Batlle administration. In fact, during the crisis there was a trade-off between printing money and, hence, increasing inflation to finance certain public programs and declaring a lack of funds for those programs. In this case, the government opted for the first of these two options in order to preserve fiscal stability.

Until 2005, this kind of discretion was the source of important political conflicts in two different arenas. On the one hand, the lack of cash availability triggered a conflict between the executive branch and particularly the ministry of finance and labor unions. Given that the public sector employs around 20 percent of the labor force, conflicts within this sector have frequently been expensive for the state as a whole. On the other hand, these conflicts have had political consequences, since government and opposition have been confronted with the way in which the administration creates a de facto mechanism for automatically adjusting public expenditures when it lacks resources to finance the budget bill. Notice that inflation is more likely to be controlled, but at the cost of violating important legal obligations set up in the budget bill. The problem, however, was that the budget bill approved in the year 2000 did not have a medium-term fiscal program behind it.

Second, the process of monitoring is also influenced by political developments and particularly the dynamics of party politics and governmental coalitions. One of the most interesting cases during recent years has been that the Blanco and Colorado Parties or coalitions of these two parties that control the executive branch have been the majority in those institutions responsible for controlling and monitoring the budget execution. This has been an important source of inefficiency in fiscal management, as well as a permanent source of doubt regarding transparency in public expenditures. Furthermore, in cases in which the Tribunal de Cuentas de la Nación (TCN) identifies illegal expenditures or discrepancies between public offices and the TCN, the legislature is the final judge.[4] However, given that the legislature was controlled by the same coalition of parties joining the executive cabinet, the TCN has been reluctant to enforce sentences against the executive branch and most subnational governments under the political control of the same parties (Nacional and Colorado). Under the FA, the TCN currently re-

---

[4] The TCN is an independent state agency dedicated to controlling the legality of budget allocations and execution. This agency is composed of six members, nominated by the executive branch but endorsed by a two-thirds majority of the Senate.

mains with the same members designated by past governments because government and opposition have been unable to achieve an agreement involving a two-thirds Senate majority. Yet it is arguable that the lack of agreement over new nominations between government and opposition can redound in better controls over public expenditures, particularly when the party in office has a majority in Parliament.

EXPLAINING SUSTAINABILITY, EFFICIENCY, AND REPRESENTATIVENESS

Drawing Hypotheses

From the previous two sections it is possible to observe that some actors and political institutions are extremely important in terms of the entire negotiation and decision-making process. In other words, the influences of interbranch relations, the type of government (coalitions, single parties, and minority governments), and the number of parties and factions with legislative representation are crucial to the level of *sustainability* and *representativeness* of public expenditures. However, the same is not necessarily true for the level of *efficiency*. In this case, enforcement technologies in the form of information and human resources to deal with complex processes during execution and monitoring are far more important than political factors in explaining *efficiency* levels in public expenditures.

Within this context, this chapter proposes five hypotheses to be developed in the next section. Hypotheses 1 and 2 relate to the level of *sustainability* of public expenditures, whereas political institutions and actors are linked to fiscal performance. Hypotheses 3 and 4 focus on the level of *efficiency* in public expenditures, and Hypothesis 5 deals with the level of *representativeness* of public expenditures.

Hypotheses

1. Public expenditures fluctuate with the electoral or presidential cycle. A primary consequence of this is that electoral years have shown a clear tendency towards fiscal imbalances since 1922. This leads only to short-term sustainability problems in public expenditures,

because the second years of most terms show fiscal adjustments to counterbalance the previous electoral cycle.

2. Given that transaction costs are expected to increase with the number of political agents with veto power over the budget bill, the larger the number of veto players, the larger the size of the fiscal imbalance (Hypothesis 2a = parties, Hypothesis 2b = factions).
3. Internal and external budget controls focus on legal and accounting aspects. Therefore, their results are not used as inputs in order to increase efficiency in the public administration.
4. Efficiency problems during the execution stage are partly due to the fact that there is no legislative influence over this process. Legislators and the legislature as a whole have almost no influence after the budget has been approved.
5. Interest groups and labor unions are relevant actors only at the approval stage of the budget process, where they can exert public pressure over parties, factions, and the executive branch. This pressure is oriented toward changing the original bill proposed by the executive branch.

Recent Trends in Fiscal Outcomes

During the late 1980s, the economy recovered from the 1982 crisis, but high levels of inflation persisted, and the average deficit for the decade was 5.5 percent of GDP. This was connected to an improvement in the situation of the region as a whole, a fall in oil prices, a rise in internal demand, and a fall in interest rates. Income increased thanks to economic expansion and a reduction in the weight of debt interest payments, which resulted from the first renegotiation of the debt and a fall in interest rates. Nevertheless, the fiscal balance was still in deficit. The possibilities for financing it were limited, given the high level of accumulated debt and the high inflation rates. Additionally, there was a constitutional reform in 1989 that linked social security expenditures to past inflation rates, and this severely compromised the fiscal balance for the future.

In 1990, a new stabilization plan came into operation and a considerable fiscal adjustment took place, basically aimed at increasing income from taxation. Expenditure did not decrease very much because allocations to the social security system were particularly rigid.

However, expenditure on interest payments fell as a consequence of Uruguay joining the Brady Plan. As a result of the fiscal adjustment, the primary surplus was 3.1 percent of GDP, while the conventional deficit fell from 6.9 percent to 3.1 percent of GDP. Another adjustment took place in 1992, including a partial reform in the social security arena. In 1995—with the increase in expenditure on social security—there was a new fiscal adjustment, which involved a new increase in income from taxation and restraint in expenditure. Also in 1995, a reform of the social security system was passed (this is described in more detail in the appropriate section), which ended the upward trend in expenditure on social security that had been making fiscal policy untenable. In 1996, a plan to reduce the number of public employees, which was aimed at reducing costs in this area, was introduced.

The primary deficit during the mid-1990s was always above what was necessary to stabilize the debt-product ratio of the previous year and there was the possibility of financing the deficit with external resources, given that there was access to these funds (Borchardt, Rial, and Sarmiento, 1998; Rial and Vicente, 2004). Additionally, the predominant view within the private sector was that the state would continue to be solvent, so fiscal policy seemed to be sustainable and solvent during the period (Rial and Vicente, 2004). In spite of this, fiscal policy appeared to be potentially vulnerable in the face of big fluctuations in one of its fundamental determinants, the gap between devaluation and inflation. Vulnerability to the other relevant factors, interest rates and product, does not seem to have been significant (Rial and Vicente, 2004). Towards 1999, problems began to emerge, making the vulnerability of the situation apparent. A general deterioration in the regional situation took place; for example, Brazil devalued its currency in 1999, and Argentina was hit by devaluation and recession in 2001.

In the face of these shocks, there was no big adjustment in the Uruguayan economy, and in particular there was no serious devaluation. But there was a primary deficit of 1 percent after a decade of positive results. The deficit stood at around 4 percent of GDP around the year 2000. Since there was no problem accessing credit, the deficit was financed in that way, and the gross debt rose from 40 percent to 55 percent of GDP, while the net debt increased from 27 percent to 36 percent of GDP around 2002. In this context, solvency indicators fell rapidly. Hence, for example, the primary surplus necessary to maintain the same level of debt as the previous year rose to 8.5 percent of GDP, while the increase in income needed for this same purpose came to 5 percent of GDP. These figures were difficult to reach, given that fiscal pressure after the successive fiscal adjustments was 31 percent of GDP, the highest in South America. Given that fiscal adjustment on the side of expenditure was not possible either, owing to rigidity problems already mentioned, there did not seem to be any real solutions on the fiscal policy side to maintain exchange rate policy.

In 2002, the fixed exchange rate policy was abandoned, and the exchange rate was allowed to float freely. The fiscal deficit was maintained at 4 percent of GDP, and there was a considerable increase in debt, which was no more than the manifestation of the latent risk mentioned above. The immediate consequences were that the country lost investment grade status, and there was a big rise in the cost of financing. Besides, the banking crisis led to the execution of contingent liabilities (the implicit deposit insurance) amounting to the equivalent of 15 percent of GDP, which was covered by increased indebtedness to multilateral organizations. Since 2005, the new left-wing party has been extremely prudent in fiscal policy by maintaining a primary fiscal surplus of 3 percent of GDP and a medium-term fiscal program based on conservative macroeconomic assumptions.

Overall, almost all items on the spending side of the budget are essentially rigid and nondiscretionary. Broadly speaking, half of public expenditures go to social security and one-fourth goes to wages. Interests and debt repayment are also outside the government's control. Therefore, the "adjustment variable" for expenditures in regard to the evolution of fiscal income (which is also very procyclical) is public investment. The volatility observed in this item is a byproduct of the absence of countercyclical mechanisms in the remaining items of public spending, in a context in which the tax burden does not allow new increases to be imposed.

SUSTAINABILITY IN PUBLIC EXPENDITURES: LOOKING AT POLITICS AND INSTITUTIONS

This section presents tests of the effects of political institutions and party politics on the level of sustainability in public expenditures in Uruguay. The first test analyzes the extent to which fiscal imbalances are more likely during electoral years (Hypothesis 1). The rationale behind this hypothesis is that politicians tend to be opportunistic, and electoral years give them an excellent opportunity to deliver public goods (in both a universal and a particularistic fashion) in order to advance their political careers. While evidence of this hypothesis has been found in cross-country studies for Latin America and Western democracies (Alesina et al., 1996; Alesina, Roubini, and Cohen, 1997), there is less evidence within cases or across time for particular cases. Furthermore, a test of this particular hypothesis in the Uruguayan case is particularly interesting, because of its democratic tradition and the strength of its political parties in the long run.

As can be observed in Figure 8.1, the electoral cycle in Uruguay has been remarkable. Data on fiscal performance were gathered for the 1942–1999 period, and electoral years are simply codified as 0, –1 for preelectoral years, and values of 1 and 2 are subsequent post-electoral years (Aboal and Moraes, 2003). The evidence shows that during electoral years (year = 0), governments are more likely to enact fiscal imbalances, while postelectoral years are systematically used to perform fiscal adjustments to counterbalance electoral years. In other words, over the long run, Uruguayan governments have used public spending in an opportunistic fashion, in order to gain reelection or to buffer electoral losses. In terms

FIGURE 8.1 Electoral Cycles and Fiscal Performance in Uruguay (1942–2000)

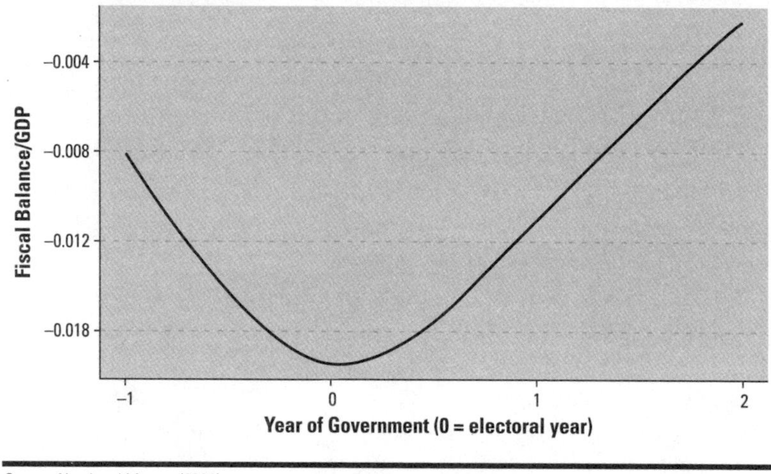

Source: Aboal and Moraes (2003).

of sustainability of public expenditures, this behavior is mostly associated with short-term problems, given that in the long run these imbalances are compensated for. That is, short-term imbalances in electoral years are compensated for by surpluses in post-electoral years.

The second test examines the extent to which the number of veto players in the party system affects transaction costs and—by extension—fiscal performance (Hypotheses 2a and 2b). As previously argued in this chapter, the number of parties and factions has increased, particularly since the emergence of the FA in 1971.[5] According to data of the analysis herein, an increase in the number of parties does not directly affect fiscal performance. Moreover, the transition from bipartism to multipartism has a relatively positive effect on fiscal behavior (see Moraes, Chasquetti, and Bergara, 2005: 28 for details on this point). However, the total number of factions in the party system has a negative effect on fiscal performance. Interestingly, the numbers of parties and factions are intertwined in the sense that an increase in the number of parties yields an increase in the number of factions. Yet, according to Figure 8.2, the effects of these two variables are substantially different for fiscal performance.

Efficiency: Looking at the Budget Execution and Monitoring Stage

In order to tackle Hypotheses 3 and 4, dealing with the overall level of efficiency in budget execution, it is important to look at the extent to which the executive branch actually executes the provisions made in the original bill endorsed by Parliament. This process is regulated by constitutional and legal provisions through the Ordered Text of Financial Accounting and Administration (Texto Ordenado de Contabilidad y Administración Financiera, hereafter referred to as TOCAF), which regulates in a unified fashion the administrative procedures for the execution and monitoring of the budget.

Within the framework of a global administrative reform, a new regime of financial control was established in 1996. Under the relatively

---

[5] In this case, we use the *effective* number of parties and the *effective* number of factions, which is an application of Laakso and Taagepera's formula that uses the number of lists to the Uruguayan Senate as the best proxy of a faction (see Buquet, Chasquetti, and Moraes, 1998).

FIGURE 8.2 The Impact of the Effective Number of Parties and Factions on the Fiscal Balance

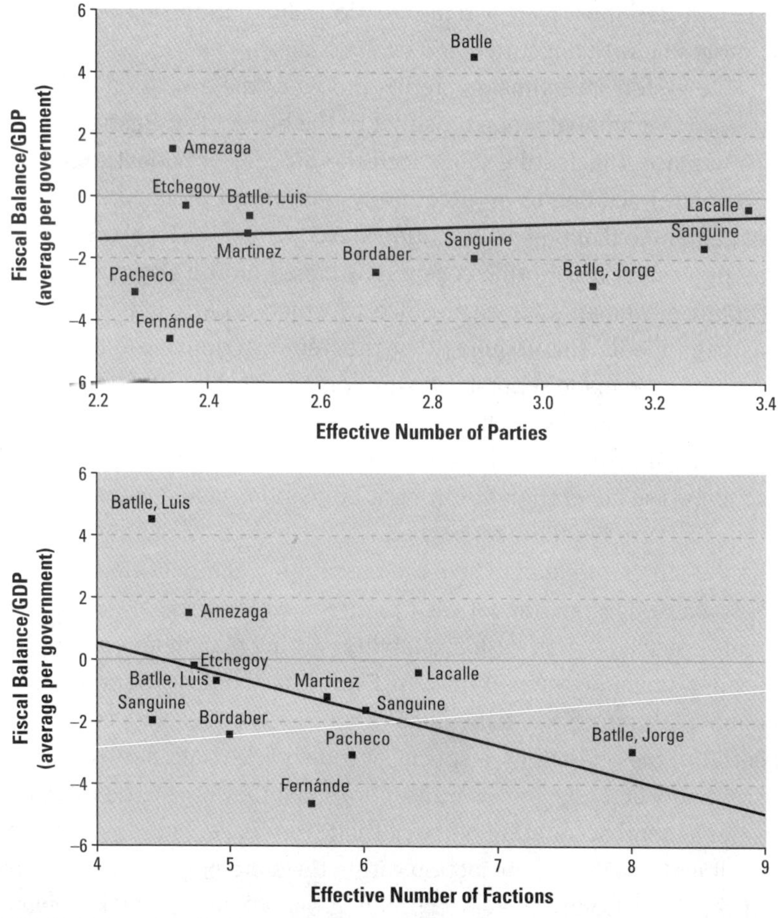

Source: Moraes, Chasquetti, and Bergara (2005).

new Integrated System of Financial Information (Sistema Integrado de Información Financiera, hereafter referred to as SIIF), every unit within each ministry is responsible for all the execution phases: the authorization of budget credits and their modifications, commitments, obligations, and payments. Before the implementation of the SIIF, public administration was characterized by several drawbacks. Since the general budget covered a five-year period, all administrative units operated with estimated credits. This system led the annual budget revisions to stimulate actual new budgets, since the constitution allowed the change of global amounts; the reallocation of investment expenditures and wages; and the creation, elimination, or modification of programs with a justified and explicit cause.

The system of estimated credits produces the execution of higher and/or lower amounts than those set by the budget law. Before the SIIF was in place, this feature influenced the process of budget execution and control, leading to an excessively centralized procedure that did not guarantee that budget execution stayed within the legal previsions. The process of monitoring is generally based on the analysis of bank account movements for each office to which a particular allocation has been made. This requires that the item discrimination of the expenditures be made separately using complex checking procedures. In general, there are no mechanisms for coordinating the pace of budget programming and control. Indeed, the cash flow administration does not allow the generation of payment obligations vis-à-vis the budget-authorized credits to be monitored.

The SIIF is intended to help the execution and monitoring process. The system uses an annual cash program, which seeks to make payments consistent with cash availability, setting maximum amounts to spend by unit and expenditure item. Every unit should elaborate its own annual plan, which has to be negotiated with the Treasury. In order to centralize the operations, a special account of the National Treasury is used. Every unit registers its transactions, but they have to be validated by the general accounting office of the MF. As a general rule, it is not possible to make any transaction within the state or government without the validation of the corresponding budget credit. The key point, however, is that cash availability depends on overall macroeconomic performance. For instance, during the economic crisis of 2002, the gap between funds allocated by law and cash availability reduced efficiency levels in most governmental programs as a result of the lack of governmental resources to execute the budget.

Figure 8.3 shows the gap between allocated expenditures made in the original budget law and overall execution for the central administration (13 ministries plus the presidency), the decentralized organisms, and the debt services for the period 2000–2004. As can be observed, the 2002 economic downturn had an impressive impact on the levels of budget execution. Also, it is important to note in the figure that in

FIGURE 8.3 Difference between Programmed and Executed Expenditures by Program: Uruguay
(constant pesos = 2003)

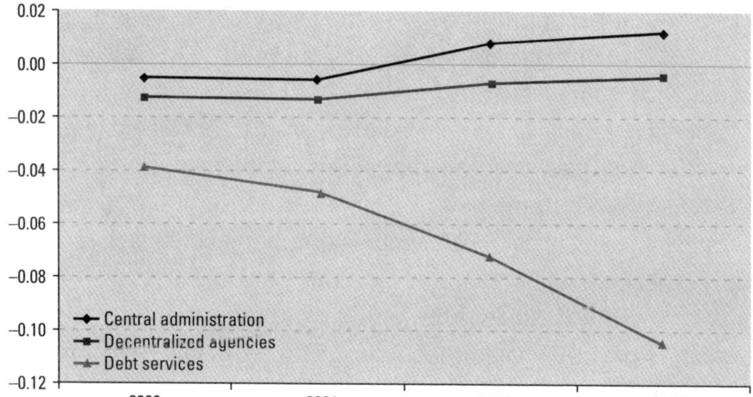

	2000	2001	2002	2003
—◆—	–0.005	–0.006	0.008	0.012
—■—	–0.013	–0.013	–0.007	–0.005
—▲—	–0.039	–0.048	–0.072	–0.105

Source: MEF/ICP (see Appendix 2 in Moraes, Chasquetti, and Bergara, 2005)

order to overcome the economic crisis of 2002, the vast majority of unallocated funds were allocated to pay for debt service.

The evidence depicted in Figure 8.3 reveals the coordination problems caused by the type of execution performed during the 2002 economic crisis. The executive's decision to avoid executing programmed expenditures creates a coordination problem between spending programs and the Treasury, which is in charge of authorizing credits. Since this office depends on the MF, most of its actions are based on tax revenues and public debt, making the budget execution dependent on the evolution of the macroeconomic financial program. Overall, the budget has been used as a mere fiscal tool, which makes it extremely difficult to evaluate how efficiently public expenditures are used.

In terms of control, the SIIF lacks the ability to develop proper auditing activities. The "delegated auditors" of the Tribunal de Cuentas monitor the units' operations, but they cannot ban the execution of expenditures, particularly in the case of subnational governments (Filgueira et al., 2002). Periodically, the Tribunal de Cuentas reports its formal and substantial observations to Parliament, but in fact legislators rarely use this information to punish irresponsible administrators.

Representativeness

As stated in Hypothesis 5, interest groups and labor unions are relevant actors only at the approval stage of the budgetary process. It is within the legislative arena that these actors can exert public pressure over parties, factions, and the executive branch. Indeed, the approval process in Parliament takes place within a participatory frame, where budget and finance committees work together, receiving interest groups and labor unions interested in the new bill. Since the legislature works with the executive proposal, cabinet members and bureaucrats systematically inform these committees about programs and related expenditures. Thus, numerous sessions are joined by core committee members, members from other committees affected by particular decisions under discussion, cabinet members, and interest group leaders (generally in the form of corporate business or labor union representatives).

In general, interest groups and labor unions are extremely important during the approval stage, largely because during the preparation process the executive sets the agenda according to its macroeconomic program and the policy preferences of the governing party or coalition of parties. Once the executive branch sets the priorities and the bill is delivered to Parliament for approval, interest groups and civil society mobilize to advance their interests or veto the executive's proposal on specific policy areas.

The fact that presidents have had to form coalitions has made this political arrangement the natural place to negotiate the content and passage of the budget bill. As previously mentioned, this process takes place at the elite level among faction leaders (generally senators and some cabinet members) who, given the features of the Uruguayan electoral system, are able to discipline most—if not all—deputies. Since 2005, the evidence shows exactly the same process under majority party. In both cases, before and after the FA took office in 2005, key negotiations for budget allocations have taken place outside the legislature, and particularly before the budget has reached Parliament.

As can be observed in Table 8.1, a 2004 survey of Uruguayan elites reveals that 50 percent of surveyed legislators perceive a weak level of legislative influence in budget design. Even those who have a positive opinion of their own jobs in terms of monitoring the executive branch have a negative perception of their ability to influence the budget

TABLE 8.1 Legislative Influence on Budget Design
(percentages)

	Occupation				
	Legislator	Executive official	Entrepreneurs	Labor unions	Total
NA	—	—	2.6	—	0.5
Not influential	6.6	—	2.6	13.2	6.0
Somewhat influential	44.3	42.1	20.5	39.5	37.5
Very influential	32.8	39.5	28.2	28.9	32.9
Extremely influential	16.4	18.4	46.2	18.4	23.1
Total	100	100	100	100	100

Source: Buquet (2004).
Note: $n = 146$.

proposal. A very similar perception is observed among labor union members, about 53 percent of whom observe a weak positioning of Uruguayan legislators during the budget design. This group has been critical of most economic policies implemented since the early 1990s and particularly of the fiscal policy contained in budget laws. Inversely, bureaucrats and business organizations have a rather positive perception of the extent to which the legislature shapes the budget bill. These two sectors and particularly business organizations have been critical of the workings of the legislature on budgetary issues, given its tendency to increase public expenditures.

Budgets, Representation, and Public Policy Reforms

The extent to which interest groups and civil society are involved in the budgetary process depends to a large extent on the contents of the budget bill delivered by the executive branch to Parliament. Since the budget has frequently been used to introduce important policy reforms, it has been an important source of political conflict and particularly a source for activating the veto power of some interest groups with important electoral connections. Indeed, since the democratic restoration in 1985, the budget bill has become a comprehensive law in regard to the kind of regulations included in it (Filgueira and Moraes, 1999). Part of the explanation for this tendency comes from the fact that parties and factions know in advance that cooperation periods are short, particularly when presidents are politically weak within and outside their parties. In this case, the budget becomes an important window of negotiations for those who are not in government, but who have votes to support the coalition or the president's party.

Since the budgetary process in Parliament is relatively open to the participation of interest groups, the fact that budgets have become mostly omnibus bills has opened channels for activating the demands of certain groups to block important policy reforms. Going forward, the extent to which the government will be successful in passing its reforms depends on how presidents link different political resources to block the pressure of some interest groups with strong electoral ties. In particular, there are four important policy reforms that have displayed the abilities of interest groups and civil society to influence the budgetary policy process in the past.

First, one of the most striking policy reforms during recent decades was introduced in 1992, within a yearly budget revision. Since President Lacalle took office in 1990, he had to face the fiscal cost of a social security reform passed in a plebiscite in December of 1989. This reform implied that all social security payments would be adjusted every four months based on past inflation rates. In this context, Lacalle attempted several times to reform the social security system in order to reduce the relative size of this sector within public expenditures. Since Lacalle failed to reform the system in two consecutive bills delivered to Congress in 1990 and 1991, he used the 1992 yearly revision to introduce a pension reform. The content of this reform was not structural, but entailed an important adjustment in the retirement age and in payments according to different income thresholds. The reform quickly activated (again) the Association of Pensioners and Retirees, which was finally able to collect the required number of signatures to have the reform revoked in 1994. The association had the support of all parties competing in the national elections, and an additional prohibition on introducing new social security reforms within budget bills and yearly revisions was included.

Second, the education reform passed within the 1995 budget bill is an example of successful linkage of political resources made by the president to obstruct the movement of unionized teachers (Filgueira and Moraes, 1999). The president was able to hold all coalition members tightly and convinced some legislators from opposition parties that the reform was technically and politically convenient. The only potential—and to some extent natural—political support for the teacher's unions was the FA Party, which was relatively divided in its support for this particular reform. The new policy was strongly promoted by its own creator, the former chair of the Economic Commission for Latin America and the Caribbean (ECLAC) in Uruguay, German Rama, and had very diffuse costs and benefits. This was a facilitating condition for defending the proposal within the electorate, given that the reform introduced an extension in public services at the primary, secondary, and technical education levels. The reform was finally passed after a strong technical and political battle by all coalition members that isolated the labor movement of teachers without consistent technical and political support. Indeed, the reform was endorsed by a majority of legislators from the opposition party in addition to all coalition members.

Third, within the same paradigmatic budget bill of 1995, the same government put forward a reform of health care in public services. The reform was also strongly promoted by its own creator, Health Minister Solari (Filgueira and Moraes, 1999). However, unlike the education reform mentioned before, this case had clear concentrated costs with diffused benefits. Who was supposed to endorse the project? The minister was unable to use the political resources provided by the coalition. Furthermore, instead of negotiating within the coalition, Solari "went public" without a clear argument determining who was supposed to win with his reform plan. Solari's reform attempted to create a set of legal instruments for improving efficiency in budget transfers to the private sector. Essentially, the reform was intended to curtail public subsidies to the private health care system, and the subsector located in the interior of the country was perceived as the most (potentially) affected by the new reform.

Uruguayan doctors are represented by one of the most powerful interest groups in the country. The strategy used by this interest group in the most affected region was very efficient for blocking the reform. Essentially, the lobby focused on deputies from the interior of the country, and given that 11 out of 19 districts elect their deputies in binominal districts, exerting pressure over this set of representatives was not a difficult task. It was enough to achieve the status quo, and these deputies finally blocked the reform. The health committee started to work with the reform delivered by the executive, and the number of changes to the proposal was large enough for the committee to be afraid of a potential executive veto, unlikely to be withdrawn. Thus, modifying the original proposal had an implicit veto threat, but withdrawing the key articles including the reform did not. This is what the health committee basically did in order to block an ambitious health care reform, in which a powerful corporation won the battle.

Finally, the budget bill approved in 2000 is a relevant example of an influential policy reform. In this case, the executive branch delivered a bill with an ambitious reform in the telecommunications sector. This policy area is almost entirely a monopoly controlled by the state. After President Lacalle's attempt to privatize the National Telecommunications Administration (Administración Nacional de Telecomunicaciones, ANTEL) in 1992, there were no serious attempts to discuss privatizations in Uruguay. Lacalle attempted to privatize public firms and particularly the telecommunications sector, but lost his battle in a plebiscite with 82 percent of the population against his plan. In the year 2000, President Batlle attempted again to reform part of this sector via the budget bill. In this case, Batlle introduced a plan to sell part of the company dedicated to cellular telephony (ANCEL) under control of ANTEL. However, the labor movement (PIT-CNT) again activated its veto power by collecting signatures to call for a new plebiscite in case the plan would be approved by Parliament. The FA immediately supported the initiative as the major opposition party, with a clear chance to win the 2004 elections. Anticipating a clear defeat at the polls, the coalition of Blancos and Colorados withdrew the articles privatizing part of ANCEL, and the plebiscite did not take place.

Overall, interest groups exert pressure at the approval stage in Parliament. Through the description of four policy reforms, this section attempts to reinforce the notion that interest groups remain important only at this stage of the budgetary process, and not within the political system as a whole and during the budget preparation stage. Indeed, Uruguayan elites generally perceive that organized groups are not very powerful actors in determining policy outputs. Their strength and veto power over public policies and the budget bill in particular depends on the policy area under consideration, the party or parties in office, and how groups are able to link their interest to a broader set of interests with an electoral connection.

CONCLUDING REMARKS

This chapter argues that the budgetary process in Uruguay determines the *sustainability*, *efficiency*, and *representativeness* of public expenditures. In order to understand why the budget process has such a powerful influence, it has been argued herein that not only institutional but also political factors are crucial to understanding public expenditures. In terms of *sustainability*, it is arguable that political factors dealing with the number of actors and the scope of political or electoral competition are a more powerful predictor of fiscal results than procedural legislation regarding the budgetary process. The timing of presidential and parliamentary elections and the effective number of factions in the party system appear to be crucial factors affecting fiscal *sustainability*.

In terms of *efficiency*, the chapter shows that budget execution is the key stage for understanding the way in which public expenditures are actually allocated. In particular, it has been demonstrated that the executive branch has low levels of internal and external control and monitoring during the execution stage. Since the budget is generally used as a mere fiscal program, the extent to which the executive executes the budget bill depends on public resources or cash availability. In this context, the economic crisis of 2002 shows how the executive prioritized fiscal outcomes regardless of the budget allocations made by Parliament in the year 2000. Given that the budget process as a whole was not based on an appropriate medium-term fiscal program, the economic crisis of 2002 caused severe problems regarding the availability of cash to finance several state programs, producing efficiency problems for state bureaucracies and citizens.

Additionally, the oversight performed by Parliament is poor, not only because Parliament does not have the institutional power and resources to perform such functions, but because coalition governments with legislative majorities have conspired with the fiscal orientation of elected presidents. The new left-wing party in office since 2005 has the double advantage of having outstanding economic performance with a medium-term fiscal program revised yearly. In this context, a possible negative shock can be prevented or buffered through efficient regulation or adjustment mechanisms rather than by simply declaring a lack of cash availability to pay the bills.

In terms of *representativeness* in the budgetary process, this chapter argues that the legislature has a weak influence during the preparation process. This stage is in the hands of the executive branch, and particularly, coalition members during the last three governments and the majority party in office since 2005. Once the bill reaches Parliament, the new budget proposal generally activates the demands of different interest groups and civil society as a whole. The power of these groups to veto the executive proposal regarding particular policies will depend on the executive's ability to hold a tight legislative majority in Congress to support the bill. However, the extent to which those groups link their preferences to a broader political or electoral context is also a factor determining their chances to succeed. Overall, most interest groups and civil society intervene during the approval process in Parliament, given that the executive branch is in charge of setting spending priorities and designing policy reforms.

Is there any trade-off between *sustainability*, *efficiency*, and *representativeness*? To a certain extent it is arguable that increases in *representativeness* can affect both *sustainability* and *efficiency*. Indeed, Uruguay is an interesting case in which to observe this trade-off, since some institutional devices like referendums and plebiscites have been widely used to veto executive proposals or advance the demands of specific groups within the electorate. In some cases, plebiscites and referendums have implied an increase in public expenditures, as in the case of the constitutional reform promoted by pensioners and retirees in 1989. In order to pay for the reform, the Lacalle administration had to implement an important fiscal adjustment with severe costs for some state programs. Thus, it is arguable that variations in the level of *representativeness* can affect the *sustainability* or *efficiency* of public expenditures.

Similarly, *efficiency* is not costless. In other words, it is unlikely that the Uruguayan state can afford certain enforcement technologies that can improve the overall level of *efficiency*. If it can, it will be a long process to assimilate performance indicators to be considered as a part of new budget allocations. Part of the efficiency problem can be observed in the number of lawsuits that the state faces every year as a result of chronic inefficiencies, ranging from the most absurd administrative problems to some complex reforms that affect individual and collective interests. Increasing levels of efficiency have a cost in terms of administrative reforms with enforcement technologies that the Uruguayan state cannot easily afford in the short run.

Finally, the newly elected government deserves a separate comment. Since March 1, 2005, the Frente Amplio has been in office and has approved its quinquennial budget, plus three yearly revisions. This party holds majority status in Parliament, but it is important to note that it has almost double the number of factions of the Blanco and Colorado parties (now in the opposition). That is, the fact that the FA Party has majority status in Parliament does not necessarily imply that it has low transaction costs within the party. Rather, the number of factions negotiating the budget has been a source of tensions within the FA every time the budget has been under consideration.

For once, the fact that a former minister of finance (Senator Danilo Astori) was only one out of five faction leaders in the cabinet implied that he had to negotiate most budget allocations with his own peers. On the other hand, budgetary policy on the whole has been subject to a fiscal program endorsed by the president's own cabinet in the year 2005, prior to the approval of the quinquennial budget in Parliament. Since then, every yearly revision and new expenditure allocation has been based on the fiscal program previously endorsed by the cabinet. In this context, President Tabaré Vázquez has been a fundamental actor supporting the policies put forward by the finance minister. Thus, an adequate fiscal policy does not necessarily require a legislative majority, but it does require a sense of responsibility and the political support of presidents with disciplined parties.

In this trend, the new government approved a new set of budgetary rules during the 2007 yearly revision (endorsed in 2008) that regulate the first steps of the negotiation process within the executive branch. This small set of rules also mandates that finance ministers approve their medium-term fiscal program in a plenary session of the cabinet before designing the budget, and certainly before the final bill is delivered to Parliament. Since this program includes the fiscal space or available amount of funds for the entire budget, the medium-term fiscal program will become the basis of the new budgetary policy of elected governments in the years to come.

REFERENCES

Aboal, D., and J. Andrés Moraes. 2003. Economía política en Uruguay: instituciones y actores políticos en el proceso económico. Montevideo, Uruguay: Trilce.

Alesina, A., R. Hausmann, R. Hommes, and E. Stein. 1996. Budget Institutions and Fiscal Performance in Latin America. NBER Working Paper No. 5586. National Bureau of Economic Research, Cambridge, MA.

Alesina, A., N. Roubini, and G. Cohen. 1997. *Political Cycles and the Macroeconomy.* Cambridge, MA: MIT Press.

Altman, D. 2002. Popular Initiatives in Uruguay: Confidence Votes on Government or Political Loyalties? *Electoral Studies* 4: 617–30.

Baldez, L., and J. Carey. 1999. Presidential Agenda Control and Spending Policy: Lessons from General Pinochet's Constitution. *American Journal of Political Science* 1: 29–55.

Bergara, M., A. Pereyra, R. Tansini, A. Garcé, D. Chasquetti, D. Buquet, and J. A. Moraes. 2006. Political Institutions, Policymaking Processes, and Policy Outcomes: The Case of Uruguay. Research Network Working Paper No. R-510. Washington, DC, Inter-American Development Bank.

Berreta, N. 2006. Government Strategic Planning Systems and Determination of Budget Priorities. Program to Implement the External Pillar of the Mid-Term Action Plan for Development Effectiveness (PRODEV). Inter-American Development Bank, Montevideo.

Borchardt, M., I. Rial, and A. Sarmiento. 1998. Sostenibilidad de la política fiscal en Uruguay. Inter-American Development Bank, Washington, DC.

Buquet, D. 2004. Encuesta Uruguaya de Elites. Study conducted for the Instituto de Ciencia Política, Universidad de la República—Facultad de Ciencias Sociales, Montevideo, Uruguay.

Buquet, D., D. Chasquetti, and J. Andrés Moraes. 1998. Fragmentación política y gobierno en Uruguay: un enfermo imaginario? Instituto de Ciencia Política, Facultad de Ciencias Sociales, Universidad de la República, Montevideo.

Chasquetti, D., and J. A. Moraes. 2000. Hipotesis para una Teoria del Ciclo Politico Uruguayo. In J. Lanzaro, ed., *La segunda transición en Uruguay.* Montevideo: Fundacion de Cultura Universitaria.

Cox, G., and M. McCubbins. 2001. Structure and Process: The Political Economy of Institutions. In S. Haggard and M. McCubbins, eds., *Presidents, Parliaments, and Policy.* Cambridge, UK: Cambridge University Press.

Cox, G. and S. Morgenstern. 2001. Latin America's Reactive Assemblies and Proactive Presidents. *Comparative Politics* 33(2): 171–90.

Filgueira, F., H. Kamil, F. Loernzo, J. A. Moraes, and A. Rius. 2002. Fiscal Discipline in Subnational Governments: The Bailout Problem in Uruguay. Research Network Working Paper No. R-459. Inter-American Development Bank, Washington, DC.

Filgueira, F., and J. A. Moraes. 1999. Political Environments, Sector Specific Configurations, and Strategic Devices: Understanding Institutional Reform in Uruguay. Latin American Research Network Working Paper No. R-351. Inter-American Development Bank, Washington, DC.

González, L. E. 1991. *Political Structures and Democracy in Uruguay.* Notre Dame, IN: University of Notre Dame Press.

Kingdon, J. 1984. *Agendas, Alternatives, and Public Policies.* Boston: Little, Brown.

Koolhas, N. 2002. Disciplina partidaria y presupuestos en Uruguay. Instituto de Ciencia Política, Facultad de Ciencias Sociales, Universidad de la República, Montevideo.

Latinobarómetro. 2007. Informe-Resumen. Corporación Latinobarometro, Santiago, Chile.

Lora, E. 2001. Structural Reforms in Latin America: What Has Been Reformed and How to Measure It. Research Department Working Paper No. 466. Inter-American Development Bank, Washington, DC.

Mainwaring, S. 1999. *Rethinking Party Systems in the Third Wave of Democratization: The Case of Brazil.* Stanford, CA: Stanford University Press.

Moraes, J. A. 2008. Why Factions? Candidate Selection and Legislative Politics in Uruguay. In P. Siavelis and S. Morgenstern, eds., *Pathways to Power: Political Recruitment and Democracy in Latin America.* University Park, PA: Penn State University Press.

Moraes, J. A., D. Chasquetti, and M. Bergara. 2005. The Political Economy of the Budgetary Process in Uruguay. Economic and Social Study Series RE1-05-009. Inter-American Development Bank, Washington, DC.

Moraes, J. A., and S. Morgenstern. 1998. Instituciones y política pública: el proceso político presupuestario en el Uruguay. In Gerardo Caetano and Romeo Pérez Antón (eds.), *Parlamento y presupuesto*. Montevideo: CLAEH/OAS.

Morgenstern, S. 2001. Organized Factions and Disorganized Parties: Electoral Incentives in Uruguay. *Party Politics* 2: 235–56.

Rial, I., and L. Vicente. 2004. Fiscal Sustainability and Vulnerability in a Small Open Economy: The Uruguayan Experience. Public Finance Workshop, Banca d'Italia, Research Department.

Shugart, M. S., and J. Carey. 1992. *Presidents and Assemblies: Constitutional Design and Electoral Dynamics*. Cambridge, UK: Cambridge University Press.

Spiller, P., and M. Tommasi. 2003. The Institutional Foundations of Public Policy: A Transactions Approach with Application to Argentina. *Journal of Law, Economics and Organization* 2: 281–306.

Tsebelis, G. 2002. *Veto Players: How Political Institutions Work*. Princeton, NJ: Princeton University Press.

Umansky, I. 2006. Planificar y presupuestar en Uruguay: los avatares de un presupuesto quinquenal. Serie de Gestión Pública, Instituto Latinoamericano y del Caribe de Planificación Económica y Social (ILPES), Santiago, Chile.

9 

Oil Wealth, the Changing Political Structure, and the Budget Process: The Case of Venezuela

José Manuel Puente, Abelardo Daza, Germán Rios, and Alesia Rodríguez

THE CONTEXT OF THE BUDGET PROCESS IN VENEZUELA

Venezuela, along with other countries in Latin America, suffered a severe fiscal contraction during the period 1974–1999. Public spending as a share of GDP fell from 35 percent in 1974 to less than 24 percent in 1999—a proportion that is equivalent to the decrease registered in the 1970s prior to the oil shock of 1973–1974. The decline in per capita terms was even more drastic, equivalent to 23 percent in the 1990s alone. In contrast, during the period 1999–2004 public spending grew significantly, reaching 34 percent of GDP in 2004, a level equivalent to the percentage registered during the oil shocks of the 1970s.

During the same period, the emergence of large fiscal deficits was notable, leading to the rapid accumulation of public debt. Venezuela's debt growth has been one of the highest in Latin America. Paradoxically, it increased significantly between two oil booms, rising from 9 percent of GDP in 1970 to more than 30 percent in 2004. Similarly, since the 1990s, debt servicing has appeared as an important component of the public budget (around 24 percent of total spending).

In addition, several measures and studies point to important problems in terms of budget outcomes. In this regard, there are doubts about the sustainability of public finances and also important issues regarding expenditure efficiency in several areas of public action. Moreover, there is evidence that fiscal policy lacks flexibility, and according to several indicators, the budget process seems to have little representativeness. Consequently, the bases of Venezuelan budgets have become encumbered with programs that are unsustainable, nonadaptable, inefficient, and inequitable/regressive, and the allocation of resources tends to reflect the preferences of interest groups.

It is also possible to observe larger changes in budget composition over time and frequent adjustments in the allocations of public expenditure in response to political and economic changes. In the first part of 1999, for example, the budget suffered seven different adjustments equivalent to 1.5 percent of GDP. At the same time, the government increased spending on salaries within the public sector, in universities, and for pensioners by the same amount, 1.5 percent of GDP.

These facts give rise to a number of questions: how is it possible to explain such variations in the level and composition of the budget across time? Are these changes associated only with variations in the main economic variables? What are the political and economic determinants of budget (re)allocations and fiscal performance? Who makes budgetary policy in Venezuela? What is the role of different actors and institutions in explaining budget outcomes?

This chapter is structured as follows: the subsequent section describes the political economy of the oil rent model and budgeting in Venezuela. The third section deals with the characterization of the budget outcomes, and the fourth section analyzes the features of political institutions, actors, and the policymaking process, with a focus on the period between 1974 and 2004. The fifth section provides an empirical assessment of the budget amendments in the approval and implementation stages and discusses the coefficients of interaction between the executive and legislative branches. Finally, some concluding remarks are presented in the last section.

THE POLITICAL ECONOMY OF THE OIL RENT MODEL AND BUDGETING IN VENEZUELA

Specialized literature often describes most of the governments of oil countries as "rentier states," since they derive a large fraction of their revenues from external rents. Venezuela is an example of this model of development par excellence. The state has been the owner and administrator of oil rent, and in the last three decades, oil has accounted for more than 80 percent of total exports, 90 percent of total foreign assets income, and 50 percent of total fiscal income. At the same time, oil has a clear political dimension. A large concentrated rent source in national income can mold a country's social and political institutions. Therefore, it is not possible to understand Venezuela's budget policy without accounting for the deep impact that oil has had in the main areas of its economy, political institutions, and society. Oil has been the single most important factor shaping budgetary policy in the country. This section leads to a greater understanding of the political economy dynamics discussed in the rest of the chapter.

According to Terry Karl (1999), actors in oil states do not behave in the same way they do elsewhere, because they simply do not have to. When oil is the key source of wealth for a state, this revenue alters the framework of decision making. Oil creates a perverse incentive structure that shapes the behavior of actors in the budget process. Oil shapes preferences, perceptions, and attitudes and provides a main explanation of why fiscal deficits, high public debts, and other disappointing budget outcomes are likely even during a boom. The exploitation of Venezuela's oil has laid the basis for a rentier state and, in general, a rent-seeking society. This rentier state has been constructed on a principle of distributing rents in which the state has maintained the citizens, and not the citizens the state.

In particular, both private sector and government have rested on the dual capacity to extract rents and distribute those internally using political criteria as a central mechanism of allocation. Politically powerful interest groups attached directly to public spending, such as political elites, bureaucrats, and public and private sector unions (e.g., Confederation of Workers of Venezuela, CTV, and the Venezuelan Federation of Chambers of Commerce, FEDECAMARAS), have systematically tended to capture the state. Consequently, governments have charged the lowest tax rates in Latin America and supported some of the continent's highest profits, wages, price controls, and subsidies.

There are two specific direct mechanisms through which oil rents can shape budget policy. The first is fiscal income: taxation. When governments derive sufficient revenues from the export of oil, they are likely to tax their populations less heavily or not at all (Ross, 2001: 332). A second mechanism by which oil rents can shape budget policy is through spending: oil wealth may lead to greater and more inefficient spending. Oil income has provided Venezuelan governments with budgets that have been exceptionally large and unconstrained despite the country's low internal fiscal income. In turn, and as a consequence of these two mechanisms, citizens lack the incentives to demand budgetary transparency and accountability from their government.

In the rentier scenario that prevailed in Venezuela, especially after the first oil boom of 1974, politicians were more electable if they promised to provide more public goods and services without asking for the raising of taxes to cover their costs. Between 1970 and 1981, public expenditure increased by more than 11 percentage points, from 16.3 percent to 27.4 percent of GDP; this was accomplished almost without increasing the tax ratio in the same period. This was possible because of the huge oil fiscal income and the large share of the expenditure that was financed through government borrowing. The citizens did not perceive the costs of increased spending in many areas or programs because "oil paid the bill." Since the state never had to compel its populations to accept taxes as regular and necessary levies on private interests to be used for public purposes, governments never created a clear separation between public and private resources, and the relation between spending and taxes was very weak. Therefore, in place of augmenting domestic productivity and internal tax income, governments sustained oil-subsidized activities whilst avoiding taxation. Thus, oil booms institutionalized a budget structure that almost inevitably led to rent-seeking behavior on the part of the state, citizens, and society in general.

The deeply ingrained belief that Venezuela was rich, as a result of many years of growing revenues and massive oil booms, undermined any efforts to demonstrate the contrary. Fiscal dependence on oil developed the notion of a wealthy state without budget limits. At the same time, oil revenues—and the extraordinarily high level of public expenditure that they facilitated—hid the institutional weakness and inefficiencies of the public administration for a considerable period. Furthermore, during the period governed by the Pact of Punto Fijo, traditional parties used budgetary resources extracted from the oil industry as a key element for modifying payoffs and sustaining political cooperation for many years. Various authors discuss this relation between political institutions, oil, and its effects on the party systems. Terry Karl (1987) argues that oil was the economic factor that allowed the country to create the modern social conditions required for the formation of a cohesive party system. This explains the continuing support for the institutional pact that solidified the democratic transition after 1958. According to this argument, without oil there would have been little chance for democracy in Venezuela at the time (Monaldi et al., 2006: 10).

After the oil shocks of the 1970s and the huge income of "petrodollars," it was a fairly simple process to distribute oil revenues through the budget among different "rent seekers" in Venezuelan society. However, as oil rent faded and society became increasingly complex, the distribution process started to collapse, either for lack of resources, or for failure to reach important parts of the population, or for the evident incapacity of the political parties to deliver. In particular, the decline of oil prices during the 1980s and the consequent drop in oil fiscal income were the origin of the rentier state fiscal crisis. This decline in oil fiscal income, sustained for more than two decades, represented the demise of the oil rent model of distribution that had been the basis of political stability for many years. Riots, attempted coups, electoral abstention, decay of the traditional political parties, and the general collapse of the political system have all been the most obvious manifestations of the decay of the model.

CHARACTERIZATION OF THE BUDGET OUTCOMES

This section presents different measures related to fiscal performance in terms of sustainability, efficiency, adaptability, and representativeness of public expenditures. It shows that several measures point to problems of sustainability of public finances and that there are important issues regarding expenditure efficiency in several areas of public action. The section also argues that fiscal policy lacks flexibility and, using several indicators, that the budget process shows little representativeness.

TABLE 9.1 Debt and Deficit Indicators, 1970–2004
(percentage of GDP)

	1970s	1980s	1990s	2000–2004
Fiscal balance[a]	–0.3	–3.8	–3.2	–3.7
Public debt, total	18.9	48.8	44.1	33.9
Public debt, internal	5.5	6.5	6.2	12.1
Public debt, external	13.4	42.3	37.9	21.8

Source: Venezuelan finance minister.
[a] Excludes capital revenues.

Sustainability

Besides having shown high volatility as a result of heavy dependency on oil revenues, fiscal policy in Venezuela has also shown signs of being unsustainable. Several studies carried out during the mid-1990s and the first part of the twenty-first century, using a wide variety of fiscal sustainability indicators, illustrated that the country's debt cannot be repaid in the future without radical changes in economic and fiscal policy. Since the 1970s, public debt has grown considerably and fiscal deficits have become chronic. For example, between 1990 and 2002, the overall fiscal balance of the Nonfinancial Consolidated Public Sector registered five surpluses and eight deficits, which ranged from 7.2 percent of GDP to –13.2 percent of GDP. In addition, total public debt went from 23 percent of GDP in 1998 to 35 percent of GDP in 2002, mainly because of an important increase in domestic debt. Table 9.1 shows fiscal deficit and public debt for the periods studied.

Efficiency

Efficiency of fiscal policy is measured as the capacity to achieve the goals established by the government in its different plans through the set of tools available (revenues, expenditures, debt, etc.). To assess the performance of the public sector, it is also important to analyze how far the authorities' actions are from the best way to deliver public goods and services in terms of costs and output. Given the array of public goods and services, herein the analysis of efficiency is carried out using specific examples in the areas of capital and social expenditures. More specifically, the cases of infrastructure and education will be presented.

Venezuela has one of the best infrastructure networks in Latin America. For example, the country fares well in the region regarding indicators such as the extension of highways and roads and the number of ports and airports per capita (CONAPRI, 2002). However, investment in infrastructure has declined considerably in recent years, and lack of maintenance has deteriorated many of the public goods and services in this area. According to CONAPRI (2002), investment in infrastructure went from a maximum of around 3.5 percent of GDP in 1977 to close to 0.5 percent of GDP in 2000. The main reasons for this have been the worsening in the economic situation since the 1980s and the perverse incentives for policymakers and legislators to cut capital expenditures rather than current expenditures in times of crisis and fiscal adjustment.

Regarding education expenditure, within the total social expenditures, those for education represent the largest share, reaching an average of around 5 percent of GDP since 2000 from a mean of about 4 percent of GDP in the 1990s. Despite high expenditures in education, a study by the World Bank (1998) shows that key indicators such as primary and secondary enrollment and dropout rates are below Latin American standards. In addition, most of the expenditures are allocated to pay wages, salaries, and administrative outlays, while there are important gaps in the provision of other inputs, such as teacher training, books, and other materials that are an integral part of a good education system.

These cases exemplify serious problems of efficiency and equity in the allocation and execution of the Venezuelan budget. Many of the issues described here can be generalized to other areas of public sector action and translate into inadequacies in budget design and implementation. Clearly, the provision of public goods and services is far from sufficient based on the goals set forth by the government and contributes little to improving living conditions of Venezuelans.

Adaptability

To measure the adaptability of the Venezuelan budget, two aspects are taken into account. First, the response of fiscal policy to economic cycles could shed light on the capacity of government to mitigate GDP contractions or expansions. In general, it is desirable that the government keep a countercyclical fiscal policy stance to ease unexpected economic shocks. Secondly, the main legal and political budget rigidities are accounted for to determine what portion of the budget the executive can freely use.

If a fiscal policy is countercyclical, then the government can save resources in periods of economic boom and use the saved funds in times of recessions. For the case of Venezuela, Rios (2003) isolates the fiscal accounts from economic cycles and changes in oil prices to obtain a structural fiscal balance. He finds that even when the main sources of shocks are suppressed from the fiscal accounts, they remain very volatile, which could be an indication of a procyclical fiscal policy. This confirms that fiscal policy in Venezuela is almost always procyclical. Other studies, such as Garcia et al. (1997) and World Bank (2002), obtain similar results.

The second aspect to consider is the share of the budget that can be assigned freely once legal requirements and current expenditures that are very difficult to cut (for political or financial reasons), such as public employees' wages and interest payments, are subtracted from the budget. For example, in the 2003 budget, legal and contractual preallocations amounted to 52 percent of the budget, and if wages and salaries for civil servants and allocations for interest payments are added, then the margin for fiscal management is even more limited.

The evidence presented here shows that the Venezuelan budget lacks adaptability when confronted with unexpected changes in economic conditions. This is because most of the time fiscal policy is procyclical and the government exacerbates shocks to economic activity. Moreover, budget expenditures required by law and difficult-to-reduce current expenditures amount to a considerable share of the total budget, which impairs the government in attempts to adjust fiscal policy when facing a changing economic environment.

Representativeness

There are several definitions of representativeness of fiscal policy that can be found in the literature. One definition refers to the extent to which the allocation of resources reflects the preference of the population at large or of organized interest groups. Another definition relates to the planning process through which public resources are allocated. Finally, it can be associated with the regional allocation of resources depending upon factors such as population, income, and poverty rates.

With respect to the first definition, in Venezuela the preferences of the population are canalized through the electoral system, although particular interest groups influence resources allocation by lobbying at the executive and legislative level. Some regional governments have implemented participative budgets, and citizens can have a say in budget matters, especially those that affect their communities. However, this practice has been rather limited. In addition, every new government is obligated to present at the beginning of its term a national plan that includes the priorities and policies that were promised during the electoral campaign. However, many times this is a conceptual exercise with little participation by civil society or organized groups. Additionally, there is no formal evaluation of the implementation of the plan.

Powerful interest groups can influence the allocation of resources for their benefit. Such is the case of universities. One important feature of education expenditure in Venezuela is its concentration on higher education. In 1999, preschool and elementary education, which accounted for 80.9 percent of all students enrolled in the education systems, received only 11.5 percent of the total budget for education. For its part, higher education accounted for only 12.6 percent of enrolled students during the same period and received as much as 40 percent of the budget (Puente, 2005). The high and growing concentration of education expenditures over the last two decades has resulted in such expenditures having a highly regressive component. This situation is very difficult to change because of powerful universities and organized interest groups.

THE BUDGET PROCESS IN VENEZUELA: INSTITUTIONAL SETTINGS AND ACTORS

Since budget policy may depend on the intricacies of decision making, it is important to comprehend the whole process of budget formation. In particular, it is important to be aware of the structure, operation, and actors involved, with a focus on the relation these actors have with each other, the formal and informal powers they possess, and how they tend to exercise them throughout the different stages of the budget process. The institutional settings through which these actors operate also have an influence as to the dynamics that underlie the whole budget process and its results.

Venezuela's economic dependency on oil has impacted the institutional setting, policymaking processes, and public policy outcomes —especially the budgetary process and its outcomes—as the budget is one of the main mechanisms through which oil revenue is distributed. Notwithstanding, changes in the economic and oil revenue conditions are not the only explanation for modifications in the different stages of the budget process, as changes in the rules of the game, functioning of the political institutions, political incentives, and constraints have also played a significant role in the trends and quality level of outcomes.

The analytical framework that adjusts to the distinctiveness of the Venezuelan case, the study period 1974–2004, is separated into three subperiods (1974–1988, 1989–1998, and 1999–2004) and is broadly characterized in Table 9.2.

First Period (1974–1988)

The institutional framework during the period 1974–1988 was embedded within the Pact of Punto Fijo and the 1961 constitution (Monaldi et al., 2006). A constitutionally weak but informally powerful president guaranteed the main party leaders veto power over major policy changes. High degrees of interparty cooperation, incentives for centralized and disciplined parties in the electoral system, presidential elections held concurrently with all legislative elections, lack of regional elected officials, and lack of expertise of legislators in the decision-making process are other traits of the fundamental institutional framework of this period.

This period comprises the last 15 years of democratic consolidation in Venezuela, and it can be typified as having an environment conducive to political cooperation, given the participation of few political actors, stable actors (repeated play), and low stakes of power. Stability was privileged over flexibility or efficiency, and a two-party cartel-like political arrangement, which had evolved since 1958 between the two major parties (AD and COPEI), became a scheme that by the end of the period 1974–1988 was exacerbated. It was common

TABLE 9.2 The Policymaking Process Setting for the Budget Process

1974–1988	1989–1999	1999–2004
• **Institutionally cooperative policymaking and budget process** • **Low number of key players**—allowed budget consultation with very limited actors • President • Leaders from the two main political parties (AD and COPEI) • Leaders from peak unions (CTV and Fedecámaras) • **Stable actors** (repeated play) • **Powerful president**—constitutionally weak but informally powerful, important power in budget process, and strong partisan powers, control over high oil rents, rights to appoint cabinet members and regional governors • **Political arrangement**—two-party cartel-type • **Party system**—highly centralized, disciplined, and nonfragmented • **Party leaders**—long tenures, with control over congressional nominations, and many were members of Congress • **High interparty cooperation** • Marginalized legislature—mainly controlled by the two main political parties	• **Decline and breakdown of cooperation**—political fragmentation • **Volatile budget process** • **Higher number of fragmented and polarized actors**—new actors: newly elected regional authorities and new political parties with significant participation in Congress • **Higher transaction costs** • **Weaker president**—loss of control over budget and governors, reduced influence in Congress, need for political coalition; oil income decline • **Party system**—decline in discipline, fragmentation • **Institutional instability** • **Stronger legislature power**—despite fragmentation and polarization	• **Weakening of cooperation**—political fragmentation, instability, partisan policymaking, and increased confrontation • **Higher transaction costs** • **Strong president**—constitutionally and informally powerful with strong concentration of powers and important role in the budget process • **Many changes in formal and informal powers** • **Weakening of institutions and accountability** • **Governance quality declined**—increased cabinet turnover • **Weakening of the legislature**—given stronger role of the president and strong discipline within the government party members

for Congress to delegate legislative authority to the president. The marginal role of the legislature and the disciplined party delegation resulted in a reduced number of actors taking part in policy consultation (only the president, national party leaders, and peak corporatist groups), which had an effect on the flow of political agreements being stamped into law.

The favorable oil scenario during part of this period made the distribution of oil revenues a key political element, influencing also the budget process. The oil booms shaped political distortions as the abundance made the executive branch more powerful and the increased stake of power triggered deviations from cooperative behavior, amplifying incentives for inefficient behavior and corruption.

The stability, coherence, and tentative building of policy capacities observed before 1974 started to decline between 1974 and 1988. Notwithstanding, a number of key areas, such as the oil industry and the central bank, still preserved relatively good-quality policymaking capacities.

From the budget process perspective, the president had broad and significant powers, which, combined with a bipartisan political agreement within a corporativist arrangement, resulted in a limited number of actors interacting throughout the different stages of the process. To maintain political cooperation, presidential power was strongly exercised in the allocation of budgetary resources, but eventually it became an unsustainable scheme. Presidents who wanted to maintain budget discipline in the 1970s and during an important part of the 1980s could achieve this goal to the extent that they could depend on extensive and disciplined support in Congress. However, these same conditions, paradoxically, helped other presidents to accelerate spending.

Second Period (1989–1998)

During the period 1989–1998, democracy in Venezuela started to unravel and cooperative agreements began to decline. The previously prevailing political arrangement fractured and led to greater political fragmentation, weaker presidential power, and stronger congressional influence in policymaking, particularly in the budget process. Transaction costs increased and budget outcomes significantly deteriorated. Thus, multiple actors (subnational actors, among many others), high electoral volatility, and institutional instability characterized this period.

Presidential power weakened, and the introduction of regional elections in 1989 activated the formal federal system that had been historically dormant and increased the number of electoral arenas and competition. The nonconcurrency between regional and presidential elections and the possibility of reelecting governors and mayors gave new regional political actors the opportunity to gain independence vis-à-vis the national authorities. Despite the modifications in the legislature system in 1993 from pure proportional representation to a mixed-member system of personalized proportional representation, the system continued to be globally proportional; incentives for political fragmentation grew; and the decline in party discipline, political instability, and weakening of cooperation were every time more evident. With varying degrees of formal and informal powers, new key actors—such as the military, civil society groups, and regional authorities—appeared in the political scenario.

The greater number of relevant policy actors led to a substantial increase in transaction costs for making informal agreements. While the overall policymaking process deteriorated, the legislature played a more significant role during this period, and with closer electoral connection of legislators to their constituents, more independent legislative groups emerged separate from consolidated political parties. Incumbent governors could shift partners more easily to ensure reelection, increasing their independence from their original parties.

The decline in presidential powers was strongly influenced by the introduction of regional elections, and it was evidenced by loss of executive control over part of the budget (given the constitutional allotment to the regions) and over the discretionary appointment and dismissal of governors. Also, the political currency of presidents was reduced by the combination of declining oil fiscal income and market-oriented reforms.

Third Period (1999–2004)

Hugo Chávez's revolution and the 1999 constitution characterized the 1999–2004 period, with a significant effect over the institutional and political landscape, which was shaped by the presence of a constitutionally powerful president, greater concentration of power, increased stakes of power, weakening of accountability, political instability, polarization, acceleration of political confrontation, partisan policymaking, and weakened political cooperation. Despite greater polarization, power was consolidated within one political party. Many formal and informal powers changed during this period, and a decline of civilian control or relevance over the military became one of the most salient features after the election of Chávez.

Congress's power in the budget process declined, and while presidential powers were strengthened and the executive branch regained its stronger role over the budget process—compared to the first period—this time the president exercised his power within a noncompetitive political context.

Governance and institutional quality declined, which was reflected in many cases by the reversal of reforms implemented during previous administrations, an increase in cabinet turnover, and a deteriorated perception of many public institutions.

During the second and third periods (1989–1998 and 1999–2004), the progressive deterioration in the quality of public policy features became evident, given the increase in volatility, incoherence, and disinvestment in many policy capacities.

The Actors and Their Roles in the Budget Process

In the case of Venezuela, there are three main global actors: the executive branch; the legislative branch; and a set of diverse informal actors, interest groups, and subnational governments.

The Executive Branch

In the broad sense, the influence of the executive branch includes the power of the president and the cabinet and of different institutions of the executive: the Ministry of Planning and Development (CORDIPLAN), the Ministry of Finance, the National Integrated Tax Administration Service (SENIAT), the Central Budget Office (OCEPRE), budget units of the public sectors offices, the Central Office of Personnel, and the Central Office of Statistics, among others. Nonetheless, in the elaboration of the budget proposal by the executive, important interactions take place between the executive and other public sector institutions, such as the Venezuelan Central Bank and public sector companies (for example, the oil company PDVSA, which plays a very influential role in the estimation of oil revenues and oil prices in the budget proposal stage).

The President and the Cabinet

In the budget process, the executive has the formal power to submit a budget proposal to Congress, which—after possibly making amendments to the proposed budget—approves it. Particular voting procedures establish who has influence on the final budget document, as well as when and how. Therefore, the proportion of seats controlled by the government party—or coalition group—was essential during the phase of increased number of effective parties in Congress (1989–2000). Until 1989, the president—though constitutionally weak—had strong power in policy matters, but a shift in the distribution of power in the legislature curtailed the president's influence, particularly over the budget process. Nonetheless, the executive branch has the formal power to put a default budget into force in the case that Congress does not approve the proposal.

As for the cabinet, besides CORDIPLAN and the Ministry of Finance—which have an active formal and informal role in the whole budget process—other ministries also have a formal role, mostly through the fact that they are required to submit the projects of their ministries that might need external funding. Also, there is the informal influence of certain ministers over the finance minister or OCEPRE's analysts, which affect the final allocation among ministries, as well as the minister's credibility within his or her ministry and among his or her colleagues, affecting his or her political stance.

After deliberations in the economic cabinet, the president in the Council of Ministries has the responsibility for approving the final budget proposal and settling any unresolved conflicts regarding expenditure allocations that could arise between individual agencies and the OCEPRE. The power of the president in the formulation stage of the budget process is also paired with the influence of key ministers, given their specific functional roles and their self-interested concerns with political survival, reappointment, or career advancement.

The constitutionally and informally stronger figure of the president after 1999, combined with an almost hegemonic Congress—represented by the government political party—has implied an almost rubber-stamped approval by the legislature of the executive budget proposal or amendments.

Main Ministries: Finance and Planning

The Ministry of Finance is one of the principal actors in the coordination of the budget process. CORDIPLAN—the planning ministry—is mainly responsible for preparing the Country Development Plan (Plan de la Nación) during the first year of a given administration. The plan describes the general guidelines embedded in the budgetary policy. Given that the necessary forecasts of macroeconomic variables and systematic strategic use of macro projections underlying the budget are the exclusive responsibility of the executive, the heads of CORDIPLAN and the Ministry of Finance team up to estimate such projections. The Ministry of Finance sets the estimates of tax revenues.

Even though the Ministry of Finance is formally the central figure in coordinating the budget process, during 2002–2003 CORDIPLAN played a more central role in the process. During this period, though the objective was to use the budget as a medium-term planning tool, the political context—based on a commanding presidential figure—altered certain dynamics between actors and made the budget more of an accounting tool with a stronger political influence. Given the political agenda, budget composition tended to be significantly influenced by the president's preferences on social programs and other spending requirements rather than by certain analytical criteria for spending efficiency, effectiveness, and sustainability. In this case ministers would go directly to the president to request additional funds rather than go through the Ministry of Finance and CORDIPLAN.

The Legislative Branch

All the legislative action on the proposed budget starts with the Finance Committee. The president and members of this committee are powerful actors who may have the greatest influence in shaping the final budget. Although other committees may have a say in budget issues regarding their particular topics, usually they do not get involved directly in the budget discussion. In general the Finance Committee takes budgetary decisions without consulting thematic committees, which means that one of the biggest political negotiations carried out among parties once a new Congress is elected is the choice of president and other members of this committee.

Congress has the power to change priorities and add or cut public works, but it cannot alter overall spending levels. Also, legislators can object to revenue estimates and macroeconomic forecasts and request that the executive review or adjust them. This pattern was more common during periods when Congress had a stronger stance. Supplementary budgets may be enacted by the legislative, and given that these tend to be less carefully scrutinized during legislative debates, they are a channel for excessive expenditure and budget indiscipline.

During the period 1974–1988, the government party had a majority in Congress and also led the presidency of the Finance Committee. Such control, paired with strong party discipline, evidenced a period of weak legislative power. Prior to the decentralization process in 1989, the Senate had no significant veto power in policymaking, but even after 1989, the power of the Senate was still very weak. In the budget process, the Senate would usually ratify—after any necessary debate—the lower chamber's approval of the budget.

From 1989 until 1999, the role of the legislature was strengthened over the budget process and spending composition, due in part to the weaker link between the government political party with majority in Congress, and over the Finance Committee. After the 1999 constitution was adopted, the change from a bicameral to a unicameral legislature and the almost hegemonic control of the government party in Congress and in the Finance Committee changed the dynamics. Inter- and intrapolitical party collaborations varied with a weakening of cooperation among political parties, but there was greater intraparty cooperative behavior within the government party.

Interest Groups

Many interest groups looking to protect their "rent" in the budget allocation have diverse degrees of power over the composition of expenditure levels, which significantly affects the inertia and rigidities present in the budget allocations. Informal actors, such as government employees and others perceiving benefits from the budget, exert pressure politically for large increases or to avoid reductions of resource allocation, adding steam to any political tension or unresolved conflicts at the different stages of the budget process.

There are strong lobby groups in the legislature and they mostly operate through three large groups: the unions, the political groups with general influence and enough electoral weight, and political authorities, especially in AD (Democratic Action Party) and COPEI (the Social Christian Party) during the first two periods analyzed and later on in the MVR. The use of "additional credit" is often due to pressures of diverse interest groups for application of extra funds to activities that might have been curtailed in certain areas during the budget proposal and approval stages.

The Subnational Governments

The shift from a scheme based on governors "appointed" and freely removed by the president (1958 to 1989) to a scheme of "elected" officials (since 1989) increased the significance of subnational governments and reduced their stigmatization as agents of the central government. The introduction of direct elections for governors had a profound and unintended effect on the Venezuelan party system, as it diminished the power of national party leaders of the two traditional political parties—AD and COPEI. Part of the increased power of these officials—gained by elected governors over time—is that they have become leading contestants for presidential elections.

The influence of subnational governments in Congress, particularly through the Senate, is enhanced where districts for elections of senators and governors are the same—as was the case in Venezuela until 1989. Nonetheless, as expressed in Monaldi et al. (2006), the 1999 constitution changed the institutional framework that could promote such connections, as it changed the legislature from bicameral to unicameral and limited the possible concurrency of elections.[1]

[1] As presidents have a six-year term, congressmen a five-year term, and governors a four-year term.

BUDGET AMENDMENTS IN THE APPROVAL AND IMPLEMENTATION STAGE: AN EMPIRICAL ASSESSMENT

This section quantifies the executive's proposed budget and the final budget allocated and executed by the government during the period between 1973 and 2004. Particular attention is paid to changes in specific years, programs, and areas of the budget. Such analyses serve to present additional empirical evidence about the pattern of interaction between the main actors in the budget process. In particular, the aggregate differences between executive budget proposals and the final legislation approved and executed illustrate four important points: first, Congress, even without altering the overall spending levels, has altered the composition of spending proposed by the executive in the approval stage of the budget. Next, consistent with the analysis conducted in this chapter, the empirical evidence presented serves to identify two different patterns of congressional activity between 1973 and 2004: two periods (1973–1985 and 1999–2004) characterized by a relatively low level of congressional involvement in the budget process and a third characterized by a high level of involvement (1986–1998). Third, the high number and level of supplementary budgets have contributed to the erosion of budgetary discipline and congressional fiscal controls regarding and have also increased spending. Finally, these differences show evidence regarding the power of specific interest groups in the executive-Congress budget process.

The Approval of the Executive Budget Law in Congress

This phase, consisting of the passage of the executive budget law through Congress up to its final approval, calls for three crucial observations. First, can the scope of the amendments, for example, increase spending and/or reduce revenues? Second, and more generally, what is the strategic relation between the executive and Congress at this stage? Third, how important is the influence of different interest groups on the budget approval process?

In particular, this section measures and explains the percentage of deviation between aggregate spending proposed by the executive and that approved by Congress. The absolute value of the difference between the president's budget request and the congressional appropriations (calculated as a percentage of the executive request) is one measure of the distribution of congressional activity. The average annual absolute difference between the president's request and Congress's allocations supplies a useful summary index of congressional activity for the period under consideration. If Congress has made no changes in a particular budget category or public office in the 31-year period, the index of activity will be equal to zero. Large or frequent congressional changes (increases or decreases) in the executive's requests will yield larger values for the index (Kanter, 1972: 133). In particular, three measures of congressional activity are employed: firstly, the increase or reductions in the executive's overall budget; secondly, the presence or absence of changes in the president's budget by office; and thirdly, the average frequency of congressional changes in the different budget items by year. As will be shown, the three measures indicate that congressional activity has been concentrated in particular budget categories and years.

In terms of the period of focus in this section, 1973–2004, the aggregate spending level of the budget law was on average –1.3 percent of the initial executive proposal for the period 1973 to 1985, 5.8 percent for the period 1986 to 1998, and –0.55 percent for the period 1999 to 2004. The average percentage of variation of the aggregate spending level across the whole period was 2.3 percent. From 1973 to 1985, almost all the changes that Congress made in the budget were reductions, whereas in the rest of the period the majority of changes were increases in the total budget request. Since 1985, the tendency to increase the initial proposal has been higher. For example, in 1986 and 1987, in the Jaime Lusinchi government, the final budget entailed increases of 13.8 percent and 22.4 percent, respectively. In more recent years (1993, 1996, 1997, 2002, 2003, and 2004), the aggregate spending figures for proposals and the final budget were identical.

The fact that overall spending increased or decreased in some cases would appear to contradict Article 229 of the Venezuelan constitution regarding the prohibition of congressional amendments to total spending. As has been explained above, the Venezuelan legal framework allowed the composition of the expenditure or revenue plans to be changed but not the global total. Thus an important question is, where did the appropriations increases come from, given that Congress was prohibited from initiating them?

At least two factors were at play in the executive budget increases and decreases during the period of focus, one having to do with budget estimates within the executive and the other with interoffice bargaining. First, Article 229 clearly establishes that the executive unilaterally determines revenue estimates and that only these figures can be used in budgeting. However, legislators can object to the revenue income, because this is usually overestimated. In consequence, in some years legislators requested that the executive update its revenue and spending estimates, by adjusting its proposed bill and even sponsoring some amendments designed to serve the legislators' interest during that time. Similarly, according to Article 22 of the Organic Budget Law, the executive budget proposal was originally submitted in the second half of June. However, in some cases during the weeks following this deadline, as fourth-quarter tax receipts and economic projections took shape, the executive itself inevitably wanted to make changes to fine tune its budget projections. The systematic bias in the economic and fiscal forecast of the Venezuelan governments increased the necessity for congressional changes in the executive budget request. Therefore, under these circumstances, it is clearly unrealistic to attribute responsibility to Congress for all alterations in presidential spending on request.

After the submission of the proposal to Congress, legislators began lobbying for increases as well as enlisting executive officials to sponsor the necessary amendments, because no legislator could initiate such changes without executive sponsorship. The ministers and other executive officials who testified before the Finance Committee were also very influential. Congress could increase or decrease total spending only with executive approval. This was one of the phases of the process in which political negotiations between the Finance Committee, parties, and the executive occurred. Legislators made suggestions and proposals and the executive proposed them itself, because Congress could not make changes in the level of total spending. This congressional influence is an additional factor that explains how the final budget bills can appropriate more money than proposals, despite the formal restrictions on congressional amendments.

Changes in Budget Composition during the Congressional Approval Phase

Given the unequal prerogatives between the branches of government and data measuring the legislative balance of power between the executive and Congress, there is a strong temptation simply to conclude that Congress was insignificant in the legislative process between 1973 and 2004, as much literature on Latin American legislatures has suggested. In particular, the conventional wisdom that holds that the Venezuelan Congress has been unwilling to address the budget in policy terms could be a consequence of analyses based on highly aggregated data. An exploration of changes in the budget law by individual office or aggregate changes in a year suggests that the legislature has had more impact in some areas than in others and, more importantly, that congressional budget activity has been concerned with more than increasing or reducing the total level of expenditure.

A measure that is able to distinguish budget categories by year or public office in which there were small or infrequent—or large or frequent—changes in the president's budget can obtain a more complete picture. This suggests that the legislature is more influential than a concrete reading of the Venezuelan constitution, the Organic Budget Law, or the internal laws of Congress would suggest. Therefore, Congress has had a more substantial impact on the budget process in Venezuela than many readers might think, as a result both of the relatively nonconflictive treatment of the budget in Congress and of the legal and constitutional rules portraying Venezuelan governments as extremely executive-dominated. To the contrary, this section provides additional evidence of congressional influence on the budget process during the period 1973–2004.

Table 9.3 shows the average change in budget law for a sample of public agencies and offices as a percentage of the initial executive proposal submitted to the Congress every year during this period.[2] Some public offices systematically increased their allocation in the budgetary process in Congress. For example, the National Electoral Council was the component with the highest average variation. This budget increased from 1977 to 1998 by an average of 39.9 percent. However, it is important to mention that this average was associated fundamentally with periods immediately prior to electoral years. Equally, the presidency office increased its proposals in almost every year, and over the period the average increase was 17.6 percent. The resources allocated to this

[2] For a more detailed analysis see Puente et al. (2007).

TABLE 9.3 Congressional Changes in Executive's Initial Budget Proposal by Public Office, 1973–2004

(average for the period, as a percentage of total budget proposal)

Public office	1973–2004	1973–1998	1999–2004
National Electoral Council (1977–2004)	29.60	39.91	–8.21
Ministry of Industry (1977–2004)	14.65	21.83	–11.67
Presidency (1978–2004)	15.64	17.61	8.73
Congress (1977–2004)	14.14	16.91	3.96
Ministry of the Environment (1978–2004)	10.44	14.90	–5.16
Ministry of Transport and Communications (1978–2004)	14.13	13.34	16.88
Supreme Council of Justice	7.70	9.31	0.73
Ministry of Urban Development (1978–1999)	7.60	8.37	8.01
Ministry of Agriculture (1973–1999, 2003–2004)	6.01	7.79	–9.38
Public Prosecutor	6.27	7.46	1.11
National Comptroller	4.81	6.86	–4.07
Ministry of Family (1973–1999)	7.21	6.86	16.31
Ministry of Justice (1973–1999)	6.54	6.69	2.57
Ministry of Defense	5.12	6.13	0.72
Judiciary Council (1977–2000)	5.13	6.05	–5.02

Source: Authors' calculation based on national budget data from 1973–2004.

ministry had the particularity that they were available and were used to a high degree at the executive's discretion.

As has already been explained in the analysis of interest groups, in the 1970s and the first part of the 1980s the Venezuelan state grew rapidly to comprise approximately four hundred entities in the decentralized public administration. The independent legal status of the offices of this administration gave them substantial degrees of autonomy with respect to income and expenditure (Crisp, Levine, and Rey, 1995: 154).

Likewise, an important proportion of the external debt was owed or guaranteed by the public sector, including those offices of the decentralized public administration that lacked adequate control and oversight mechanisms. The lack of control mechanisms on the part of either the executive or Congress meant that many state agencies were left free to incur external debt on their own initiative. When attempts were made to institute needed controls, decentralized offices began to borrow from public financial institutions, which, in turn, increased their own overseas borrowing (McCoy and Smith, 1995: 271). Thus, as a consequence of huge amounts of borrowing, the budget allocations to the decentralized public administration in the 1970s and part of the 1980s were even larger.

Not surprisingly, Congress itself also increased its budget by more than 16.9 percent during the period studied. Other offices that systematically increased their share of the total budget in the congressional budget approval were the Ministry of Transport and Communications, the Ministry of the Environment, the Ministry of Agriculture, and the Ministry of Defense.

This distribution of changes made by various public offices in the executive budget during the congressional approval phase is consistent with the hypothesis that, during the period of study, Congress as a whole had a programmatic as well as a fiscal orientation towards particular areas of the budget: namely, its judgments regarding specific programs and their relation to legislature and party interests, rather than an exclusive concern with reducing spending, eliminating waste, or preserving budget discipline. For Congress, and in particular for the members of the Finance Committee, budgeting was their purpose and one of their powers.

Moreover, with the exception of 1983, 1996, and 1998 (the years of the COPEI and the Convergencia parties), the executive branch achieved the passage of the budget in the constitutionally mandated period. In doing so, the executive had to take into account the wishes of Congress in the approval stage of the budget to a much greater extent than had been the case in those years in which it had employed the previous year's budget (*presupuesto reconducido*). This factor generated a further incentive to make agreements that benefited the constituencies or interest groups close to legislators. Members of Congress, like spending ministers, could propose such amendments, but failed to internalize the budget costs associated with these measures.

Thus, the cross-sectional variations in congressional activity support the view that congressional average increases in the president's budget were concentrated in a group of public offices and ministries. One may conclude from these results that congressional activity and, inferentially, congressional interest was concentrated on those sectors. Certain budget categories appeared to attract more congressional interest than others.

Patterns of Congressional Activity: Some Explanations

The interaction between the executive and Congress is very important in terms of budget allocations because both political authorities have to approve budgetary decisions. The question arises as to what happens when the two authorities have arrived at different decisions. According to the data, especially between 1986 and 1998, there was no clear consensus between the executive and the legislative on how to address the problem. As can be seen in Figure 9.1, congressional activity was relatively high between 1986 and 1998, while during the periods between 1973 and 1985 and 1999 and 2004 there were somewhat fewer or smaller changes made by Congress, which is evidence of the fact that Congress accepted and ratified the budget decisions of the executive.

Interesting also is the aspect that, in those periods, the budget approved by Congress was lower in some years compared with the executive request. From 1973 to 1985, Congress's allocation varied from the presidential request by an average of less than 5 percent per year. From 1986 to 1998, three annual appropriations involved changes of less than 5 percent, six more than 26 percent, and one (1986) more than 36

FIGURE 9.1 **Average Congressional Changes in President's Budget Requests by Year, 1973–2004**
(in absolute terms)

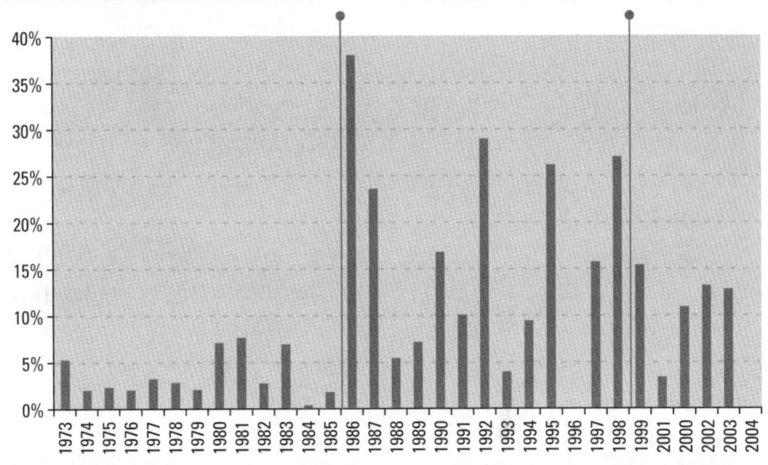

Source: Authors' calculations based on national budget data from 1973–2004.
Note: The average is calculated using the absolute value.

percent. When compared to the average changes per year in the previous period and the period that followed, congressional alterations or redistributions in the president's budget request were large between 1986 and 1998. Consequently, and consistent with the analysis made above, it is possible to identify three different patterns of congressional activity between 1973 and 2004 (Figure 9.1): two periods are characterized by a relatively low level of congressional involvement in the budget process (1973–1985 and 1999–2004), and the other by a high level of involvement (1986–1998).

Consequently, the above aggregate figures, especially from 1986 to 1998, somewhat understate the extent to which executive proposals were amended. In contrast to the vision of an insulated executive power, the data on congressional activity show that, on average, Congress modified more than 20 percent of the legislative initiatives of the executive (amendments to the presidential budget). In various ways the budget was formulated to contain "something for everyone" to ensure passage through Congress and benefit sectors of interest for the legislator (Drazen, 2000: 706).

At least two forms of bargaining were used by the Venezuelan Congress to build majority coalitions to make decisions about budget allocations and, in consequence, to bring about redistribution of resources across programs, public offices, and areas: logrolling and compromise. Logrolling was an exchange of voting support on different budgets by different members of Congress. It was an effective means of coalition building because members were rarely equally concerned about all public-spending distributional decisions. Second, compromise, unlike logrolling, built coalitions through negotiation over the content of legislation. Each party agreed to modify policy goals on a given bill in a way that was generally acceptable to the other. A middle ground was often found.

Explanations for the dramatic change in congressional activity observed may be divided into two general classes: firstly, considerations of domestic politics are reflected in presidential and congressional budget processes; secondly, the variations in budgetary activism may also reflect Congress's changing assessment of the executive's handling of economic policy.

As has been shown, the dramatic increase in congressional activity occurred in the period of Jaime Lusinchi and then continued through successive periods under the administration of Carlos Andrés Pérez, the transitional government of Ramón J. Velazquez, and the presidency of Rafael Caldera. There was a high level of congressional activity in this period (1986–1998), which in many cases took the form of important increases in the executive budget. These budget changes in this period may be seen as a response to the changing perceptions of domestic political conditions. In particular, two political factors are important in explaining the change in pattern: firstly, the increase in party fragmentation, and secondly, the visible decay of tight party discipline.

In the 1980s and 1990s, the major parties AD and COPEI and the organizations that represented specific interests, such as FEDECAMARAS in the business sector and CTV for unions, started to lose their capacity to aggregate, channel, and manage the demands and interests of the sectors they supposedly represented. Moreover, trust in these institutions deteriorated, and within each of them internal discipline declined, leading members to question the leadership and reducing the margins for action and representativeness. This increased the number and differences among the actors involved, fractionalized the sectoral leadership, and generated more complex, costly, and less predictable patterns of negotiation (Kornblith and Levine, 1995: 93). Power began to be fragmented, resulting in a systematic incapacity to form viable governing alliances. Party discipline and party-government coherency decayed, with serious implications for the ability of either the executive or Congress to act effectively and with reasonable dispatch in public policy and particularly in budgetary policy.

In particular, party fragmentation rose very significantly at the end of the 1980s. The Venezuelan political system became more atomized, with more parties represented in Congress; this fragmentation was an important factor in explaining the increase in congressional activity in Venezuela. Conventional wisdom argues that the lower the number of parties (e.g., the larger the government's majority party in Congress), the lower the transaction cost of redistributing and allocating budgetary resources for the president. The hypothesis comes from extensive literature claiming that party fragmentation in the legislature tends to be inversely associated with the size of the president's party (Jones, 1995; Mainwaring and Scully, 1995; Mainwaring and Shugart, 1997; Linz and Valenzuela, 1994). Thus, a president with a smaller party contingent or facing many legislative parties would have to compromise and distribute patronage and pork barrel among the opposition in order to gather a legislative majority willing to pass his budget proposal.

Equally, party discipline has been proposed as an important factor contributing to a president's legislative success: in this case, the proportion of a president's budget that wins approval in Congress without amendments. The Venezuelan democracy—before the dramatic erosion of its parties at the end of the 1980s—was a system with strong party discipline, whereas the period of low levels of congressional activity between the 1970s and most of the 1980s was still characterized by oppositions and critiques and counterproposals. However, the winning factors of an AD and COPEI majority and relatively strong party discipline ensured that the deals made between the executive branch and Congress were—for the most part—respected, and the number of amendments of the budget very low. It would therefore be a mistake to infer from the relatively smooth passage of the president's budget in Congress that the budget was totally executive-dominated during that period. Rather, the absence of conflict is explained in particular by two factors: first, a relatively disciplined AD and COPEI legislative majority that allowed for bargaining over the budget to be conducted in an intraparty and less public setting; and second, the fact that most serious negotiation over the budget between legislators and the executive branch normally took place prior to the formal submission of the budget to Congress.

In conclusion, the potential for governability in Venezuela was poor at the end of the 1980s. Compared to its highly governable nature in the past, society was more polarized and Congress was fragmented and divided. The period between 1989 and 1998 was generally characterized by the decline and eventual breakdown of cooperation and a volatile budget process. At this time, there were also more fragmented and polarized actors in the policymaking process and, in general, higher transaction costs (Monaldi et al., 2006). Venezuela suffered the initiation of a period characterized by weaker presidents, a decline in party discipline, increasing levels of party fragmentation, and electoral abstention. Consequently, it was a period characterized by weak presidential control over the budget process, which led to confrontation between the executive and Congress over economic policy and, in particular, over budget policy.

In contrast, an institutionalized cooperative budget process with a low number of key players generally characterized the period from 1973 to 1988.[3] This allowed the presidents during these years to conduct budget policy consultation with a very limited number of actors. It was, in general, a period of a highly centralized, disciplined, and nonfragmented party system (closed list, no regional elections, etc.); a low level of abstention; a marginalized legislature; and a controlled delegation to a predominant president with control over regional governors. The result was the development of an executive branch with important powers in the budget process.

Budget Amendments in the Implementation Stage

The formulation of the budget in the executive and its approval in the legislature together comprise only one part of the budget process. If one defines budgeting in the broader sense as the allocation of the resources available to the government, it is evident that several other decision-making processes must also be taken into account. These include supplementary budgets, rescissions of unspent funding (*insubsistencias*), transference of resources between budget chapters, and other budget amendments during the implementation stage of the budget. In particular, supplementary budgets represent an additional point of budgetary interaction among the actors involved, and patterns in the use of those appropriations may be related to regular appropriations. In consequence, they may illuminate the budgetary bargaining between the executive and Congress and the influence of different interest groups. This subsection presents additional empirical evidence about this implementation phase of the budget.

In the Venezuelan case, modifications to the budget during the implementation stage can be made only on the initiative of the executive, and only Congress can approve them. In consequence, supplementary budgets have been in the first instance an executive initiative; however, during the initiation, approval, and execution of these budgets, in one way or another, the two main actors (executive and Congress) in the budget process have been involved.

---

[3] However, as was shown above, in strict budget terms it has been possible to verify a different pattern of congressional activity since 1986.

However, the main questions that arise in this subsection are, between 1973 and 2004, what was the percentage deviation between allocated and actual aggregate spending in the annual Venezuelan budget process, and what was the total amount actually spent at the end of the budgetary year?

Figure 9.2 provides data that describe the difference between budget law and the "agreed + modifications budget" (including supplementary budgets and other budget amendments) between 1973 and 2004. The first observation to be made is that, with a few exceptions, the Budget Office has underestimated the final budget. The second is that the errors, particularly in years of oil booms, have been very high. The flows of amendments, especially supplementary budgets, appear to follow the level of oil prices, increasing during oil booms and dropping thereafter. It has proven more difficult to reduce supplementary budgets in years in which revenue has been strong as a consequence of a typical boom in oil prices (e.g., 1974, 1980, 1984, 1989, 1996, and 2004). In many cases, the Venezuelan experience has shown that high oil prices are the perfect excuse to increase public expenditure through supplementary budgets.

As a consequence of the oil boom and a testament to lack of planning, these supplementary budgets reached an astonishing 192 percent in 1974 and averaged 30 percent of the initial budgets during the next four years. Once President Carlos Andrés Pérez had permitted the 1974 budget to triple, there was no turning back. In the 1970s, spending expanded throughout the bureaucracy, initial government goals and plans were deemed too modest, and public offices were actually asked to revise their budgets upward so that the government could spend more money more quickly. As a consequence, public offices increasingly relied on supplementary budgets, which had the additional advantage of being partially removed from congressional scrutiny.

This pattern did not change when presidential power shifted from AD to COPEI, despite President Herrera's pledge not to repeat the mistakes of the past during his term between 1978 and 1983. During the second oil boom, between 1979 and 1981, actual spending was on average more than 25 percent of the original budget approved at the beginning of the year. In 1989, during the second Carlos Andrés Pérez government, supplementary budgets represented a whopping 74 percent of the initial budget and more than 9 percent of GDP (Figure 9.2). This

FIGURE 9.2 **Difference between Budget Law and "Agreed + Modifications Budget," 1973–2004**
(percentage change)

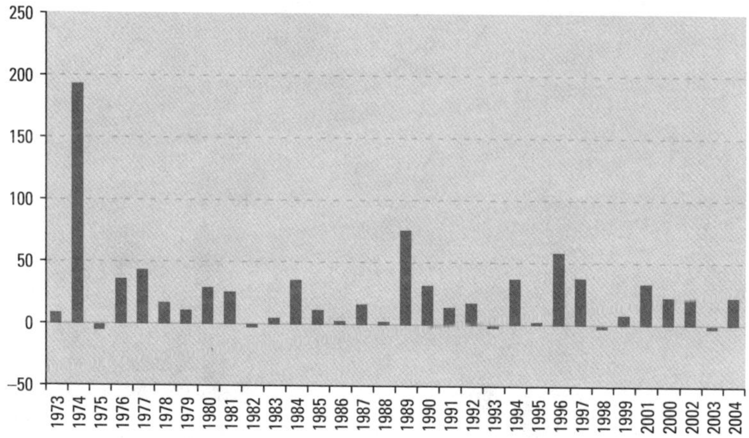

Source: Authors' calculations based on national budget data from 1973–2004.
Note: "Agreed + modifications budget"/budget law.

implies that the final budget had almost doubled as a consequence of multiple supplementary budgets. From these data it is evident that Congress routinely approved executive requests for supplementary budgets. It can be inferred from this simple relationship that Congress found it politically difficult or inconvenient not to approve an executive request, whether or not it was made on an emergency basis.

In summary, the total spending level as a consequence of supplementary budgets was on average 29.3 percent higher than the budget law throughout the period 1973 to 2004, and in all the years the budget increased as a consequence of the supplementary budgets that Congress approved. Therefore, a review of budget patterns in Venezuela indicates that actual spending was largely at variance with budget priorities established in the original budget law approved at the beginning of every year, contributing substantially to the fragmentation of the budgetary process and the weakening of spending control.

Executive and Legislative Interaction Coefficients

Additional evidence about the patterns of the executive and legislative interaction in the budget process can be shown. Following the methodology of Chapter 2, this subsection estimates the relative magnitude of changes in spending composition introduced in different stages of the budget process. The following coefficients were calculated:

$$\text{Stage 1: } C_{BL} = \frac{\sum_{i=1}^{N} |B_i - L_i|}{2}, \text{ for each year;}$$

$$\text{Stage 2: } C_{LV} = \frac{\sum_{i=1}^{N} |L_i - V_i|}{2}, \text{ for each year;}$$

$$\text{Stage 3: } C_{VD} = \frac{\sum_{i=1}^{N} |V_i - D_i|}{2}, \text{ for each year;}$$

where:

B_i is the participation of item *i* in total spending presented in the executive budget proposal;

L_i is the participation of item *i* in total spending approved in the budget law;

V_i is the participation of item *i* in the total of effective credit;

D_i is the participation of item *i* in the total of executed expenditure.

The coefficients C_{BL} and C_{LV} represent the yearly changes in the composition of spending in the approval and execution phases, respectively. C_{VD} on the other hand is a crude indicator of budget efficiency, since it measures the extent to which planned expenditures are actually executed.

The results for the coefficients are presented in Figure 9.3. Only in four years (1984, 1986, 1991, and 1997) did Congress play a more important role than the executive in defining budget outcomes. This is once again consistent with the argument that the executive branch is the leading actor in the budget process; however, budget allocations and particularly budget reallocations are also the product of legislators' power.

As shown above, important negotiations do go on in Congress, even if most of the action occurs at the executive level. Ministers, public managers, and interest groups who failed to include their budget needs in the planning phase in many cases influence reallocations in the approval and implementation phase of the budget. Furthermore,

FIGURE 9.3 **Coefficients 1 (Approval Stage) and 2 (Execution Stage)**

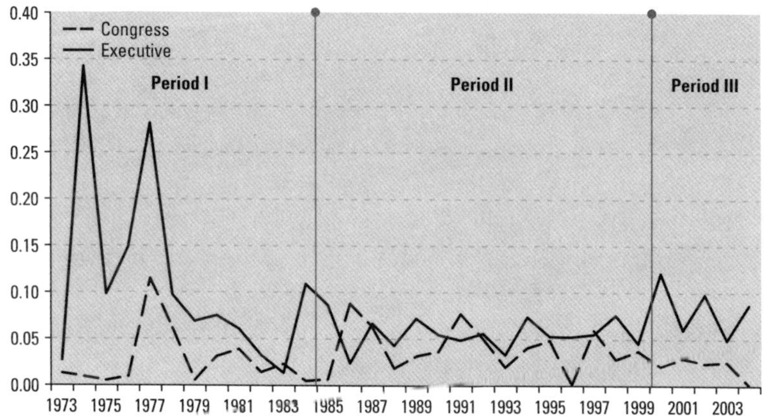

Source: Authors' calculations.

legislators attempt to increase pork for their districts and groups or sectors of interest.

Equally, consistent with the analysis already offered in this chapter, the coefficients presented serve to identify two different patterns of congressional activity between 1973 and 2004: two periods (1973–1983 and 1999–2004) were characterized by a relatively low level of congressional involvement and a clear power of the executive in the budget process. A third period (1984–1998) was characterized by a high level of congressional involvement with a more balanced sharing of power between the two main actors, including four years in which Congress even played a more important role than the executive in defining budget outcomes.[4]

CONCLUSIONS

The main conclusions of this chapter are as follows: firstly, from the general policymaking as well as budget-making perspective, three dis-

[4] For additional econometric evidence about how the relative strength of the executive and Congress, with some other factors controlled for, affects fiscal performance, see Puente et al. (2007).

tinctive subperiods within the years 1974 and 2004 have been identified using both a qualitative and a quantitative approach, displaying the following main characteristics:

- First period (1974–1988): strong presidential power within a cooperative system strongly influenced by a corporative arrangement in a political context of limited competition.
- Second period (1989–1998): weakened presidential power and stronger Congress within a noncooperative system and a fragmented political context.
- Third period (1999–2004): constitutional and informally powerful president with no political competition.

Secondly, in general the executive branch has been the leading actor in the budget process. The executive has a number of bargaining advantages over Congress during the process. However, budget allocations have also been the product of legislators' pursuit of (re)election and power, as well as of the demands of interest groups.

In particular, Congress has altered the overall composition of spending proposed by the executive in the approval stage of the budget. Cross-sectional variations in congressional activity support the view that legislature increases in the executive's budget were concentrated in a group of public offices and ministries. One may conclude from these results that congressional activity and, inferentially, congressional interest was concentrated in those sectors.

Likewise, the high number and level of supplementary budgets approved between 1973 and 2004 have been an important source of fiscal indiscipline and a source of power of specific interest groups in the executive-Congress budget decision process. In particular, the evidence indicates that supplemental funds have been routinely used as instruments to maintain the budgetary status quo and preserve the budget allocations of some important groups in Venezuelan society, as well as to compensate those sectors for low levels of funding in the approval stage process. Therefore, a review of budget patterns indicates that actual spending was largely at variance with budget priorities established in the original budget law approved at the beginning of every year of the period studied, contributing substantially to the fragmentation of the budgetary process and the weakening of spending control and fiscal discipline.

Thirdly, as has been shown by the political economy literature, political institutions affect the "rules of the game" under which different actors interact by placing constraints on the whole budgetary process and distributing power and responsibilities among different actors.

REFERENCES

CONAPRI (Venezuelan Council for Investment Promotion). 2002. El Costo Venezuela: Opciones de política para mejorar la competitividad. CONAPRI, Caracas.

Crisp, B., D. Levine, and J. Rey. 1995. The Legitimacy Problem. In J. McCoy et al., eds., *Venezuelan Democracy under Stress*. Edison, NJ: Transaction Publishers.

Drazen, A. 2000. *Political Economy in Macroeconomics*. Princeton: Princeton University Press.

García, G., R. Rodríguez, L. Marcano, R. Penfold, and G. Sánchez. 1997. La sostenibilidad de la política fiscal en Venezuela. Working Paper Series No. R-317. Research Department, Inter-American Development Bank, Washington, DC.

Jones, M. 1995. *Electoral Laws and the Survival of Presidential Democracies*. Notre Dame, IN: University of Notre Dame Press.

Kanter, A. 1972. Congress and the Defense Budget: 1960–1970. *The American Political Science Review* 66(1).

Karl, T. L. 1987. Petroleum and Political Pacts: The Transition to Democracy in Venezuela. *Latin American Research Review* 22(1): 63–94.

———. 1999. The Perils of Petroleum: Reflections on the Paradox of Plenty. In *Fueling the 21st Century: The New Political Economy of Energy*, special edition of *Journal of International Affairs*, 53(1) Fall.

Kornblith, M., and D. Levine. 1995. Venezuela: The Life and Times of the Party System. In S. Mainwaring and T. Scully, eds., *Building Democratic Institutions*. Stanford, CA: Stanford University Press.

Linz, J., and A. Valenzuela. 1994. *The Failiure of Presidential Democracy in Comparative Perspective*. Baltimore: Johns Hopkins University Press.

Mainwaring, S., and T. Scully, eds. 1995. *Building Democratic Institutions: Party Systems in Latin America*. Stanford, CA: Stanford Univeristy Press.

Mainwaring, S., and M. Shugart, eds. 1997. *Presidentialism and Democracy in Latin America*. Cambridge, England: Cambridge University Press.

McCoy, J., and W. Smith. 1995. From Deconsolidation to Reequilibration? Prospects for Democratic Renewal in Venezuela. In J. McCoy et al., eds., *Venezuelan Democracy under Stress*. Edison, New Jersey: Transaction Publishers.

Monaldi, F., R. González, R. Obuchi, and M. Penfold. 2006. Political Institutions, Policymaking Process, and Policy Outcomes in Venezuela. Research Network Working Paper No. R-507. Latin American Research Network, Inter-American Development Bank (IDB), Washington, DC.

Puente, J. 2005. The Political Economy of the Budget-Making Process in Venezuela, 1974–1999. D.Phil. diss., University of Oxford.

Puente, J., A. Daza, G. Ríos, and A. Rodríguez. 2007. The Political Economy of the Budget Process in The Andean Region: The Case of Venezuela. Working Paper No. CS-103. Inter-American Development Bank, Washington, DC.

Ríos, G. 2003. Sostenibilidad fiscal en un contexto de alta volatilidad. Corporación Andina de Fomento, Caracas, Venezuela.

Ross, M. 2001. Does Oil Hinder Democracy? *World Politics* 53 April: 325–61.

World Bank. 1998. *Public Expenditure Management Handbook*. Washington, DC: World Bank Institute.

———. 2002. Sostenibilidad y manejo de la deuda pública Venezolana. World Bank, Washington, DC. Unpublished.

10

The Budget Process as a Political Arena

Mark Hallerberg, Carlos Scartascini, and Ernesto Stein

This volume explores the interplay between institutions and politics in Latin America. The individual chapters focus on the budget process in different Latin American countries. Understanding how the budget process works is important for several reasons. First, it determines the level of public goods for a given population. Second, together with monetary and exchange rate policy, fiscal policy is one of the three tools governments may use to affect the domestic economy. Finally, an understanding of how fiscal policy is made is instructive in regard to the more general economic policy. Budgets also have important political connotations. Political actors may seek to address the needs of many sectors in society, but there are inevitably scarce resources that must be distributed in some way. Budgets encapsulate the trade-offs political actors must make on different policy priorities and, by extension, on different groups in society.

The overall framework in which these actors interact with one another is what Stein et al. (2008) call the policymaking process, and the chapters in the book build explicitly upon this approach. The studies in Stein et al. (2008) argue that the ability of actors to cooperate with one another and to guarantee that such bargains are honored in the future affects the quality of public policies. Cooperation is more likely when actors expect to collaborate repeatedly and over fairly long periods of time. In such situations, actors can strike intertemporal bargains with one another.

Whether such intertemporal bargains are honored, however, depends very much on the institutional makeup of the policymaking process. Institutions affect the likelihood that actors will indeed interact with each other repeatedly; for example, bargains on policy struck between two individuals will likely no longer be valid after an individual leaves public office. On the other hand, where political parties are strongly institutionalized, interactions among parties are likely in the future. This means that bargains struck among stable political parties that remain in the political arena after successive elections have a better chance of being complied with and thus of being offered in the first place. This temporal element means that political parties based on programs rather than the appeal of one individual are more likely to cooperate with one another. Stein et al. (2008) provides empirical evidence, moreover, that public policies tend to be of higher quality in countries where the policymaking process encourages such intertemporal cooperation.

The chapters in this volume, which complement and add to Stein et al. (2008), distinguish the actors that matter most in the budget process. This makes it possible to expand on some of the themes in Stein et al. (2008) by examining just one policy area. The volume as a whole also reinforces Stein et al.'s argument that knowing the actors and what they want is not enough to predict what they get—the institutional context, which in this volume means the way that governments make and execute budgets, has concrete effects on outcomes.[1] To test whether the rules that structure the interactions between a given set of actors matter requires an understanding of those rules. A fundamental strength of this volume is that it brings together economists and political scientists from several Latin American countries, many of whom have substantial policy experience, to document these rules and examine how they have evolved in each country over roughly a three-decade period. The chapters in

[1] The assertion herein that institutional attributes affect a tool of economic policy in the Latin American context is not uncontroversial. In two of the best-known studies of central bank independence, Cukierman (1992) and Cukierman, Webb, and Neyapti (1992) assert that the formal rules that structure monetary policy in OECD countries are not effective in developing countries because governments are unlikely to abide by them. Their measure of central bank independence for developing countries, therefore, is an average of the term of the central bank governor.

this volume, in fact, provide the first detailed evidence on the type of fiscal rules, institutions, and norms in place in each country, both formally and in practice.

Yet to state that "rules matter" as a fundamental message of this volume would be incomplete for two reasons. First, if budget rules do matter, it is important to understand what they matter for. In other words, what dimensions of fiscal outcomes do the rules and institutions that regulate the budget process affect? This volume explores budget outcomes along four dimensions. *Fiscal sustainability* is a gauge of the state of budget balances and debt levels, and it is usually the only measure that more traditional studies of fiscal policy consider Fiscal sustainability is certainly critical in the budget process, and it is difficult to achieve other goals if it is not maintained. Yet it is not the only relevant measure when a particular budget process is judged. First, the relative *adaptability* of a given budget is also important. Most countries covered in this volume have relatively small open economies, which are subject to important external shocks. Changing conditions abroad may require changes in domestic fiscal policy. If most of the budget cannot be readily changed because of excessive rigidities, countries may have to resort to inefficient adjustments, or become more vulnerable to crises. Another way to judge budget outcomes is to consider the *efficiency* of expenditures, that is, the extent to which public resources are allocated to the most important needs and are used in a cost-effective manner (e.g., Schick, 1998; Herrera and Pang, 2005). The final way to measure performance is to look at the overall *representativeness* of the budget. To determine whether all sectors in society are represented in a given budget by looking at spending allocations and tax burdens is difficult, and instead the focus in this volume is on an inherently process-centered definition, that is, a budget is more representative if the budget process allows for the representation of most interests and does not over-represent any given interest.

Second, the "rules matter" line does not reveal much about *why* or *when* the rules matter. This chapter argues that they matter when at least some of the actors with some power over the budget process benefit from their enforcement. While this point will be revisited later, it is important to note that the formal institutions themselves are not "causing" the outcomes, and indeed, as the discussion of Congress below will indicate, there is no guarantee that policymakers will follow those rules.

The chapters in this volume also have lessons for the fiscal institutions literature. Budgetary rules and institutions are embedded in a broader policymaking process. As the next section argues, it is important to look closely at how these rules and institutions are used in order to understand them. Also, if one ignores the actors and their incentives, one cannot predict whether a given fiscal institution, such as a balanced-budget requirement, will have any practical effect.

In the remainder of this chapter, these themes are developed in more detail. To focus the analysis on one particular set of institutions for illustrative purposes, one institutional relationship in particular is examined, that between Congress and the president. The countries discussed in this volume are presidential democracies, and there have been differing accounts in the literature about the possible trade-offs of having a "strong" or "weak" president vis-à-vis Congress. The next section indicates that not all rules are as they may seem once one looks closely at how they are used, and it reinforces the message that there may be trade-offs in the types of goals that a given budget institution may be able to promote. The third section investigates in a comparative context a specific set of fiscal reforms, which were commonly introduced as fiscal responsibility laws. The previous chapters indicate that most of the laws have failed on their own terms; that is, governments have not stuck to the goals they set themselves. Herein it is argued that these reforms work best when there is a supportive underlying policymaking process. The fourth section presents a broader examination of the relationship between the policymaking process and the budget process and shows evidence of feedback between the two processes. Using a general review of the case study evidence, it can be argued that certain conditions of the policymaking process matter for the sustainability of fiscal reforms. Also, the reforms to fiscal institutions may have unintended consequences for the policymaking process. The cycle may be positive. Fiscal reforms that address a weakness in the overall policymaking process may improve both fiscal policy and the overall policy environment.

TRADE-OFFS AMONG DIFFERENT GOALS: REEXAMINING THE RELATIONSHIP BETWEEN CONGRESS AND THE PRESIDENT

The legislative branch lies at the heart of representative democracy. In addition to its lawmaking responsibilities (and the responsibility to elect the government in the case of parliamentary democracies), it has an oversight function to keep the executive honest. Also, citizens directly elect the legislative members, which provides them with a device to reward or punish legislators. The overall powers of legislatures vary considerably in Latin America (e.g., Morgenstern and Nacif, 2002), but there is often a sense that a strong legislature is a key component of a strong democracy. If one cares about the representativeness of a budget (i.e., the match between budget allocations and preferences of the population), presumably one would like input from this body that the people directly elect.

Yet curiously, this branch of government has often received a bad name in the fiscal institutionalist literature, which focuses mostly on fiscal sustainability. The reason is that the legislature is considered an arena especially likely to have an endemic "common pool" resource problem. In the model presented in Weingast, Shepsle, and Johnson (1981), legislators care only about the health of their electoral districts. In fiscal terms, this means that legislators consider the benefits of spending in their district, but only in terms of the taxes that their district must pay. The taxes, however, ultimately come from the general revenue base, or the "common pool" of resources. Legislators therefore vote for more spending than they would if they considered the full tax effects of their spending. If legislators simply aggregate together their spending proposals in one big logroll, there will be too much spending. The president and the finance minister, in contrast, worry about the financial well-being of the whole country (Hansen, 1998; Persson and Tabellini, 1999) and thus consider the full tax burden when making decisions. Fiscal rules that benefit the president in his relationship with Congress are then expected to lead to better fiscal outcomes. Restrictions on Congress are more effective, moreover, the greater the common pool problem in Congress, which varies according to the incentives that the electoral system creates (Hallerberg and Marier, 2004). Comparative empirical work on Latin America has reinforced this point. Alesina et al. (1996) find that countries with institutions that make the budget process more hierarchical have lower deficits and debts, and one of their measures is related to the power of the president vis-à-vis Congress. In more sophisticated studies in terms of measuring the effects of institutions and covering more years, Filc and Scartascini (2006, 2007) similarly find that countries with more hierarchical procedures and more stringent rules have higher fiscal balances. Once again, one component of these studies focuses on restrictions on Congress. In an empirical study that is especially wide-ranging in the number of countries it covers, Wehner (2008) examines spending levels in 80 countries and finds that states where there are restrictions on what Congress can change in the executive's budget have lower public expenditures than countries where such restrictions are absent.

The country studies in this volume do reinforce the message that fiscal rules that centralize the budget process have improved fiscal sustainability. Budget deficits have been high under less restrictive fiscal rules, but have shrunk in countries like Ecuador and Peru, after those countries have imposed additional restrictions on the role of Congress. Countries such as Chile that have always had restrictive rules also do well in terms of fiscal sustainability.

Yet, the chapters also lead to two further conclusions that are not evident in the more "macro"-level studies of fiscal institutions and fiscal rules. First, despite the more "macro" evidence on fiscal sustainability, the reality of the budget process is not always the same as what one would expect from a reading of the laws on the books. Second, as suggested by the discussion of representativeness above, fiscal rules that successfully address one goal of fiscal policy—such as sustainability—may affect adversely other goals. To return to the example above, a setting that restricts the ability of Congress to increase the overall size of the budget during approval limits common pool resource problems, which enhances fiscal sustainability. But congressional involvement in the allocation of spending and taxation may enhance allocative efficiency, as well as the representativeness of the budget process. However, these reforms do not work in isolation. The incentives of the actors at each stage are determined by their prerogatives in the overall budget process and their incentives and abilities in the general policymaking process. Therefore, restrictions should be placed on both actors at different stages. Of course, as will be demonstrated in the section that discusses the existence of feedback effects between the budget and policymaking processes, these restrictions should be compatible with their needs in the general policymaking process. In some cases, restricting the discretion of the executive might lead to a more fruitful relationship with Congress. In others, this discretion might undermine the executive's possibilities for relating to Congress.[2] These topics, in turn, are treated with reference to the relationship between the president and Congress in this section.

The Roles of Congress and the President during the Stages of the Budget Process: Matching Latin American Practice with the Theoretical Ideal

To make these points empirically, the discussion is organized around an "ideal" relationship between these two branches of government that includes a focus on the extent to which the countries in the sample approximate this ideal. Table 10.1 summarizes the expected involvement of a given actor at a given point in the budget process. In most presidential democracies, the president prepares the draft budget and proposes this budget to Congress. This stage includes the presentation guidelines for the upcoming budget year, such as estimated revenues and expenditures, and one would expect these estimates to be unbiased to facilitate planning by all concerned.

At the next stage, Congress passes the budget and is certainly the main actor. As the literature cited above emphasizes, the ability of the legislature to make unlimited amendments to the budget can undermine fiscal sustainability. At the other end of the spectrum, a Congress that

TABLE 10.1 Expected Role of the President and Congress in the Budget Process

Stage of budget process	President	Congress
Draft	Main actor	Does not participate
Appropriations/passage	Secondary actor	Main actor
Execution	Main actor	Secondary actor
Control	Main actor	Main actor

[2] Filc, Scartascini, and Stein (2005) compare the case of Brazil (included in this volume) with the case of the Dominican Republic to argue this point.

does nothing at this stage is also not desirable. Congress generally represents more parts of society than the president, and some congressional input at this stage increases the representativeness of the budget process and—depending upon the execution of the passed budget—the allocative efficiency of the budget as well. In terms of formal restrictions on Congress, this discussion suggests that a rule that allows changes to the budget that do not increase overall spending or decrease taxes (known as "offset" rules) would be appropriate, although, as discussed below, the fact that such rules are in place does not mean that they are honored.

Once the budget has passed, the president clearly will have primary responsibility for executing it, but Congress nevertheless should play a secondary role as well. An executed budget will have lower allocative efficiency if the president spends money only on his or her pet projects and ignores the preferences of Congress. Finally, Congress should serve an important "watchdog" function at the control stage to ensure that the executive properly allocates the resources. Executive agencies can play a similar role.

To what extent do countries in this volume fit this ideal model of the role of the players at the different stages of the budget process? To begin with the **budget preparation stage**, in all countries the executive formulates the initial budget proposal. The anticipated interaction between president and Congress at future stages of the budget process affects the president's budget proposal in two ways. First, the executive surely anticipates what type of proposal, at a minimum, is required to obtain the approval of Congress. One would expect that the content of this proposal would vary to some degree based on the ability of Congress to amend the budget, as well as the relative impatience of each player (Tsebelis and Money, 1997). Indeed, the president has different formal legislative powers in different countries—powers to set the legislative agenda, to veto the decisions of Congress, or to legislate by decree.

In Chile, for example, the president controls the legislative agenda through the use of *urgencies,* which force Congress to vote on a given bill within a specific time frame (usually three, 10, or 30 days). According to Tsebelis and Money (1997), this means that the president can force Congress to be impatient, which weakens its bargaining power. The president in Chile can also call an extraordinary session of Congress to determine what bills are to be considered, which gives him or her agenda-setting power. Congress, on the other hand, only has the power to approve the budget and cannot change the content of what the president proposes.

In contrast, in Paraguay there is a general time limit for passing the budget, but the president does not have the power to shorten this consideration period. Moreover, Congress can change the budget as it wishes during the approval stage. Even formal rules meant to give the executive some agenda-setting power, such as the requirement that the finance minister make any changes to the government's budget proposal, are generally ignored in practice. These institutional differences, in turn, have practical implications in terms of changes in the budget—while Congress does not increase the president's budget proposal in Chile, this is common practice in Paraguay.

The second way the interaction between president and Congress affects the preparation stage is through expenditure and revenue estimates. Beginning at the formulation stage of the budget, as indicated by the chapters in this volume, the executive's estimates for revenues and expenditures are routinely—and systematically—biased. Some countries, such as Brazil, Bolivia, and Paraguay, have executives that regularly overestimate revenues, while other countries, such as Argentina and Venezuela, have executives that regularly underestimate revenue.

The explanation for the under- or overestimation of specific accounts is likely the way the negotiation process is conducted in each country. In countries where the executive has more discretion during the execution stage, there is a tendency to overestimate revenues during the approval stage.[3] In Brazil, for example, the president has discretion to cut projects during the execution stage as long as actual revenues are below estimated revenues. The discretion to cut legislators' favorite projects gives the president bargaining power when he or she needs to pass key legislation. The president has this discretionary power only if actual revenues are below estimated revenues, and hence the executive consistently overestimates revenues. In Argentina, the economic context has affected the relevant set of actors and the incentives for biased estimates. Prior to 2004, the main government priority was to

[3] Having the discretion to execute (or underexecute) the budget at will means that the executive has the ability to cut expenditures if revenues fall short of the estimates. Therefore, under those conditions the executive has an incentive to overestimate revenues and include legislators' pet projects in the budget, in order to ensure that he or she can build a coalition of legislators and obtain a quick approval of the budget in Congress.

present optimistic market forecasts. Since 2004, however, the economic context has improved, and presidents do not want to suggest that they have additional funds at their disposal when they are renegotiating their debts. Moreover, the executive, through the body known as the Jefatura de Gabinete, has the power to decide on the allocation of revenues that exceed estimated revenues. Revenues have since 2004 been strategically underestimated. In a related case, in Venezuela the price of oil is consistently underestimated, which is useful to the president because he or she can spend the "unanticipated" revenues when the price of oil turns out to be higher than initially assumed.

Moving on to the **approval stage** of the budget process, Congress clearly has a direct role in this stage. That role, however, is often limited formally in ways that fit with what the general literature would advocate to reduce common pool resource problems. For example, in all countries discussed in this volume, aside from Argentina and Paraguay, there are formal restrictions on the ability of Congress to change the president's budget. In some countries, such restrictions include barring legislators from increasing expenditures, while in other countries legislators are formally required to identify additional sources of financing for any proposed additions to the original budget, which is known as an "offset" rule.

Once again, one finds that there are rampant examples of members of Congress getting around the intention of the formal rules. As is the case for the preparation stage, manipulation of estimates is common before Congress passes the budget. Take, for example, the previously mentioned offset rule. This measure responds to the necessity of legislators having to internalize the political cost of raising taxes that the increases in expenditure demand; that is, it is a response to the common pool resource problem that is described at the beginning of this section. However, in practice legislators circumvent this rule, in some countries by increasing estimated revenues above those estimated by the government and in others by strategically shifting the allocation of the budget in a way that eventually leads to greater overall expenditures.

In Bolivia, for example, Congress has increased effective government expenditure by raising debt or by overestimating revenues. In 1998, the Bolivian Congress raised the expected efficiency of the tax collection and customs agencies by 50 percent in order to have a greater estimation of revenues. However, those efficiency increments did not take place, and the deficit for that year was increased by 4 percent, even though the government spent 3 percent less than what was authorized in the budget. Similarly, in Ecuador and Colombia expenditures are sometimes shifted from debt service or amortizations to other expenditures. Since debt services have to be met, this shift effectively increases the total size of the budget.

In addition to the formal powers that structure the relationship between the president and Congress, there are also important political factors that matter at the approval stage. In particular, countries differ in the extent of the president's partisan powers in Congress, that is, the size of the groups of legislators that support him or her. The president has more power when he or she has majority support in Congress from one party, which has been the case over most of the time period covered herein in Argentina. However, in countries such as Brazil with highly fragmented party systems, the president has comparatively less power when there are many parties whose support is needed.

During the **budget execution stage**, while in most countries Congress legally has a role in limiting the discretion of the executive to make unilateral changes to the budget, in many countries legislatures do not actually play that role in practice. In Argentina, for example, formal rules stipulate that the executive requires the approval of Congress in order to add any expenditure to the budget or to shift investment expenditures to current expenditures. In practice, however, the executive makes these changes unilaterally, usually by executive decree. Congress is supposed to oversee these decrees, but in practice the commission in charge of doing so has not yet been constituted. Bolivia, as well as other countries discussed in this volume, experiences similar situations in which the government's decision is supposed to be subject to legislative approval whenever there are changes to the budget during the execution stage. Yet in practice the executive makes unilateral changes throughout the year and, at the end of the budget year, Congress just "rubber-stamps" the decisions of the executive. This is why the executed budget ends up looking quite different from the one approved by the legislature, both in terms of total spending and in terms of the allocation of expenditures among competing programs.[4]

[4] Scartascini and Stein (2004) indicate that on average some agencies end up spending 30 percent more than what was originally assigned to them and others spend 30 percent less. In terms of each item, in some years spending is twice the amount of the original budget, while in others, it is as low as 5 percent.

During the **control stage**, in most Latin American countries Congress plays a less significant role than what is stated by the formal rules. In Argentina, the law establishes that Congress must approve the investment account each year, at which time Congress also is supposed to review what was spent the preceding year. However, the investment account is never approved on time, and sometimes it is approved three or four years later. This does not allow legislators to use what is learned each year about the budget process in the following year. In Paraguay, something similar occurs. Congress is supposed to make, evaluate, and approve the annual expenditure plan, but this plan is always accepted as the comptroller has delivered it, without major analysis done by the legislators (Chapter 2).

One reason for this lack of control may be the resource disparity that structures the relationship between the president and Congress, with the president having unparalleled technical resources in all of the cases discussed in this volume. Countries do differ substantially with regard to the technical capacity of the legislature, which is related to the extent of legislative experience of the legislators; the extent to which these legislators specialize in committees; and the availability of technical advisors, as well as outside technical support from "think tanks" and other organizations.[5] Yet in general, the differences in technical capacity between the executive and legislative branches are large. On the one hand, most central budget offices in the executive have more than 40 employees.[6] On the other, very few countries have specialized budget offices in Congress, and the existing offices are usually staffed with less than 10 employees.[7]

---

[5] The technical capacity of Congress in regard to budget-related issues depends partially on the existence of technical advisor teams. Even though the legislators on the relevant committees may have experience with this topic, the rest of the legislators do not have incentives to acquire knowledge of budgetary procedures. Most Latin American countries do not have an adequate office of technical advisors. In a 2003 survey of 12 countries designed by the World Bank, IDB, and OECD, it was found that only seven countries had a technical advisor's office. Out of these offices, four had fewer than 10 employees. Exceptions include Brazil, where there is an office of technical advisors with more than 500 employees, and Chile, where there is the support of several think tanks with strong partisan links.

[6] Out of 14 Latin American countries, Uruguay had less than 40 employees in its central budget office. Meanwhile, countries such as Argentina, Brazil, and Mexico had more than 200 employees (source: OECD/WB/IDB database, http://www.oecd.org/document/61/0,2340,en_2649_34119_2494461_1_1_1_1,00.html).

[7] Only Mexico and Costa Rica have more than 50. Large countries such as Argentina do not even have a specialized budget office in Congress.

In sum, the role of Congress in the budget process is fundamental. A setting that restricts the ability of Congress to increase the overall size of the budget during approval limits common pool resource problems, which enhances fiscal sustainability. However, congressional involvement in the allocation of spending and taxation enhances allocative efficiency, as well as the representativeness of the budget process.

FISCAL RESPONSIBILITY LAWS

While the previous section covers the relationship between two sets of actors in the budget process, this one considers a particular type of fiscal reform that several countries in Latin America have introduced during the past two decades: fiscal responsibility laws. These laws have touched all parts of the budget process and are designed to improve fiscal sustainability.

As the previous section suggests, these laws are generally placed on top of a preexisting policymaking process. This process, in turn, affects whether such laws are implemented in practice. A core finding of this volume is that governments are most likely to comply with such laws when there are powerful actors who are interested in their success. When there are no strong political backers in a country, the law may be only partly implemented or ignored entirely.

Of the 10 countries covered in this volume, six have introduced fiscal responsibility laws: Argentina, Brazil, Colombia, Ecuador, Peru, and Venezuela.[8] Moreover, Chile recently passed into law a structural balance rule that codified a practice that the Lagos administration had introduced in 2001, and this requirement is consistent with fiscal responsibility laws. The exceptions that remain are Bolivia, Paraguay, and Uruguay. In Venezuela, the FRL was introduced in 1999, but it was never actually implemented. Of the remaining cases that did implement such laws, the country studies indicate that—based on the period covered in the book—only in Brazil did the government succeed in reaching the targets established by the law. To explore why such laws generally fail to meet their goals and to learn something from the one

[8] See Filc and Scartascini (2007) for a detailed account of budget institution reforms in Latin America and the Caribbean.

success story, this section examines the examples of Argentina and Brazil (further detail on Colombia, Ecuador, and Peru will be provided in the following section).

Argentina's Fiscal Solvency Law

The main objectives of the fiscal solvency law implemented in Argentina in 1999 were to contain public spending, reduce fiscal deficits, and increase fiscal transparency. The main components of the law were a countercyclical fund, fixed numerical rules on the deficit and expenditure, rules on budgetary procedures, and measures to increase transparency. As Emmanuel Abuelafia, Sergio Berensztein, Miguel Braun, and Luciano di Gresia indicate in Chapter 2, the targets fixed in the law were not met. In 2000, 2001, and 2004 the budget law explicitly granted the executive the right to exceed the targets, while in 1999, 2002, and 2003 so-called "decrees of necessity and urgency" (*Decretos de Necesidad y Urgencia*) were used to achieve the same goal. The targets were clearly exceeded in 2001: the deficit was at 3.5 percent of GDP, which was almost 15 percent higher than the new limit of 2.5 percent and over six times the limit of 0.5 percent of GDP established for that year in the original law.

The technical reason for this failure was the attempt to use permanent fiscal rules—which were designed to improve medium- and long-term fiscal performance—for a short-term adjustment in response to the crisis, combined with doubts about the sustainability of the convertibility regime and Argentine fiscal solvency.[9] There is also an important political story that gets to the heart of the lessons from this volume. Even though the law covered only the national level—another design flaw in a federal country in need to restrict deficits—the national government needed to get the provinces behind the reform. In Argentina, deputies and senators are elected in province-wide districts and respond to the governor. The national government consequently agreed to finance a larger portion of a deficit that had developed in the provincial pension system in order to garner the support of the governors (Chapter 2). Yet, once the law was in place, the national government itself did not find it beneficial to comply. There were no

[9] This exchange rate regime set Argentine $1 equal to US$1. It required having enough reserves to match the monetary base.

important actors in the policymaking process that had a stake in the fiscal responsibility law, and the national executive violated its terms every year from 1999 to 2004.

Brazil's Fiscal Responsibility Law

While the Argentine law targeted only the national level of government, the Brazilian fiscal responsibility law passed in 2000 targeted all levels of government, and thus would seem to face even further hurdles. Given this ambition, its success is even more remarkable: it has restrained spending at the federal, state, and municipal levels. As Lee Alston, Marcus Melo, Bernardo Mueller, and Carlos Pereira indicate in Chapter 3 of this volume, the consolidated public sector moved from a budget balance of –3 percent of GDP in 1997 to 4.3 percent in 2004, while only two states had any fiscal deficits by 2002. This restraint, in turn, has contributed to low inflation in a country that had experienced bouts of hyperinflation in the past.

Why did the Brazilian law work so well while the Argentine one did not? One reason is that the law changed some aspects of the policymaking process by bringing additional players into the budget process that supported the law, such as the Tribunais de Contas, which had not had a budgetary role before. Most importantly, the actors themselves in the process had an incentive to see the law succeed. For the states, the law gave the executive enforcement mechanisms to address the common pool resource problem. The governors of the states were better off if they all cooperated under this arrangement than if all of them defected. While this was also generally the case in Argentina and explains the passage of the law in both cases, only the Brazilian case included the enforcement mechanisms. Moreover, unlike in Argentina, the executive in Brazil wanted to see the reform succeed because it meant the end of routine executive bailouts of the provinces. The fact that the law was more comprehensive than the Argentine law means that there were greater incentives for the executive to maintain it.

Consequently, a change in the rules is not a sufficient condition for modifying the results when they come into conflict with the rules of political interaction of the agents involved. However, in some cases, changes in rules can have an impact because they substantially change the political game. In Brazil, the introduction of the fiscal responsibility law improved fiscal results. This improvement was not so much a direct effect of the deficit limits put into place by the law, but took place because the law also changed the power relationships in the political process, especially between the federal and subnational governments.

A Case of Policy Diffusion?

Before moving on, it is important to comment on the implications of this discussion for the literature on policy diffusion. Weyland (2005) discusses the spread of the privatization of social security in Latin American countries. He indicates that Chile was the first country to initiate this reform in the early 1980s. For a decade, no other country followed this path, but by the end of the 1990s, nine countries had also privatized, to varying extents, their social security systems. He suggests that decision heuristics—that is, the fact that a close neighbor implements the reform and that the reform seems to be a success—drive the waves of reforms one observes in a short period of time across a set of geographically contiguous (or close) countries. A similar wave seemed to take place with regards to fiscal responsibility laws. While the first attempts to introduce these laws in the region owed some intellectual lineage to New Zealand's Fiscal Responsibility Act of 1994, the true leader in this context was Brazil.[10] As Chile was an exemplary leader in the social security case, Brazil was the country that seemed to get its fiscal house in order quickly after it adopted legislation with this name. Without going into further details (see, however, Filc and Scartascini, 2007, for a deeper analysis), this pattern fits well with what Weyland (2005) describes. The findings in this volume supplement the diffusion approach by examining whether the diffusion of such reforms leads to changes in practice within a particular country. Something that could not be diffused out of Brazilian experience was the support of critical actors in the policymaking process for seeing

---

[10] There are some differences between the New Zealand and Latin American fiscal responsibility laws in form. While the New Zealand version introduced a medium-term fiscal framework based on five guiding principles (Scott, 1995), the laws in Latin America have been more detailed and have usually combined numerical targets (such as balanced budget requirements or limits on the growth of expenditure) with procedural rules (such as whether Congress can increase spending amounts in the president's budget proposal). There have also been efforts in Latin America to increase the transparency of the budget process with such laws.

the reform implemented. As this section illustrates, in settings without such actors, the reforms crumble when they are tested, or they are not implemented at all.

THE RELATIONSHIP BETWEEN THE POLICYMAKING PROCESS AND THE BUDGET PROCESS: ARE THERE FEEDBACK EFFECTS?

The chapters in this volume consider the main political actors in the policymaking process. They also indicate how those actors then fit into the budget process and whether the sets of actors are the same in each stage. The previous two sections, moreover, indicate that the policymaking process influences whether or not formal rules in the budget process are followed and what effects these rules have. This discussion brings up a series of questions about the relationship between the two processes. In particular, does the relative quality of the policymaking process affect, or even predetermine, the quality of the budget process? If one begins instead with the budget process, can reforms of the budget process feed back into the overall policymaking process? Guidance on such questions can be found in Filc, Scartascini, and Stein (2005), which presents case studies of decentralization in Venezuela and of the role of the Brazilian and Dominican presidents in fiscal policy decisions. The authors find that feedback effects in other policy arenas are often unanticipated by the original designers of a reform. This chapter argues that the budget process is a fundamental element of the overall policymaking environment. Successful changes in this arena may lead to change in other policy areas as well.

Fitting Budget Making into the Overall Policymaking Process

Looking at the country studies, there is certainly considerable overlap in the quality of the two processes.[11] This is evident especially for the

[11] While this volume includes only eight countries, this section summarizes work on ten countries in the region. In addition to the countries covered in the chapters, papers were commissioned for Bolivia and Chile as well that have appeared as working papers, and we include information from those papers in what follows.

countries at the extremes in terms of the quality of the policymaking process—that is, those countries with environments that most facilitate cooperation and those that least facilitate cooperation.

As Cristóbal Aninat and Joaquín Vial (2005) indicate, **Chile** is a case in which the policymaking process is especially robust. On the fiscal front, Chile has established two innovative fiscal rules. The first is a structural surplus rule introduced in 2001, which dictates that government should maintain a surplus of 1 percent of GDP over the cycle. The second is a Copper Stability Fund introduced in 1985 and first implemented in 1987, which is meant to smooth the effects of changes in the price of one of Chile's main exports. The Chilean government has successfully complied with both rules, so much so in fact that the country ran a surplus that equaled 8 percent of GDP in 2007. The government's adherence to the rules continues despite criticism that the government's estimation of copper prices is too low and despite the behavior of governments in other Latin American countries (e.g., Venezuela) that take natural resource price changes as permanent and continue to have budget deficits. The Chilean government is also active in evaluating its own fiscal performance, and it has introduced a wide-ranging performance-based budgeting system. In the Chilean case, a policymaking process that instills cooperation goes hand in hand with a well-functioning budgetary process.

On the other end of the spectrum, the case of **Paraguay** provides evidence for how well-intentioned fiscal rules may not function well when the policymaking process does not engender cooperation. In Chapter 6, José R. Molinas, Aníbal Pérez-Liñán, and Mark Hallerberg explain that Paraguay has experienced an increase in the number of formal and informal veto players in the policymaking process. These new players want to increase spending for their constituencies, but are reluctant to bear the costs. In Paraguay, the president and the Ministry of Finance have fairly weak roles in the policymaking process in relation to Congress; their power comes from de facto control of the disbursement of funds after the budget passes. This power is not that effective—while it is relatively easy for the finance minister to strike clear pork barrel projects, he has political difficulty in striking higher wages. Knowing this, Congress diverts spending to exactly this item in the budget. In terms of implications for the budget process, this case provides a warning about relying too much on a "strong finance minister" to maintain fiscal discipline. This option will not work if political actors do not have an incentive to support such a position. As one would expect from this setup, fiscal outcomes have not been good in Paraguay. The budget balance has been volatile, and large deficits are common. Spending is inefficient, and the reliance on the executive to cut what it can after Congress passes the budget means that the budget is not that representative.

The case of **Bolivia** reinforces the importance of the relationship between the policymaking and budget processes and suggests that fiscal reforms are unlikely to succeed on their own without an overall supportive policymaking process. As Scartascini and Stein (2004) indicate, Bolivia has introduced many of the customary budget reforms, but results did not change much, as political actors were able to circumvent—at least in their spirit, if not in regard to the exact letter of the law—the new rules and regulations. Also, presidents fail to propose budgets on time, governments do not stick to the budget that is initially passed, and revenues are systematically overestimated. Existing controls come through cash management, which means that the final decisions on allocations usually take place outside of the public eye. Moreover, the fiscal deficit has traditionally been high, resources do not necessarily flow to the most efficient uses, and the use of public monies does not sufficiently reflect citizen preferences. Increases in revenues from higher gas prices and from the introduction of new taxes have contributed to an improvement in sustainability in recent years, but weaknesses in the budget process remain.

In **Colombia**, problems with the policymaking process have had unfortunate implications for the budget process. As Mauricio Cárdenas, Carolina Mejía, and Mauricio Olivera explain in Chapter 4, the nature of the relationship between Congress and the president has meant that the president has made increasing use of so-called forward allocations, which commit the government to spending certain amounts over the medium term. Historically, Colombia had performed well in terms of fiscal sustainability, but from 2000 to 2005 the budget deficit was consistently near 5 percent of GDP. The country also has fairly inefficient spending patterns.

Argentina may be the most exemplary case of the importance of the policymaking process of those discussed in this volume. In Chapter 2, Emmanuel Abuelafia, Sergio Berensztein, Miguel Braun, and Luciano di Gresia document that the country introduced formal fiscal rules that many observers would consider exemplary. Yet the structure of the policymaking process, which gives the provinces control over many of the decisions that are taken in practice, means that less than half of the budget is decided under the formal budget process. The important story that emerges from this case is that changes in the formal budget process are not so effective if much of the budget is decided outside of that process.

There are, however, two cases in which fiscal reforms have had some success when the respective policymaking processes have been weak: **Ecuador** and **Peru**. Andrés Mejía Acosta, Vicente Albornoz, and M. Caridad Araujo provide evidence in Chapter 5 that Ecuador generally has had a weak policymaking process. However, the rules of the game underwent a series of changes, including a major constitutional reform in 1998, dollarization in 2000, and the implementation of a fiscal responsibility law in 2002. Overall, fiscal sustainability improved, although the reforms did make the budget more rigid. Overall the impression the authors provide of these changes is a positive one. Luis Carranza, Jorge F. Chávez, and José Valderrama indicate in Chapter 7 that there have been a series of important institutional changes in **Peru**. The country's 1993 constitution barred the central bank from financing the government's budget and strengthened the power of the executive in the budget process. A fiscal responsibility law passed in 1999 set a positive fiscal balance over the economic cycle as a goal and introduced ceilings on the deficit and on expenditures. More recent legislation has increased the transparency of the process and has created new regional governments that received some fiscal powers. The reforms have contributed to the turnaround of fiscal performance in terms of sustainability—budget deficits in the 1980s were high, averaging 9 percent of GDP, but they fell to only around 2 percent in the 1990s and around 1 percent for the period 2001–2006. Political business cycles, fairly common in the 1990s, vanished in the last electoral cycle in Peru.

At the same time, these cases also illustrate the limits the policymaking process places on such reforms. First, as the narratives above illustrate, in each case there is some adjustment of the policymaking process. Second, the respective authors argue that there are still significant problems with the policymaking process and they are affecting the budget process. In Ecuador, Congress and the president weaken the fiscal responsibility law prior to elections, while the short tenure of the finance minister in practice (about seven months in office on average) undermines the additional powers in the budget process that come with the office. In Peru, political parties are still highly fragmented and pork barrel projects are often needed to buy political support. Success in sustainability also masks other developments. The budget has become more rigid over time, and the public sector remains inefficient.

Correcting Flaws in the Policymaking Process: The Role of the Budget Process

The conclusion so far is that one needs a supportive policymaking process to have successful fiscal reforms. Yet an intriguing finding from another set of countries is how parts of the budget process seem to be designed to address clear weaknesses in the overall policymaking process. This means that there is some scope for fiscal reforms even where the policymaking process is not ideal. Take, for example, the situation in **Uruguay**. There, the policymaking process includes one of the few established political party systems in Latin America. The powers of the president and Congress are clear, and the two are able to check one another. Yet as Juan Andrés Moraes, Daniel Chasquetti, and Mario Bergara persuasively show in Chapter 8, fiscal rules and actors' incentives and interactions with one another are structured around pronounced electoral cycles. As elections near, parties and presidents seek to increase their profile with voters. At the beginning of the term of the president and Congress, cooperation among political actors is high. At this time, the government passes a five-year budget plan, which becomes the default budget if the players cannot agree on a budget in future years. Indeed, as elections approach, the coalition among actors usually breaks down. Nonetheless, this budget plan ensures some fiscal discipline even if the rhythm of the policymaking process means that cooperation among the political players is difficult to achieve in some periods.

A similar story can be told for **Brazil**. Lee Alston, Marcus Melo, Bernardo Mueller, and Carlos Pereira suggest in Chapter 3 that the budget process is at the core of the policymaking game because it provides the president with the exchange mechanisms to survive in a contested political arena. It also has other features worth exploring, such as an electoral system that encourages legislators to cultivate a personal vote through allocation of spending to their constituencies. At the same time, the president has strong powers in the budget process, including, most critically, the ability not to spend money that the legislature has allocated. The president has used these powers extensively to compensate for the incentives the electoral system creates for the behavior of representatives in Congress.

The overall message is clear. Well-intentioned fiscal reforms can fail because of bigger failings in the overall policymaking process. At the same time, the budget process can sometimes address issues that are not resolvable at the level of the broader policymaking process. When designing reforms, policymakers should take into account the feedback effects between the two processes.

FUTURE RESEARCH

This volume has established that one needs to have a good understanding of the underlying policymaking process to explain how the budget process works. The evidence for this argument comes from case studies conducted for 10 countries in Latin America, eight of which are discussed in detail in this volume, and two that are examined herein through previous working papers.

One question to ask is how well the lessons drawn in this volume transfer to other countries. A reasonable expectation is that the lessons would be the same for the countries in Central America and the Caribbean that are not included herein, even though they do have somewhat different histories, party systems, and the like. Preliminary work done in the Dominican Republic seems to confirm that the lessons are transferrable (IDB, 2005). This and other countries are Spanish-speaking presidential democracies with some levels of economic development. The lessons from the big country in the region that is not discussed in this volume—Mexico—should be similar to those for Argentina and Brazil. There is nothing about the framework that restricts its applicability to Latin America, and one would learn more about the limitations of the model by testing it empirically in other worldwide settings.[12]

[12] See, for example, Pereira and Singh (2008), which applies the model to policymaking in Portugal.

Another avenue of future research would be to take some themes that authors touch upon in this volume and then expand the data set to include countries from outside of Latin America. For example, regarding the theme of natural resources, three countries in the data set used for the discussion herein have what one can characterize as an abundance of such resources—Chile has copper, while Ecuador and Venezuela have oil. The literature often treats such abundance as a "curse." On the economic side, such a curse translates into a "Dutch disease" for some countries. If a country is afflicted with this disease, the natural resource becomes the main export item, society reallocates resources to this sector, and there is a squeeze in particular of the other tradable and manufacturing sectors (e.g., Bruno and Sachs, 1982). On the political side, the curse is on democracy. Extractive industries require economies of scale, and elites have no reason to encourage education or specialization (Frieden, 2006). Democracy is then stillborn.

The chapters on Chile, Ecuador, and Venezuela discuss how the respective countries deal with the fiscal consequences of natural resource abundance. They indicate that the price of such goods can vary widely on world markets, which presents significant challenges to government budgets. The chapter on **Venezuela**, for example, illustrates that the drop in the oil price in the 1980s had a dramatic effect on the health of the state finances. The three countries have adopted different strategies of late to deal with their natural resource wealth. Chile has imposed a Copper Stability Fund that has functioned well. Ecuador, for its part, has set up formal rules to establish what to do with additional oil revenue, but increases in revenue have nevertheless been spent on particularistic projects. Venezuela has not implemented the measures it passed regarding oil revenue. There are parallels to these cases in other parts of the world—such as in Norway, Saudi Arabia, and Indonesia—that could be usefully compared to the cases in this volume.

When considering the development of future budget policies in Latin America, analyses will likely need to consider a broader set of actors in the process. The chapters presented herein indicate that courts are increasingly important in countries like Brazil and Colombia. As these democracies continue to age, courts may be called upon in a wider group of cases to settle disputes and to make rulings that affect the budget. Similarly, central banks were not a major actor over the time period that was studied for this volume, but recently they have become more active in the setting of macroeconomic policy.

More work also should be done on why reforms are successful in some contexts but not in others. One can imagine similar studies on regulatory policy, for example. In the country studies of focus for this volume, the fiscal results that are discussed are the end of a complex process in which many actors (Congress, the executive branch, and subnational governments) interact in an environment only partially determined by the formal fiscal rules. The budgetary process is determined by a larger set of elements such as the historic legacy and political institutions (e.g., constitutions, electoral rules). These elements, in turn, shape the incentives of the different actors involved in the process and the ways in which they seek agreements. In order to design reforms, it is necessary to understand the dynamics of the process in question and the complexity of the decision-making process. Some questions that lead one in this direction are: Who are the actors involved in the budgetary process? What are their main incentives? What exchanges occur among them? Why are there differences between the norms in written procedures and the way things get done? What determines the role played by the main actors involved in the budget process?

Some lessons for the implementation of effective reforms are clear. As this chapter has argued repeatedly, policy reforms are not easily transferable from one country to the other. The potential impact of the reforms depends on the characteristics of the budget and policymaking process. Consequently, reforms should be tailored for each country, taking into account the incentives of the relevant actors across every policy margin.

REFERENCES

Alesina, A., R. Hausmann, R. Hommes, and E. Stein. 1996. Budget Institutions and Fiscal Performance in Latin America. NBER Working Paper No. 5586. National Bureau of Economic Research, Cambridge, MA.

Aninat, C., and J. Vial. 2005. Who Decides on Public Expenditures? A Political Economy Analysis of the Budget Process in Chile. Manuscript, Universidad Adolfo Ibáñez.

Bruno, M., and J. Sachs. 1982. Energy and Resource Allocation: A Dynamic Model of "Dutch Disease." *Review of Economic Studies* 49(5): 845–59.

Cukierman, A. 1992. *Central Bank Strategy, Credibility, and Independence.* Cambridge, MA: MIT Press.

Cukierman, A., S. Webb, and B. Neyapti. 1992. The Measurement of Central Bank Independence and Its Effect on Policy Outcomes. *World Bank Economic Review* (6 September): 439–58.

Filc, G., and C. Scartascini. 2006. Instituciones presupuestarias, resultados fiscales y el rol del Congreso en el proceso presupuestario. In M. Braun, G. Uña, and L. Diaz Frers, eds., *El Congreso y el Presupuesto Nacional en Argentina.* Buenos Aires: Centro de Implementación de Políticas Públicas para la Equidad y el Crecimiento (CIPPEC).

———. 2007. Budgetary Institutions. In Eduardo Lora, ed., *The State of State Reform.* Stanford, CA: Stanford University Press.

Filc, G., C. Scartascini, and E. Stein. 2005. Decentralization, Budget Process, and Feedback Effects. In *The Politics of Policies.* Economic and Social Progress in Latin America: 2006 Report. Washington, DC. Inter-American Development Bank and Cambridge, MA: DRCLAS

Frieden, J. A. 2006. Global Capitalism: Its Fall and Rise in the Twentieth Century. New York: Norton.

Hallerberg, M., and P. Marier. 2004. Executive Authority, the Personal Vote, and Budget Discipline in Latin American and Caribbean Countries. *American Journal of Political Science* 48(3): 571–87.

Hansen, J. M. 1998. Individuals, Institutions, and Public Preferences over Public Finance. *American Political Science Review* 92(3): 513–31.

Herrera, S., and G. Pang. 2005. Efficiency of Public Spending in Developing Countries: An Efficiency Frontier Approach. World Bank Policy Research Working Paper No. 3645. World Bank, Washington, DC.

IDB (Inter-American Development Bank). 2005. *The Politics of Policies.* Economic and Social Progress in Latin America: 2006 Report. Washington, DC: Inter-American Development Bank and Cambridge, MA: DRCLAS.

Morgenstern, S., and B. Nacif, eds. 2002. *Legislative Politics in Latin America.* Cambridge, England: Cambridge University Press.

Pereira, C., and S. Singh. 2008. Economic Performance and Political Coordination in the Portuguese "Dry" Political System. Michigan State University, East Lansing, Michigan. Unpublished.

Persson, T., and G. Tabellini. 1999. The Size and Scope of Government: Comparative Politics with Rational Politicians. 1998 Marshall Lecture. *European Economic Review* 43: 699–735.

Scartascini, C., and E. Stein. 2004. The Bolivian Budget (1990–2002): A Year Long Bargaining Process. Office of Evaluation and Oversight and Research Department, Inter-American Development Bank, Washington, DC. Unpublished.

Schick, A. 1998. *A Contemporary Approach to Public Expenditure Management.* Washington, DC: World Bank Institute.

Scott, G. 1995. New Zealand's Fiscal Responsibility Act. *Agenda* 2(1): 3–16.

Stein, E., M. Tommasi, P. Spiller, and C. Scartascini. 2008. *Policymaking in Latin America How Politics Shapes Policies.* Washington, DC: Inter-American Development Bank and Cambridge, MA: DRCLAS.

Tsebelis, G., and J. Money. 1997. *Bicameralism.* Cambridge, England: Cambridge University Press.

Wehner, J. 2008. Constitutions, Executive Authority, and Fiscal Policy. Working Paper, London School of Economics.

Weingast, B. R., K. A. Shepsle, and C. Johnson. 1981. The Political Economy of Benefits and Costs: A Neoclassical Approach to Distributive Politics. *Journal of Political Economy* 89: 642–64.

Weyland, K. 2005. Theories of Policy Diffusion: Lessons from Latin American Pension Reform. *World Politics* 57: 262–95.